WHO MOVED MY INTEREST RATE?

WHO MOVED MY INTEREST RATE?

LEADING THE RESERVE BANK OF INDIA THROUGH FIVE TURBULENT YEARS

DUVVURI SUBBARAO

PENGUIN
VIKING

VIKING

USA | Canada | UK | Ireland | Australia
New Zealand | India | South Africa | China

Viking is part of the Penguin Random House group of companies
whose addresses can be found at global.penguinrandomhouse.com

Published by Penguin Books India Pvt. Ltd
7th Floor, Infinity Tower C, DLF Cyber City,
Gurgaon 122 002, Haryana, India

Penguin
Random House
India

First published in Viking by Penguin Books India 2016

ISBN 9780670088928

Typeset in Adobe Caslon Pro by Manipal Digital Systems, Manipal
Printed at Thomson Press India Ltd, New Delhi

www.penguin.co.in

For my parents who taught me values

Contents

Author's Note

I stepped down from the office of governor of the Reserve Bank of India (RBI) on 4 September 2013. In the months before I left the RBI and for long afterwards, several people have asked me if I planned to write a book on my time as governor. I remained dismissive of the suggestion if only because I found the idea of writing a book very daunting.

In mid-2014, I took up a position as a Distinguished Visiting Fellow at the National University of Singapore (NUS). I was employed primarily by the business school although my appointment was also partly supported by the Institute of South Asian Studies and the Monetary Authority of Singapore. The job involved giving occasional lectures on issues in central banking, the financial sector and the global economy. Many faculty and students who heard the lectures urged me to put those ideas, thoughts and experiences together in a book.

Encouraged by all this urging, I decided to bite the bullet and started on the book in earnest in mid-2015. This book is an account of my term as governor during 2008–13. This was, by all accounts, an unusually turbulent period for the world and for India. The global financial crisis erupted in full blast within a week of my stepping into the Reserve Bank. Just as India started recovering from the impact of the crisis, the action shifted to combating a decade-high, stubborn inflation during 2009–11 which segued into a battle against a sharp depreciation of the rupee from mid-2012 up until the close of my tenure in September 2013. At its heart, the book is about the dilemmas I confronted in leading the Reserve Bank through a period of extraordinary economic and political challenges.

This book is not an attempt to defend my decisions as governor, so much as to explain the circumstances in which I acted. It is not an effort to reshape the narrative of that period but to convey my perspectives on the issues and challenges which shaped that narrative in the first place.

My five years at the Reserve Bank also marked an intellectually vigorous period for central banking around the world. Not only has the global financial crisis tested the policy force of central banks but it has also raised several questions about the tools of their trade, their forays into communication, the limits of their autonomy and the limitations of the manner in which they render accountability. Much of the debate surrounding these issues has been set in the advanced economy context. I have endeavoured to place some of these issues and debates in an Indian and emerging-market perspective.

The book is more than just about my challenges and dilemmas. It is also an attempt to demystify the Reserve Bank. Although monetary policy is the glamorous stuff that grabs the headlines, the Reserve Bank is much more than a narrow monetary authority. It has a broad mandate and a wide array of responsibilities. Yet the vast majority of people in India only have a scanty understanding of what the Reserve Bank does and how that affects their everyday lives. I have endeavoured to bridge that knowledge gap; a wider awareness of the functions and responsibilities of the RBI should help the larger public hold the Reserve Bank to account for results. Or that, at least, is my hope.

I did not keep any notes while serving as governor which ruled out a conventional memoir organized chronologically. Besides, I was more attracted to the idea of telling my stories and recounting my challenges thematically. The ordering of the chapters has, however, been informed by a rough chronological sequencing.

As I started on the book, I was apprehensive about whether I could recall the relevant details and reconstruct my experiences after a gap of over two years in the absence of any notes whatsoever. In the event, it did not prove to be as big a handicap as I feared. I depended almost entirely on press clippings, my speeches and the Reserve Bank publications of my period which helped me put together a narrative in as much detail as I wanted. Besides, the Internet was a handy and efficient resource for research and fact–checking.

Virtually, the first question that colleagues at NUS, many of them experienced authors themselves, have asked me when I told them about the book was, 'Who is your target reader?' A straightforward answer eluded me. There are economists, analysts and commentators who know the Reserve Bank but are keen on understanding how the Reserve Bank's mind operates. Then there are several times that number of educated and intelligent people who do not know much about the Reserve Bank but are eager to understand how its policies affect them. Both those groups are my target readers. To paraphrase Einstein, I have tried to make the book as simple as possible, but no simpler.

It is customary for a preface to end with a vote of thanks. If I do so now, it is not so much to pay homage to a tradition but to acknowledge many people who encouraged and supported me in this project. First and foremost, my thanks to the NUS authorities for generously allowing me the time and space to write the book in the intellectually stimulating university environment. A special thanks to Dean Bernard Yeung at the business school who attached so much value to the scholarly pursuit of a book that he kindly agreed to free me of other obligations so that I could focus on writing.

I needed specific information on certain topics from the Reserve Bank. Deputy governors Harun Khan and R. Gandhi, under advice from Governor Raghuram Rajan, supplied me notes on such topics, always on the mutual understanding that the notes they gave me could be put out in the public domain. My sincere thanks go to them and their support staff who serviced me with the quiet efficiency that is the hallmark of the Reserve Bank. Susobhan Sinha, my former executive assistant at RBI, went way beyond the call of duty to act as an intermediary between me and the notes suppliers at the RBI, with his characteristic efficiency and energy that I have so taken for granted. Alpana Killawala, chief of the Reserve Bank's communications department, kindly provided me a CD of the press clippings which were of invaluable help in constructing the basic narrative on each topic.

Indira Rajaraman read through every chapter and Anantha Nageswaran through most chapters. I profited immensely from their insightful feedback and suggestions, and was deeply touched by their generosity, patience and enthusiasm. I owe them more than they realize.

At the Reserve Bank, Janak Raj and Muneesh Kapur peer-reviewed several chapters with the same diligence and critical eye as they would have were I still the serving governor. I was deeply touched by their earnestness and enthusiasm. Others at RBI, serving and retired, who provided me thoughtful inputs or reviewed one or more chapters were, in alphabetical order: Vivek Aggarwal, S.K. Bal, Surajit Bose, Madhumita Deb, Suddhasattwa Ghosh, Meena Hemachandra, Gunjeet Kaur, Grace Koshie, G. Mahalingam, A.K. Misra, Deepak Mohanty, Gopalraman Padmanabhan, Suman Ray, Mridul Saggar, Uma Shankar and Susobhan Sinha. Being thoroughbred Reserve Bank professionals, they did not endorse all of what I said or the way I said it. My apologies to all those who I may have inadvertently missed out, and my sincere thanks to them as well as to all those who helped from behind the scenes.

I felt free to use retired deputy governors of RBI—Shyamala Gopinath, Usha Thorat, Subir Gokarn and Anand Sinha—as my sounding board on a number of issues, and they indulged me as before with their wise counsel and advice. It felt very nostalgic.

Outside the Reserve Bank, those who reviewed one or more chapters and gave constructive feedback were, again in alphabetical order: Gita Bhat, Mythili Bhusnurmath, Kalpana Kochhar, K.P. Krishnan, Amitendu Palit, V.G.S. Rajan, Alok Sheel, Venky Venkatesan and Jumana Zahalka. My thanks to Rinisha Dutt for her research assistance.

The improvement from my first drafts to the final versions that you see owes to the comments and contributions of all the above reviewers. The standard caveat that I remain responsible for the final version applies.

I am grateful to the team at Penguin—Meru Gokhale, Ranjana Sengupta, V.C. Shanuj and Anushree Kaushal, and indeed all their teammates—for leading me through the mysterious realm of book publishing with passion and professionalism.

Many authors say that their families have been their harshest and also most helpful critics. I can now vouch for that. My wife, Urmila, sons, Mallik and Raghav, and daughters-in-law, Rachita and Aditi, who have grown to be more than the daughters we didn't have, have all been my most discerning and caring critics. Their love and care is my most prized blessing.

Introduction

'May You Live in Interesting Times'

11 October 2008, Washington DC

It was a cold, rainy, gloomy October evening when finance ministers and central bank governors from the G20 countries had assembled in HQ2 Conference Hall of the international Monetary Fund (IMF) office complex in downtown Washington DC. For sure, the ministers and governors had not travelled to Washington for this special meeting of the G20; they were already scheduled to be there for the annual meetings of the IMF and the World Bank over the weekend.

The G20 meeting was a last-minute add-on, convened at short notice, to discuss 'the probable negative impacts of the present acute global financial situation on world growth'. Given the uncertainty and turmoil of the preceding few weeks following the collapse of Lehman Brothers in mid-September, the anxiety of the finance policymakers to get together to exchange notes on what had happened and what would likely happen was understandable.

Brazil was the chair of the G20 in 2008. I received the meeting notice on 9 October, shortly before catching the overseas flight out of Mumbai. On the morning of the meeting, 11 October, when I was already in Washington, I got another mail from the G20 chair asking if I could be one of the two lead speakers in the second session of the meeting which would focus on the implications of the current turmoil for emerging markets. The Brazilian finance minister and the current chair of G20, Guido Mantega, much in the news in subsequent years for his strong position on the international currency wars, was the other lead speaker.

I was just over a month into my new job as governor of the Reserve Bank of India but I was not new to the IMF and World Bank meetings which are held twice a year—the spring meetings in April and the annual meetings in September or October. As a mid-level official in the finance ministry in the late '80s, it was my task to prepare briefs to the finance minister and the finance secretary who would go for these meetings. As finance secretary myself since early 2007, I had attended these meetings as a regular delegate. The G20 was a later innovation but I was a little familiar with the set-up, having attended a couple of G20 meetings earlier that year in my capacity as the finance secretary; however, those were meetings of deputies (finance secretaries and deputy governors). This meeting, of finance ministers and governors, was a notch higher in the hierarchy. It was also, in the words of the convenors, 'an extraordinary meeting to discuss an extraordinary situation'.

I was quite irritated by this late request to be a lead speaker. I was fatigued and jet-lagged, and my schedule for the day was clogged with meetings and appointments with a lot of stakeholders who typically gather in Washington during the week of these Fund–Bank meetings—possibly wanting to get a measure of this unknown guy who had landed up as the governor of RBI. With virtually little time and even less mind space to organize my thoughts, my first impulse was to decline the request. But then ego came in the way. I was, by all accounts, a greenhorn governor, unknown to most ministers and governors; yet they chose to ask me to give the Asian perspective on what was turning out to be a ferocious crisis. I had to take on the challenge! My experienced support staff, efficient as they always were, cancelled a couple of appointments to slot a half hour to tutor me for the meeting.

An Anxious G20

Since the mid-1990s, the biannual Fund–Bank meetings have also become a high-profile venue for protests spanning a wide array of disparate causes—repressive aid conditionalities, trade imperialism, climate change, gender discrimination, child labour, poor governance and corruption, as well as a host of other issues. Just as placards, slogans and hundreds of protestors from around the world have become a standard feature of these meetings, so has tight security, with the five or so city blocks that house the offices of the World Bank and the IMF cordoned off and several layers of security to ensure access only to authorized personnel. As a central bank governor, I enjoyed privileged security clearance; even so, going in and out was always quite a hassle and I tried to stay within the security cordon all through the business day.

It is standard practice during these international meetings for the Indian delegation to park themselves in the spacious office complex of India's executive director at the IMF which is located in the HQ1 building of the IMF. The G20 meeting venue was in the adjacent HQ2. In other times, my inclination would have been to walk across to the meeting but since that would involve moving in and out of security, my staff navigated me through the basement tunnel connecting the two buildings.

By the time I entered the meeting hall shortly before starting time, I was still unsure about whether I could weave a coherent narrative from my jumbled thoughts. The meeting was organized around a large quadrangular table with the finance ministers and governors of the G20 'troika' (Brazil, the current chair; South Africa, the chair of the previous year, 2007; and UK, the chair for the following year, 2009) seated on one side while the rest of us occupied the other three sides. The ministers and governors sat in the front row with two deputies per delegation in the back row. The managing director of the IMF, Dominique Strauss-Kahn, and the president of the World Bank, Robert Zoellick, and their support staff too were present. It was a fairly large meeting with about 125 of us in there. The atmosphere was decidedly sombre with the usual pre-meeting banter unusually low-key.

After a brief introduction by the chair, the meeting rolled on with Hank Paulson, the US treasury secretary, giving an account of the hectic activity during the week and the weekend prior to 16 September when Lehman Brothers filed for bankruptcy, setting off tumultuous developments in the global financial markets. Although Ben Bernanke, the chairman of the Federal Reserve, was not listed as a lead speaker, Paulson had yielded to him. In his professorial baritone, Bernanke gave an account of the unusual measures that the Federal Reserve had instituted to inject liquidity into the financial markets which had gone into seizure, and outlined the bespoke solutions they were contemplating for some of the stressed financial institutions. The mike then passed on to Jean-Claude Trichet, the president of the European Central Bank (ECB) who explained, in his graceful, French-accented English, how the European banks, with large exposures to the US sub-prime assets and their derivatives, had come under pressure, how the contagion was spreading across Europe and what the ECB was doing to cope with the evolving situation.

The anxiety in the room was palpable. Already a lot of hands had gone up to comment or ask questions, especially directed at the US, but the chair decided that we should go on with the emerging-market perspective before opening up for discussion. Minister Mantega is reasonably fluent in English, but I noticed, after seeing him in several international meetings in later years, that he prefers to speak in Portuguese wherein he comes off more articulate and decidedly more forceful. Quite predictably, his comment, as the lead speaker, centred on the paradoxical 'safe haven' effect—capital fleeing from emerging markets back into the US even as the US was the epicentre of the crisis—which was destabilizing emerging-market economies and complicating their macroeconomic management.

My turn to speak came shortly after 7 p.m., an hour into the meeting, as the earlier speakers had exceeded their time limits. I was going to make two points. First, that the impact of the unfolding crisis on emerging markets had been more severe than was understood or acknowledged internationally. The narrative that had taken shape over the past few years that emerging markets had decoupled from advanced economies— which is to say that even if advanced economies went into a downturn, emerging markets would not be adversely affected because of their robust foreign exchange reserves, resilient banks and sound macro fundamentals—had been dented by the developments over the past few weeks. Even though emerging-market financial institutions were not exposed to toxic assets, the contagion had spread to them through the interconnections in the financial system. Second, admittedly the market situation was uncertain and unpredictable for advanced economies. But it was even more so for emerging markets which had an additional layer of uncertainty because of not knowing the precise channels through which the contagion would hit them. I suggested that it was not enough that the advanced economies acted in coordination. They had to keep us too in the loop, and on the inner track, and keep our interest in view while shaping their policies.

The G20 delegations, except the 'troika', are typically seated in the alphabetic order of countries. As it happened, the India seat happened to be close to the door, at one edge of the rectangular table. Two minutes into my comments, the door opened, and a man walked in quietly, but with self-assurance, trailed by two burly grey-suited men of stern demeanour. I am sure they tried to be unobtrusive but I was nevertheless distracted by this shuffle so close to my seat and momentarily lost my flow of thought. It struck me that the 'intruder' looked a lot like President Bush. But there had been no indication that he would join us. Besides, how could the President of the United States, by far the most heavily guarded man in the world, walk into a meeting so casually? Wouldn't the famous secret service have subjected the whole building to a high-profile security quarantine before his arrival? Wouldn't there have been security details swarming around the premises since early afternoon?

By now, I was flustered, unsure whether I should just ignore what was happening and continue with my comments or wait until this disturbance had settled down. Although I was not completely sure if it was indeed Bush, by some unconscious instinct I stood up just as he passed behind me. Quite quickly, all the people in the room caught on and stood up too as President Bush walked past two sides of the quadrangle to get to the troika table. I soon realized that everyone at the meeting, including possibly Paulson and Bernanke, was surprised by Bush's unannounced entry.

Hastily, amid mild applause, they made space for him at the troika table, and also found a seat beside him for Secretary Paulson. There was a minute of whispering at the table, possibly briefing the President on what had transpired so far and inquiring if he would like to speak. But after a very brief apology for the interruption that he had caused, Bush requested that we continue from where we had left off.

So here I was, barely weeks into my new position as governor, speaking not just for India but for all emerging markets, telling the President of the US and his team of the obligations advanced economies, particularly the US, had towards emerging markets. I was quite satisfied with my intervention; I thought it came out quite cogently and effectively, given my limited experience and even more limited preparation.

President Bush then said that he had already been briefed about the US situation, but wanted to get a first-hand account of Europe. So the ECB president, Trichet, got an opportunity to repeat what he had said earlier.

Bush spoke after that. He spoke informally, but with self-assurance. I can't recall all of what he said but one point he made stayed in my mind. He reiterated his conviction that in the American system of free enterprise, markets should be unfettered and the federal government should intervene only when necessary. He said he had agonized quite a lot over the previous few weeks whether the nature and extent of government intervention in the financial markets was the right thing to do. But the precarious nature of the financial markets post-Lehman—and importantly, the impact of that on the daily lives of the American people—had led him to believe that such intervention was not only warranted but even essential. Echoing the approach taken by Franklin D. Roosevelt in the years following the Great Depression, he added that preserving the free market in the long run occasionally required government intervention in the short run. Finally, he added that he was confident that the ministers and governors gathered around the table were more than equal to the challenge of resolving the growing market turmoil.

Bush then looked at his watch, apologized once again for his unscheduled appearance, apologized also that he couldn't stay longer since he had promised 'Laura' that he would be back home for dinner. As he started walking back the way he entered, all of us stood up; he exchanged a few words with Trichet, said something to Bernanke and acknowledged a few others with a smile or a nod. As he passed behind me, he patted my shoulder and said something to the effect that he was impressed by what I had said and he would keep my points in view as they moved on.

~

Media Interaction

The next couple of days in Washington were a blur. I was flitting from meeting to meeting during the day. During much of the night, I was on the phone with senior management back at the RBI headquarters in Mumbai—they were apprising me of the situation and seeking my approval for some 'firefighting' actions, and I was telling them about the sense I was getting from these international meetings on the growing crisis and seeking their clarifications on the inputs from my meetings and interactions in Washington.

The Fund–Bank meetings traditionally attract media from all around the world, including newspapers, magazines, wire services, network and cable TV and radio. This time round, for obvious reasons, the media were around in significantly larger numbers. Several of them, both from the international media as well as the contingent that travelled from India, were chasing me. By now, I was acutely conscious that there was growing criticism in the media back home that the new governor was not communicating enough. Over the past couples of weeks, we had taken a host of measures to restore stability in the financial markets, including pumping in liquidity, which implied reversing the tightening monetary stance that I had inherited from governor Reddy. The media view was that if the situation was so urgent and grave as to warrant such a slew of forceful measures, including a regime change in monetary policy, that too outside of the regular policy schedule, then some communication from the governor beyond just the written statement was warranted.

It was clear to me that I had to speak soon, but I was not certain whether I should do so from Washington or wait until I returned home. After consulting Rakesh Mohan, deputy governor, who was also in Washington for the meetings, and Alpana Killawala, the Reserve Bank's competent and affable communications chief, I decided that the balance of advantage lay in meeting the media in Washington. Not only would it be sooner but we would also be reaching out to the international media.

One young rookie journalist who had travelled from India was calling my staff several times a day for an exclusive interview with me. My staff told her that I neither had the time nor the inclination for one-on-one interactions. As time went by, she became increasingly desperate. At some point, she called me directly, and on the verge of tears told me that her editor had sent her all the way to Washington on the condition that she would interview the new governor, and if she failed, it would dent her career prospects. Even as I sympathized with her, I could not oblige. Given all the pressures on my time, I found it difficult to accommodate her career prospects in my priorities. When I scheduled the media conference, I told my staff to make sure to invite her too.

At the media conference which lasted maybe about ten minutes, there were questions seeking explanation for the actions the Reserve Bank had taken, and I valued the opportunity of elaborating our stance. There were questions about why India was affected by the unfolding crisis; I had a reasonable explanation for it. The questions I found most difficult to address were those concerning the future—how would the situation evolve and what actions would we take? These were in the realm of speculation, there was too much uncertainty around the world and the gloomy G20 meeting the previous evening was very fresh in my mind. I found it hard to be definitive or forthright.

As an aside, I must add that the rookie journalist has since grown into a well-regarded and knowledgeable professional in her media house. Whenever she ran into me in the five years that I was in the Reserve Bank, she would thank me for her success, always leaving me feeling guilty about this undeserved gratitude.

Frankly, I was getting increasingly uncomfortable by the hour and was eager to be back in my office. I cut short my stay by a day and took the flight back to Mumbai.

'May You Live in Interesting Times'

The Chinese have a saying: 'May you live in interesting times.' I can't complain on that account. As governor of the Reserve Bank for five years, I had more, much more, than my share of interesting times. The crisis began days after I assumed office and continued in some form or other all through my tenure without even a week's respite. The most frequently asked question of me during those early months was about when the crisis would end. I used to joke that since the folklore was that the new governor was responsible for inflicting the crisis on India, it would be logical to expect it to end only when his tenure ended. For good measure, I used to tell them when my term would end.

Many will recall that the last few months of my tenure in 2013 were marked by the pressures on the rupee as part of the global taper tantrums. As it happened, the rupee stabilized the week after I left the RBI. If there was one prediction that I would have liked to be wrong on, it would have been this one on the crisis ending with my governorship. But that was not to be my legacy!

1

From Main Street to Mint Road

Appointment as Governor

As a career civil servant, my ambition had always been to become the Cabinet secretary to the Government of India, the highest civil service position in the country. This was within the realm of possibility too since both age and seniority at the top of my batch in the Indian Administrative Service (IAS) were on my side. A lot would, of course, depend on my performance evaluation which, in the civil service, is confidential, but I was confident that my ratings were generally above average. But one can never be sure of one's career trajectory in the civil service as appointments and placements are based on a number of factors, not all of them transparent or contestable.

I was transferred from the prime minister's Economic Advisory Council and posted as finance secretary to the Government of India in April 2007. By then, I was within striking range of the Cabinet secretary's job as the position was expected to open up well before my scheduled superannuation in August 2009. The reason for this long preface is only to say that the job of the governor of the Reserve Bank was not in my career calculus.

The term of Y.V. Reddy as governor of the Reserve Bank was going to end in early September 2008. The inevitable speculation about his putative successor started several months earlier, with economic journalists compiling their own panels of candidates and evaluating the strengths and weaknesses, as well as the chances of each candidate. The trick of the trade is to write authoritatively so as to give the impression of being on the inside track. There was talk too that Y.V. Reddy would be requested to continue for a year to allow the new government, post-election in mid-2009, to make a choice on the successor. Occasionally, my name too would appear on some journalist's panel, which meant nothing beyond inquiries from my friends and colleagues to ask if it was true, and if I had indeed been sounded for the job by the prime minister or the finance minister.

I found all the speculation about being a possible candidate for the governor's job either irritating or amusing depending on my mood. To be honest, the question of whether I had the profile and experience to be the governor would occasionally cross my mind. True, compared to many of my civil service colleagues, I had long experience in public finance management, both at the state and central government levels, if only because of accident and luck in postings. My CV was also burnished by international experience at the World Bank for over five years. But all this was mostly on the fiscal side—not the main focus of central banking. Because I thought there were others who fit the bill better, I was quite dismissive of all the kite-flying by the media.

I had known Rakesh Mohan, deputy governor in the Reserve Bank, for several years—which in itself should not be surprising if only because there are few people that Rakesh does not know. That acquaintance grew into a warm friendship over the previous year because of the regular professional interaction entailed by our respective jobs. Over this period, I had grown to respect Rakesh's intelligence, competence and maturity, and agreed with the widely shared view that he was a shoo-in for the governor's job. In an informal conversation, Y.V. Reddy once told me that it had been a standard convention for the government to consult the outgoing governor on the choice of his successor, and should that convention be followed, he would certainly recommend Rakesh's name.

On 24 August 2008, Rakesh who was in the United States, attending the annual Jackson Hole Conference of central banks, called me up to say that he had got a call from the finance minister's office asking him to come and meet the minister in Delhi later that week. He asked me if I knew what it was about. I didn't, but my hunch was that P. Chidambaram was calling Rakesh to personally convey his appointment as governor before releasing the public announcement. I was quite pleased about this prospective development, since like Y.V. Reddy, my choice for governor too would have been Rakesh. Besides, I had built a comfortable professional relationship with him, which meant that we would be able to handle the inevitable differences between the government and the RBI in an objective and agreeable manner.

~

Interview for the Job of Governor

Finance Minister Chidambaram was usually the first one to check into North Block, the imposing building on Rajpath that houses the ministry of finance, every workday morning. After a few months of working with him, I realized that this early-morning slot was the best time to touch base with him if I had to discuss any urgent issue before the day's schedule engulfed both of us.

So it was that on Tuesday, 26 August, I had gone to catch the finance minister during this short morning window mainly

to tell him that I would be leaving that night for Brazil to attend
the G20 Deputies meeting. As my minister, Chidambaram had
approved my foreign travel, but that was some time ago and the
exact dates of my absence from office may not have stayed in his
mind. In particular, I needed to check if he wanted me to attend
to anything before I left.

My hunch was right as he went into some silent calculation
when I told him about my trip. He asked when I would be back
and when that date registered on his mind, he paused briefly
and asked me if I would be interested in being considered for
the governor's job. Frankly, I was surprised. Notwithstanding all
the media speculation, I thought that the prime minister and
Chidambaram had decided on Rakesh as the next governor. Even
before I replied, he offered that I could think about it and let him
have my answer by lunchtime.

Being the governor of the Reserve Bank would, of course,
be a great honour and privilege, an exciting opportunity to steer
the macroeconomic management of the country. There was
hardly any need to think through further; the decision seemed
straightforward. I immediately thanked Chidambaram for
putting my name on the shortlist and requested him to take
my candidature forward. I don't think he was surprised by my
enthusiastic response but added for good measure that the prime
minister wanted him to explicitly check with me since I was in
line to be the next Cabinet secretary.

With the big issue settled, we quickly moved into settling
the logistics. He asked me what time my flight was, which
unsurprisingly for a West-bound international flight out of India
was in the middle of the night. 'Could you then,' he asked, 'come
to my house at 8 p.m. for a chat with Dr Rangarajan and myself?
Rakesh is coming in at 7 p.m.' Dr C. Rangarajan is a former RBI
governor and at that time was chairman of the prime minister's
Economic Advisory Council.

I had a heavy schedule for the day stretching late into the evening, including a briefing session on the forthcoming G20 meeting agenda with my staff. On top of that, I now had to make space for this interview. I called up Urmila, my wife, and told her. Her reaction was typically nonchalant. 'If that's what you want, I wish you all the best.' Her only advice was that I call up Rakesh and level with him on this development. I could not reach him all through the day.

Several times during the day, it did cross my mind if I was being interviewed as a pro forma candidate just to build up the paperwork to show that the government did indeed consider a panel of candidates before making a final choice. That would be handy if the decision came under the scrutiny of any of the watchdogs, including the media. But I dismissed the thought because Chidambaram was too professional to do something like that. Besides, in the course of the day, I was not handed any formal notice of interview; no paper trail was being established.

By the time I showed up for the 'interview' at Chidambaram's house, I was exhausted but neither anxious nor tense. Coincidentally, the interviewers were my former boss in the prime minister's Economic Advisory Council, Rangarajan, and my current boss, the finance minister—two people who could evaluate my professional competence and personality traits even without an interview. In the event, the interview turned out to be a relaxed, informal discussion on a few professional topics. I can still recall a couple of issues that came up.

Chidambaram asked if I would back the idea of a Monetary Policy Committee (MPC) to decide on the Reserve Bank's monetary policy, thereby replacing the present arrangement where the governor makes the final call. Given the ongoing debate on constituting an MPC, this was prescient. We discussed the pattern in advanced countries, including the Federal Open Markets Committee in the US, the MPCs of the Bank of England (BoE) and the Bank of Japan (BoJ), and even the opaque system of the People's Bank of China. My substantive stance was that an MPC was the direction in which we must go but that the governor must have a veto, at least during the transition period until the institutional structure stabilized.

Chidambaram did not agree. His point was that the governor should see himself as the chairman of a corporate board and try to persuade the MPC members to his point of view. And if he failed to do that, he should defer to the majority view. I agreed with him but countered that the parallel with a corporate board would work only if the members of the MPC did not owe any allegiance to the government for their appointment. They might, given the institutional structures of our system, feel pressured to push the government's point of view in the MPC.

Another topic we discussed at length during the interview was bank branch delicensing. Under the regulation prevailing then, if a bank wanted to open a new branch at some place, it had to get a specific licence for that location from the Reserve Bank. Left to themselves, banks would prefer to expand in urban areas where the business is attractive, and tend to neglect rural areas. The Reserve Bank used the leverage of licensing to push banks to spread into rural areas.

I had first-hand exposure to this issue from my field postings in the early phases of my civil service career. We were handicapped in providing opportunities to the poor to improve their livelihoods because there were no banks to extend credit support. I was unfamiliar though with the pros and cons of the issue at the policy level, since banking policy issues in the ministry of finance were in the charge of the Department of Financial Services whereas, as finance secretary, I was in charge of the Department of Economic Affairs.

As the discussion rolled on, we realized that all three of us were on the same page—of balancing the efficiency of a laissez-faire regime with the equity-enhancing licensing regime. The challenge of managing the tension was most acute for Chidambaram who had to balance his reformist instinct to dismantle the licensing regime with his compulsions, as a politician, to deepen bank penetration. I would recall this conversation several times in later years as the Reserve Bank, on my watch, moved quite a distance towards bank branch delicensing.

It was well past 9 p.m. by the time the conversation ended. Chidambaram walked me to the car parked in the drive of his house and wished me a safe flight. I was touched by this gesture as few ministers would extend such courtesy when their staff came to see them at home, but then I had always known that Chidambaram was way more courteous than he is given credit for. Of course, he can't suffer fools, but that is a different matter.

At any other time, I would have rehashed the interview in my mind, thinking through where I could have put across my views better or argued more coherently. But just then, I was too preoccupied with more immediate concerns, like getting ready for the journey and all the preparation I still needed to do for the G20 meeting.

As I was driving home, I got Rakesh on the line at last and told him about my 'interview'. He was not aware that I too had been invited to an interview, and frankly, was quite flustered when I gave him the news. I got home, scurrying to pack, bathe and eat, and set off for the airport. In the middle of all this, Rakesh called back to let me know how touched he was that I levelled with him, and both of us acknowledged, in unspoken words, that no matter what the final decision, it would not affect our friendship. I was deeply comforted after connecting with Rakesh, for if I had not, it would have haunted my mind all through the trip.

My mind automatically switched off from all this as I boarded the plane for Frankfurt on my way to Rio de Janeiro.

Appointment as Governor

As my plane landed in Delhi in the early morning of 2 September, my phone started beeping incessantly with an unusual flood of messages. I was confused about the congratulations since not one of them contained any clue. I called Urmila who gave me the news of my appointment as governor and did not miss out on complaining that the previous evening she had done nothing but field phone calls from literally hundreds of people, many of them not even known to us.

~

I would be the twenty-second governor of the Reserve Bank in its seventy-three-year history—the eleventh bureaucrat to don the governor's mantle. Finance secretaries had become governors in the past too, but I would be the first finance sectary to go directly from the North Block to Mint Street without a gap in between. I would also be the first governor of the Reserve Bank born after Independence.

The news was expectedly all over the TV and print media over the next couple of days, instantly turning me from an unknown unknown to a known unknown. There was coverage of my background and career trajectory, and also extensive commentary on my reform credentials and policy biases.

In over one year as finance secretary, I had occasion to make a few statements on inflation, financial sector reforms and capital-account liberalization. At the time I made these comments, they passed off as relatively innocuous items, but now analysts, columnists and economic journalists were digging them up to evaluate my potential policy stance as the prospective governor.

Opinion and commentary were varied. Some said I would continue with Y.V. Reddy's hawkish monetary-policy stance, while others said that I would be more biased towards growth and would be of a more dovish disposition. Some said I would accelerate the financial market reforms laid out in the Percy Mistry, Deepak Parikh and Raghuram Rajan committee reports, and some others thought I would be more cautious in moving forward with reforms. Similarly, there was much speculation about my stance on exchange rate issues and balance of payments. There were questions about whether, as governor, I would fulfil my dharma of countering fiscal profligacy for which I was—some said—'at least partly responsible'. All of this amused me since this was at best informed speculation passing off as authoritative commentary. The biggest takeaway for me from all this was that there was a lot riding on the governor's policy stance and world view.

And there was advice aplenty, predictably from both ends of the ideological spectrum: slay inflation with all the policy force at the Reserve Bank's command vs recognize the paramount importance of supporting growth at a time of business-cycle downturn; leave the exchange rate to the dynamics of the market vs you can't afford to abandon the exchange rate to the vagaries of the market; open up the capital account with blitzkrieg reforms vs beware of the pitfalls of hasty capital-account liberalization; invite foreign banks with open arms vs keep in mind the sorry experience of other emerging markets which had embraced foreign banks prematurely; implement financial sector reforms with alacrity vs focus on the macroeconomy and let reforms wait.

There was the expected and predictable debate on the advisability of appointing civil servants as governors. Some thought that tried-and-tested civil servants can bring fresh thinking into what is considered to be an insular institution: an outsider like me would add value to the Reserve Bank and shake the institution out of its 'status quo'. The opposing view was that I did not have any central banking experience and this would be a handicap in providing leadership to the RBI.

There was quite a bit of commentary on what a direct transition from North Block to Mint Street would entail. Y.V. Reddy, my predecessor, had a formidable reputation for standing his ground with the government. The commentariat said that my familiarity with, and sympathy for, the government's point of view would help repair that strained relationship between the ministry of finance and the Reserve Bank. Others thought that my allegiance to the ministry of finance would make me more pliable and I would dilute the independence of the Reserve Bank. Some even suggested that I was being dispatched to implement the government's agenda from within the Reserve Bank.

The media commentary was par for the course and a pointer to the expectations and demands of the job I was getting into. The only bit that troubled me was doubts about my credentials and the suspicion that I would compromise the autonomy of the Reserve Bank. I was aware too that the only way I could counter those doubts and suspicions, and establish my credibility, was by demonstrating my professional integrity in all that I said and did, which would inevitably take time. I had no option but to be patient.

My immediate concern, where I did not have the luxury of time, was to establish my credentials with my staff in the Reserve Bank, as their trust and support would be critical to my performance and effectiveness. More than any other constituency, I had to convince them as soon as possible that all my decisions as governor would be informed by nothing but larger public interest. This would be a daunting addition to my already long list of formidable challenges on the way forward.

Transition from Delhi to Mumbai

I had barely two days to prepare—physically, mentally and emotionally—for this most unexpected turn in my career. I met the finance minister and thanked him for selecting me for this responsible and prestigious position. I called on the prime minister and the conversation went along predictable lines about how he reposed confidence in me and of all the challenges that the government and the Reserve Bank had to jointly address. The prime minster also encouraged me to brief him on the macroeconomic situation regularly, and added for good measure, 'I will always make time for you.' As I look back, I can say that the prime minister stood by his word. Not only did he always give me time no matter how pressing his schedule or the preoccupations on his mind, but he also seemed to enjoy those meetings.

There was also a strange irony in my appointment as governor. I say this more from hearsay and my own inferences rather than any hard evidence. A year and a half earlier when I was being considered for the position of finance secretary, Chidambaram did not know me and was understandably circumspect about taking me into his team. I gathered that Prime Minister Manmohan Singh, who was acquainted with me from my earlier posting in the ministry of finance in the early '90s, had to nudge him into it. And now when it came to my appointment as governor, I understand it was Chidambaram who was more actively sponsoring my candidature and it was the prime minister who had to be nudged.

I was touched by the farewell given to me by my colleagues and staff in the DEA. The DEA attracts some of the best civil service talent in the country, and over the previous year and a half, I had built valuable professional relationships and personal friendships. Together, we had launched many initiatives and several were still works in progress. They were proud that one of their own was going as governor, and I was sad to break these bonds, and apprehensive about jumping from the comfort and familiarity of the known to the fear and uncertainty of the unknown.

In the middle of the logistic nightmare of the transition that I was muddling through, Y.V. Reddy, who was also from the IAS, called me up from Mumbai to advise that I should seek voluntary retirement from the IAS before assuming office as governor. At the time, I was fifty-nine and still a year away from superannuation. Reddy's logic was that I should unequivocally be covered by the code of conduct prescribed for the governor which may be at variance with the IAS code of conduct. When I checked, I was informed by the 'rules people' not to bother since I would be deemed to have retired from the IAS as soon as I assumed office as governor. Never in the thirty-five years of my IAS career did I imagine that I would sever links with the civil service, which nurtured and defined me all through my adult life, so nonchalantly.

On 5 September 2008, I took an early-morning Air India flight from Delhi to Mumbai, a two-hour journey that would mark by far the most significant transition of my career. Even as I was drained—physically, mentally and emotionally—I couldn't keep my mind away from the potential challenges and concerns about how I might perform as the governor of the Reserve Bank of India.

2

Baptism by Fire

Battling the Global Financial Crisis

When I assumed office as governor on 5 September 2008, the dominant concern of the Reserve Bank was decidedly the persistently high inflation. In fact, the only thing I could think of saying when I was ushered in front of the media for a sound bite minutes after signing on as the governor, was that reining in inflation and anchoring inflation expectations would be my top priority. Little did I know that my top priority would change in such a dramatic way in less than a fortnight.

The advance tremors of the global financial crisis started going off in the week following my joining the Reserve Bank, sending tectonic shocks across financial markets around the world. Every day there was news of some storied financial institution crumbling under pressure. In the space of just a few days, Fannie Mae and Freddie Mac went into conservatorship; Merrill Lynch had vanished; Washington Mutual was closed down by the regulators; Wachovia was sinking, and AIG was on the brink of a meltdown. Finally, on 16 September, the big bang—Lehman Brothers collapsed, plunging the global financial sector into a near-death experience.

Quite unsuspecting of the oncoming tumult, my staff had scheduled a series of briefing meetings for me over the first two weeks to 'induct' the new governor into the world and work of the Reserve Bank. The shock and awe following the collapse of Lehman Brothers denied me the luxury of learning systematically and at my own pace. It was baptism by fire.

Reserve Bank's Immediate Response

The Reserve Bank swung into a crisis-management mode with energy, intelligence and briskness. I was impressed by the rich expertise and mature understanding of the senior management of the Reserve Bank, which was clearly evident in the way they advised me on where pressures might erupt and what our priorities should be. Within hours of Lehman Brothers filing for bankruptcy, we had issued a press release, saying: 'The Reserve Bank is keeping a close watch on the developments in the financial markets and is in touch with banks and other market participants to manage in an orderly manner any fall-out of these developments on the Indian financial markets.' With characteristic alacrity, the Reserve Bank ring-fenced the operations of both the Lehman subsidiaries in India—Lehman Brothers Capital Pvt. Ltd, a non-banking financial company (NBFC), and Lehman Brothers Fixed Income Securities Pvt. Ltd, a primary dealer—restricting their operations and prohibiting them from making foreign remittances.

Around the world, fear and panic gripped financial markets; virtually every big-name institution was engulfed by rumours of imminent collapse. Trust had dried up, banks were hoarding liquidity, and trading came to a near-complete stop. We anticipated panic in our financial markets too, mainly because of the fear of the unknown. The standard first aid a central bank administers when markets are unnerved is to shore up liquidity. So was the case in India, as on that very day, we instituted a slew of measures to ease liquidity both in the money and forex markets.

The Contagion

Over the following days and weeks, the global financial markets remained on the boil, and markets at home reeled under the onslaught of the global tremors as the contagion spread through three channels—the finance channel, the real economy channel, and importantly, as happens in all financial crises, the confidence channel.

The contagion through the finance channel was, by far, the most perceptible as external developments fed on our domestic vulnerabilities through complex and pernicious feedback loops. All our financial markets—equity market, bond market, money market, credit market and forex market—were rattled by the global developments.

The benchmark equity index, the Sensex, collapsed by over a quarter from 13,518 on 16 September to 9647 by end December 2008. The call rate in the money market zoomed by over 5 percentage points from 13.1 per cent on 16 September to a high of 18.5 per cent on 10 October, reflecting market fear and uncertainty. A complex, cascading knock-on impact played out, squeezing the money and credit markets. Edged out of foreign markets, corporates started turning to domestic banks for their credit needs even as the banks themselves were in the midst of a huge funding uncertainty. Simultaneously, corporates also started withdrawing their investments from domestic money market mutual funds; money market mutual funds, in turn, started withdrawing their investments from NBFCs; and NBFCs, reeling under the funding pressure, turned to banks, exacerbating, in the process, the stress on banks which were already struggling to cope with the additional credit demand from the corporates.

The forex market pressure reflected two main developments. First, foreign institutional investors (FIIs), who had put billions of dollars into our equity and debt markets in the pre-crisis years, started withdrawing their investments as part of the global deleveraging process. Second, as external financing dried up, Indian corporates raised funds locally and began converting those into foreign currency to meet their external obligations. The exchange rate plunged as a result, falling from ₹46.63 to a dollar on 16 September, to a low of ₹50.52 on 2 December 2008, despite the Reserve Bank's almost regular intervention in the forex market.

Since forex intervention by the Reserve Bank when the rupee is under downward pressure involves selling dollars for rupees, an incidental by-product of our forex-market intervention was that we were squeezing rupees out of the system, and thereby exacerbating the pressure on domestic liquidity. On the balance of payments front, we were also worried about a potential sharp drop in remittances from non-resident Indians (NRIs) located in advanced economies which were sinking into deeper recession and in the Gulf countries which were wobbling from a steep drop in oil prices.

The contagion of the crisis through the real channel, which manifested mainly in the form of a slump in demand for exports, was more prolonged and painful. The United States, the European Union and the Middle East, which together accounted for three quarters of India's foreign trade, were in a synchronized downturn. Not just goods export, but even services export growth started slowing as overseas financial services firms—traditionally large users of outsourcing services—were downsizing.

Beyond the finance and real economy channels, the crisis spread through the confidence channel. For sure, even at the height of the crisis, Indian financial markets continued to function in a fairly orderly manner; also, our banks continued to lend. However, the tightened global liquidity situation in the period immediately following the Lehman collapse came on top of a turn in the domestic credit cycle which heightened risk aversion, making banks wary and cautious about lending.

Crisis Management

In terms of crisis management, our strategy in the Reserve Bank was to focus on the finance and real economy channels on the calculation that if we kept the domestic financial markets functioning normally and ensured that the liquidity stress did not set off solvency cascades, confidence would automatically return to the financial markets. This translated into targeting three objectives: first, make the system flush with rupee liquidity; second, augment foreign-exchange liquidity; and third, drive a policy framework aimed at keeping credit delivery on track and arresting moderation in growth.

It is standard practice for central banks to impound a prescribed proportion of commercial banks' net time and demand liabilities (NDTL), called 'reserve requirement', as an instrument of monetary policy; but this also doubles as a safety deposit that a bank can draw upon to meet any sudden and unexpected liquidity crunch. In India, we call this the 'cash reserve ratio' (CRR). In addition to the CRR, the Reserve Bank also requires commercial banks to invest a minimum proportion of their NDTL, called the 'statutory liquidity ratio' (SLR), in government securities. We were anxious that banks should not pull back on credit flow which meant that we had to put more money in their hands. To do so, we reduced both the CRR and the SLR. To further encourage flow of credit to what we thought were stressed sectors, we extended regulatory forbearance to banks by relaxing the risk weights and provisioning norms governing bank loans to the stressed sectors. This meant I was partly reversing the countercyclical measures instituted by my predecessor, Y.V. Reddy, to restrain risky lending during the 'subprime' years.

On the forex side, we had to offset the pull-out by the FIIs by encouraging inflows of other types. Towards this end, we raised the cap on the interest rate that banks could offer to foreign-currency deposits by NRIs, substantially relaxed the norms for external commercial borrowing by corporates and allowed NBFCs and housing finance companies to access foreign borrowing. To mitigate the dent on export prospects, we extended the period of pre-shipment and post-shipment credit, and expanded the refinance facility for exports.

I announced the first interest rate cut on 20 October 2008, just a month after the Lehman collapse, reducing the policy repo rate—the rate at which commercial banks borrow overnight from the Reserve Bank—from 9 per cent to 8 per cent. The significance of this move becomes clear if you note that Y.V. Reddy had actually raised the rate as late as July in response to rising inflation. And here I was, reversing the policy stance and cutting the rate in less than three months' time, signalling that financial stability had overtaken inflation as the overriding concern. True, we had cut the CRR and SLR in the past month, and these were technically monetary-easing measures. But given the extraordinary financial market situation, they were interpreted by the markets, and correctly so, as pure liquidity-easing measures without a link to the monetary policy stance. A rate cut, on the other hand, was a decisive shift in the policy regime.

Within the Reserve Bank itself, opinion within the top management was divided on the rate cut. The majority view among my top advisers was that a rate cut was uncalled for and that we could ride out the crisis without a change in the monetary policy regime. However, I agreed with and accepted the minority view that the uncertainty and unpredictability in the markets was choking credit flow and that more than the rate cut itself, the fact that we were reversing the monetary policy regime would send a strong signal to the markets about the Reserve Bank's resolve to preserve financial stability, restore market confidence and improve credit flow.

The markets generally welcomed the rate cut, and analysts endorsed it as being consistent with our earlier liquidity-easing measures. But there was criticism in certain quarters both for its timing—just four days before a scheduled policy review—and for the way we nuanced the policy rationale by emphasizing financial stability more than growth and inflation.

I could see where the critics were coming from but could not agree with them. Sure, making a major policy shift just four days before a scheduled policy review was an unusual decision, but then we were handling an unusual situation, and my honest judgement was that waiting for another four days would be costly at a time when the markets were gripped by uncertainty and fear about developments in advanced economies. Besides, we also calculated that in the prevailing global context, the signalling impact of an unscheduled policy announcement would be substantial. Similarly, the relative de-emphasis on growth and inflation concerns in explaining the policy rationale was deliberate inasmuch as the motive for the unscheduled and hurried action derived from preserving financial stability.

Why did our critics not see it the way we did? There is always an information asymmetry between a regulator and the regulated institutions, and even more so between a central bank and the external world of analysts and markets. In the prevailing situation, there was more than the usual share of it. From within the Reserve Bank, we were getting a lot of information on the inside track. Also, my exposure to the Washington IMF and G20 meetings had given me a keener, if also a more disturbing, perception of the uncertainty and turmoil in the global economy and finance, an appreciation that differed from that of our external interlocutors.

Global Coordination and Consultation

There was no let-up in the financial market uncertainty and global economic convulsions up until December 2008. The international media ran saturated coverage of the crisis, and reams were being written on its diagnosis and prognosis; analysts were busy critiquing policy responses and offering their own advice on what should and should not be done by policymakers. This advice spanned a wide spectrum of issues—stabilizing the markets, arresting the economic downturn, coordinated fiscal stimulus, infusing capital into banks, disciplining shadow banks, punishing guilty banks and bankers, and international cooperation, just to name a few. As someone said, in an otherwise no-growth world, the only growth to be seen during this period was in the output by economists, analysts and financial sector commentators.

The crisis tested the leadership mettle of central bank governors. Even big-name governors were struggling to cope with the challenge of the biggest financial crisis since the Great Depression. For me, there was additional pressure as I was called upon to perform on the big stage even before I had time to establish my credentials and before the market had time to size me up. I was aware that the markets were struggling to interpret my actions and words. And what with all the speculation surrounding my appointment about whether I would act at the government's bidding, I also had to endure intense scrutiny for acting independently.

If advanced economy central banks were shaken by the ferocity and unpredictability of the crisis, for us in emerging markets, it was a double whammy since we had to factor in not only the uncertainty of the global market developments, but also the uncertainty of how the policy responses of advanced economies would impact our economies and our markets.

Understandably, there was greater interaction among central bank governors during the crisis than during normal times. Recall that in my intervention in the G20 meeting in October 2008, I had urged the advanced economies to keep the emerging-market central banks in the loop on financial market developments as they view them as also on their proposed policy responses. Either because of that, or more likely quite apart from that, there was regular briefing to some of us in the emerging markets—China, India, Brazil, Argentina, Mexico, Turkey, South Africa—by the US Treasury, the Federal Reserve and the European Central Bank (ECB). These would typically happen on a conference call but on occasion also be one-on-one.

Even more useful in this anxious period—when fear mounted, prices plunged and markets froze—were the Bank for International Settlements (BIS) bimonthly meetings of governors in Basel, which provided a forum for both structured and informal exchange of views among the governors. Given the centrality of America to the origin of the crisis and to its resolution, the highlight of these meetings invariably was the briefing by Bernanke, the Fed chairman. But there would also be a lot of interest in what Zhou Xiaochuan, the governor of the People's Bank of China, had to say—a sign not just of China's growing clout in the global economy, but also of how important China's prospects were to leading the world out of the Great Recession. There used to be active interest on the situation in India too, in part because we are a large economy and how India fared mattered to the world economy; moreover, some of the macroeconomic developments in India were contrarian to the global trends.

Unconventional Monetary Policy

Advanced economy central banks were stretched in terms of policy response to the crisis. The standard and conventional instrument available to central banks is the policy interest rate. Once they have brought that down to zero and find that the markets are still choked, what else can they do? They wade into unconventional policy, which is what they did by embarking on quantitative easing (QE)—large-scale asset purchases to flood the system with liquidity with the aim of repairing broken financial markets and stimulating their economies.

An interesting question was whether we, in the Reserve Bank, too were required to resort to unconventional measures. True, our policy rate, at 3.25 per cent, the lowest we had reached in the crisis, was still way above zero, but given our inflation rate, this was virtually the zero lower bound for us with not much room for further cuts. However, given the stress, and even more so a perception of stress, in segments of the financial markets, we too instituted our own version of unconventional measures. We opened a rupee–dollar swap facility for Indian banks to help them meet any shortfall in foreign funding requirement; we expanded the lendable resources available to apex financial institutors like the Small Industries Development Bank of India (SIDBI), the Export–Import Bank of India (Exim) and the National Housing Bank (NHB) so as to expand the flow of credit to productive sectors. We established dedicated lines of credit for augmenting the liquidity of NBFCs and mutual funds to provide them the cash they needed to pay off their investors.

We didn't exactly throw the rulebook out the window, but had to be quite inventive in invoking little-used provisions to stitch up bespoke solutions.

~

As the global markets remained on the brink all through the last quarter of 2008, there would be constant news from all around the world of banks failing, and pictures in the media of long lines of people outside banks waiting to empty out their savings and investments for fear that their bank was going bust. That nervousness would occasionally have a knock-on impact on India with ominous stories appearing in our media about a run on the branches of some banks in some city or some large NBFC collapsing. In the event, and to our great relief, these turned out to be false alarms.

Compounding our anxiety in those dreary months were the dastardly terrorist attacks in Mumbai on 26 November 2008. Mumbai shut down, but the world around us did not. Even as the security forces were battling the terrorists, and the police were engaged in arresting fear and panic from spreading, some of us, the senior management of the Reserve Bank and essential staff, were back in the office ensuring that we were in readiness to react and respond to both domestic and external developments. Brainstorming meetings on the eighteenth floor of the Reserve Bank central office in the Fort area of Mumbai, even as we could look out of the window and see the onion dome of the iconic Taj Mahal Palace hotel in Colaba belching out smoke, will forever remain etched in my memory as a reminder of that gloomy period.

We were anxious that there should be no contagion from the terrorist attack to the financial system. The payment and settlement system, which enables settlement of financial transactions, is the plumbing of the financial system. If it breaks down, it would cripple the financial sector, bring commercial activity to a standstill and sap public confidence. The potential for panic was frightening. A lot of experts, in fact, claim that during the early weeks of the global financial crisis when markets were seized with deep anxiety and fear, what prevented a total collapse was that even as everything around was breaking down, the global payment systems held up. Quite understandably, this was our top concern in the wake of the terrorist attack. That we were able to recommence the two large payment and settlement systems—the Real Time Gross Settlement (RTGS), National Electronic Funds Transfer (NEFT)—on 27 November, just a day after the attack, is a tribute to the commitment of the Reserve Bank staff and a testimonial to the robustness of our technological systems.

Chidambaram was on the phone several times asking when we could reopen the markets. He was particular that we must demonstrate to the world that India would not be cowed down by terrorists and that our financial markets were too resilient to be hit by anyone. I consulted Chandu Bhave, chairman of the Securities and Exchange Board of India (SEBI), which regulates the equity markets. We agreed that we must open our markets as soon as possible and do so simultaneously. By 28 November, within two days of the attack, we reopened government securities, foreign exchange, money and stock markets, and clearing houses returned to normal functioning. I must admit that Chidambaram's pressure was the motive force behind our sense of urgency and alacrity.

~

By December 2008, I had brought down the policy rate from 9 per cent to 5 per cent, in effect reversing in just three months the policy rate hike that took five years on the way up. In fact, I cut rates so regularly during this period that I was rapidly coming to be seen as a trigger-happy governor. At the launch of Rakesh Mohan's book in Delhi in February 2009, I alluded to my predicament with one of my famous hair jokes. This is what I said:

'The other day, when I was in Hyderabad, I went to my regular barber for a haircut. In the inevitable barber–client conversation, it was our practice to talk about his children, my children, local politics and Bollywood. But this time round he was seeing me for the first time after I became governor. Even as he was preparing to apply scissors to my hair, he asked, "When are you going to cut interest rates?" I was exasperated by even my barber not giving me any respite from interest rates. Clearly wanting to take my mind off stressful issues, I tried to divert the topic. But he seemed bent on dispensing wisdom and persisted with the banter on interest rates. I got irritated and snapped at him, "What do you know about interest rates and how does it matter to you at all? Why don't you just leave me alone?" He smiled and said, "I don't know much about interest rates, but I do know that if I talk about them, your hair will rise and it will be easier to cut it.'"

Government and the Reserve Bank during the Crisis

In mid-October 2008, even as the Reserve Bank was dousing the system with rupee and forex liquidity, Finance Minister Chidambaram had *suo moto* constituted a committee on liquidity management, with Finance Secretary Arun Ramanathan as the chairman. The Reserve Bank was asked to nominate a representative on the committee. I was annoyed and upset by this decision. Chidambaram had clearly overstepped into the RBI turf as liquidity management is a quintessential central bank function. Not only did he not consult me, but he had not even informed me of this before the notification was issued. Coming as it did amidst a lot of suspicion in those early weeks of my tenure that I was a government lackey sent to the Reserve Bank to act at the government's bidding, the constitution of this committee only reinforced the view.

I called up Chidambaram and let him know in unequivocal terms that his action was totally inappropriate, and requested firmly that he dissolve the committee. His argument was that when liquidity management was such a central concern, getting advice from external market participants would help us understand and respond to the ground reality in the market faster and better. I granted that, but if he wanted external experience to be tapped, he could have advised me informally to constitute such a committee rather than taking the Reserve Bank for granted. The call ended with my telling him that the Reserve Bank would not participate in the committee. This skirmish with Chidambaram, who I believed pushed my candidature for the governor's job, so early in my tenure upset me a lot. Little did I know that this set the tone for what would be an uneasy relationship between us in the last year of my term.

~

The prime minister also held several informal discussions during these months and his office was invariably kind enough to schedule these meetings to suit my convenience. Most of these would be informal, involving just the finance minister and me, and occasionally, the finance secretary; a few times, the chairman of the Economic Advisory Council, Rangarajan, and Planning Commission Deputy Chairman Montek Singh Ahluwalia were also present. I was aware that such frequent meetings at the prime minister's level were unusual and were occasioned entirely by the crisis.

In general, Chidambaram believed that the crisis demanded more aggressive easing both on the policy rate and liquidity than I was comfortable with. At these meetings, he would try and pin me down to specific actions and time frame. I would go as far as indicating the general direction in which I would go but refused to get committed to any specifics. There were no overt arguments between us, but it was clear that Chidambaram was annoyed that I was not moving as aggressively as he would have liked me to. Our relationship remained frosty.

There was one particular meeting sometime in late November 2008, larger and more formal than usual, chaired by the prime minister and also involving a dozen Cabinet ministers and secretaries to the government. The agenda was to discuss the government's response to the crisis, and I too was invited. By then, Chidambaram had moved from finance to home ministry, a transfer occasioned by the terrorist attacks in Mumbai, but he was also invited to the meeting to get the benefit of his advice.

The meeting kept clear of monetary or regulatory issues, but several ministers and secretaries took advantage of my presence and the pressure of the crisis to ask that the Reserve Bank open money spigots for all sorts of sectors and schemes, much of which had no relevance to fighting the crisis. I was amused by this attempt to use the crisis as a cover to get the Reserve Bank to relax its norms and support proposals that it had consistently resisted.

In some sense, this was vigorous democracy at play and, in fact, mirrored what was happening in another big democracy, the US. There were headline media reports on how US lawmakers were playing pork-barrel politics while debating their President's fiscal package in the Congress. They were tearing apart the package to include their own pet schemes to serve narrow constituency interests as a precondition for their support, never mind that all the pork barrelling may have compromised the basic thrust of the scheme of boosting consumer demand.

I had to say no to almost all of these proposals even as I found it difficult to disagree with friends and colleagues who were all well intentioned, but not necessarily well informed on what the Reserve Bank can or cannot do. When the meeting concluded well past 10 p.m., and all of us stood up waiting for the prime minister to leave, I recall the prime minister coming around to me, silently patting me on the back and then exiting. Vini Mahajan, joint secretary in the prime minister's office, one of my friends and well-wishers, told me as we were all walking out of the meeting that such demonstrative behaviour on the part of the prime minister was uncharacteristic and uncommon. I was deeply touched by the prime minister's gesture, which I realized was both an act of commiseration with my plight and an endorsement of my firm stand.

~

Criticism against the Reserve Bank

There was broad endorsement in the media of the Reserve Bank's policy response to the crisis although there were some outliers—some saying that the Reserve Bank was doing too much by way of crisis management and others saying that we were doing too little.

In all of this, there were two strands of criticism from the commentariat during those early months which had disturbed me. The first was that I was compromising the Reserve Bank's already fragile autonomy by allowing the government to dictate policy, confirming what some people suspected at the time of my appointment. The second criticism was that the Reserve Bank remained largely uncommunicative even as it was hyperactive on the policy front. The general refrain was that the Reserve Bank's silence was jarring, especially when set against the flurry of comments from almost everyone in Delhi—whether on the inside track or not—about what *should* be done and what *would* be done by way of policy response to the crisis.

There was not much I could do about the criticism on diluting the Reserve Bank's autonomy, not in the short-term anyway. The crisis was a black swan event, and everywhere around the world, governments, central banks and regulators were acting in concert and synchronizing their policy responses. What we were doing in India was no different from the global practice during those anxious and turbulent times. But my credentials were suspect because of my background as finance secretary and so lent credence to this criticism.

I was more sensitive to the criticism on the 'eloquent silence' of the Reserve Bank. This was by no means deliberate. In normal course, it would take at least a couple of months for the media to take a measure of a new governor, for both sides to get to know each other and for a protocol of communication to get established. The crisis did not allow us the time to go through this familiarization process at the normal pace. In part because of the lack of familiarity, I tended to neglect the communication dimension of my job in those early months.

The criticism was a welcome call for corrective action. My first response was to establish a practice of a media conference following every major crisis-response package by the Reserve Bank.

The first of this series of media conferences was on 28 October 2008, following the first quarterly policy review on my watch. I was not a novice in dealing with the press; I had in the past taken questions from reporters as finance secretary, and also given brief interviews. But facing a media conference as governor was an altogether different proposition since so much seemed to hang on what you said and how you said it. I had gone through answers to possible questions with the staff but I was still nervous. After all, this wasn't any old time; we were going through a period of acute anxiety and uncertainty, and the media was struggling to interpret my actions and understand my personality. I knew they would be more probing than usual, but would they also be adversarial?

As I entered the conference room with the four deputy governors in tow at 3 p.m., a strange calm suddenly descended upon me. The conference didn't exactly go as per script; in fact, no media conference does. But I never felt cornered or lost. I believe I gave cogent and reasoned replies to all the questions, including why I had to resort to an unscheduled policy action, that too one as significant as a regime change in monetary policy, just four days ahead of a scheduled policy review. One question that came up several times and in several formulations was whether the government was driving the Reserve Bank's agenda. Beyond a simple denial, I chose not to join issue since any elaboration would have seemed defensive and unconvincing. Time alone should establish my credibility.

The press conference lasted an hour, longer than the typical thirty–forty-five minutes of post-policy conferences under my predecessor, Governor Reddy. It seemed a success on several fronts. The explanation of the rationale for the slew of crisis-response measures gave the media an appreciation of the context in which we were operating; the media got a full, good look at me, enough to size up the new governor; and at a personal level for me, it drove away the fear of the unknown. Most importantly, it set the tone for a very constructive and happy relationship that I enjoyed with the media through my five-year term.

The criticism that I was ceding control of the Reserve Bank's crisis response to the government was weighing on my mind, but as I said, there was nothing much I could do to reverse what I thought was an ill-informed view. Time alone would have to neutralize that.

My bigger concern though was whether I was, even at this very beginning of my tenure, losing credibility with my own staff in the Reserve Bank. What if they too became prejudiced by all the talk of my inability or unwillingness to protect the Reserve Bank's turf? Instead of looking up to me for my professional competence and intellectual integrity, they would be looking at me with suspicion, and worse, distrust. This would hurt my reputation in many ways, but even more importantly, it would compromise my effectiveness, something that the Reserve Bank could not afford, least of all in a crisis situation like this.

Hopping from job to job and organization to organization is standard fare in an IAS officer's career trajectory. With thirty-five years of civil-servant experience under my belt, I was quite aware that the default relationship between a new boss and the organization that he comes into laterally is of distrust and suspicion. The new boss has to work hard early on in his tenure to tear down those barriers and establish his credentials to earn the respect of his staff. But here I was, forced to perform at peak level, under high-profile visibility even before the large majority of the senior staff of the Reserve Bank, let alone the thousands of subordinate staff, got to know me. Besides, here I was interacting with the government much more actively than the Reserve Bank staff had been used to seeing. Would they give me the benefit of the doubt and evaluate my actions in the context of the crisis? Or would they write me off as someone who couldn't stand up to pressure from the government?

The senior officers' retreat of the Reserve Bank in late November 2008 presented a much-needed opportunity for me to open up with the senior management and speak to them candidly about my concerns and anxieties, and also about my positions vis-à-vis the government. This retreat is a standard feature on the Reserve Bank's annual calendar when all the senior staff, from the governor down to the chief general manager, maybe about one hundred in all, go offsite for a couple of days to learn, understand, bond and rejuvenate.

I spoke without any notes which—as the Reserve Bank's staff would learn as they got to know me better—was very uncharacteristic of me. I also spoke without any specific narrative in my mind. I levelled with them on the process leading to my appointment, on the complexity of the crisis, and my journey up the learning curve. I drew their attention to what was happening everywhere around the world—governments and central banks were coordinating as never before to fight the crisis. What was happening in India, I told them, was in tune with that pattern. It was only the special circumstances surrounding me—my background in the government and my relative 'unknownness'— that were fuelling these misperceptions. While I could live with the negative press, I could not live with an institution that was suspicious of me. As I concluded, I requested them to help transmit this message to the entire staff of the Reserve

Bank, not all of whom were able to fully appreciate the unusual circumstances brought on by the crisis.

~

The criticism on both strands—inadequate communication and not acting independently—waned and eventually disappeared as the calendar turned to 2009. The broad thrust of the media evaluation of the first 100 days of my governorship in December 2008 was that I had handled a very turbulent period with intelligence, professional integrity and exemplary calm. Even more gratifying was the one-year evaluation of my governorship in the media in September 2009 where the broad consensus was that the Reserve Bank under my 'mature and reassuring' leadership was bold, swift and imaginative in its response to the crisis and that, in an uncertain time, I brought clarity and candour to the central bank.

What was most comforting to me was that some of the very same commentators who had earlier criticized me for surrendering to Delhi's instructions had now written that I meant business, didn't bend under pressure and steered the Reserve Bank with calm determination and quiet confidence during a time of great tumult. Writing in the *Business Standard* of 1 February 2010, Sanjaya Baru said: '[Subbarao's] leadership at the central bank through the difficult months of 2009 has, without doubt, been exemplary. As he led his four deputy governors into the boardroom last Friday, he exuded the kind of confidence that only being in charge and in control gives.'

Universal endorsement is perhaps too much to expect in a public policy job. Even in the midst of this wide appreciation, some analysts were more grudging and said that even if I may have passed the test as a crisis manager, that success didn't say anything about my competence in the bread-and-butter business of central banking—fighting inflation—and that the real test for me was yet to begin. As later developments would show, this summing-up was prophetic.

The Governor's Bungalow

Even as I was completely preoccupied with the crisis, I also had to complete the transition from Delhi to Mumbai.

The Tilak Lane house that I was occupying as finance secretary had to be vacated within three months of leaving the job or else the Central Public Works Department (CPWD) would charge me a penal rent. That itself was no problem as Urmila too had got a transfer to Mumbai as chief vigilance officer of Air India. I could hardly devote any time to the winding up, packing and shipping, but Urmila managed that with the ever-efficient logistic support from the Delhi office of the Reserve Bank.

There are many perks attached to the governor's job; among them, the colonial-era governor's bungalow on the posh Carmichael Road, since renamed M.L. Dahanukar Marg, is possibly the most valued. The location of the bungalow is itself symbolic of the sharp contrasts that are so characteristic of Mumbai. Along the road are the homes of some of the richest corporate leaders of the country with snazzy houses and flashy cars, and just down the cliff, a slum, one of hundreds in Mumbai, sheltering migrants from villages across the country who come in pursuit of a livelihood to this 'maximum city' of hope, enterprise and opportunity.

Y.V. Reddy had vacated the bungalow within a couple of days of handing over to me but I continued to stay in the Reserve Bank guest house on Nepean Sea Road as the bank's maintenance staff asked for a couple of weeks to undertake some long-pending repairs and restoration. Even as the staff got to the job with alacrity, the two weeks turned into two months as the governor's bungalow is a heritage building, and any alteration or replacement, from floor tiles to woodwork to wall colour, requires the clearance of the Bombay Natural History Society (BNHS). In the event, some chipped floor tiles remained, as our engineers could not produce a replacement 'colonial era tile' which could pass muster with the BNHS. I am not complaining though, as the BNHS surveillance ensures that the bungalow maintains its period-piece decorum and gentle charm.

Living in the bungalow was a happy and comfortable experience. What I liked most of all was its spaciousness and generous proportions. The irony of living in such a large house when it was just the two of us, as we had lived in matchbox-like government housing in Delhi when our two sons were of the running and jumping age, was not lost on Urmila and me.

I must confess that we—Urmila and I—never really got around to doing full justice to that magnificent habitation, caught up as we were in our respective jobs which involved extensive travel too. But we did try to grab every opportunity possible to invite family and friends over so that these 'outsiders' could enjoy to the full the short time they got to spend in these splendid, sylvan surroundings.

We were conscious that the place was on loan to us for the period of our stay and wanted to share it to the fullest. And so it was that, on more than one occasion, we made it available for the celebration of Diwali by the Carmichael Road Walkers' Association—the lights, fireworks and delicious Diwali food contributing to evenings filled with joy, cheer and bonhomie. On another occasion, towards the end of my tenure, we hosted the Asia Society for an evening of 'exploring the heritage' of the bungalow. An expert they brought along conducted a tour of the bungalow for us, explaining the history of the architectural design and the ancestry of every piece of furniture and furnishing. I knew I was an ignoramus on heritage issues; even so, the realization that

I was so much of a boor that I had remained indifferent to the rich heritage of the surroundings I had inhabited for nearly five years left me shamed.

In terms of actual time spent in and on the bungalow, I must confess to having been an indifferent, if not a poor, householder. But when I open my 'inward eye', I recall many a moment spent enjoying the 'atmosphere' of it, revelling in the open spaces, the fresh air wafting in through the many large windows, the cacophony of birds that converged on the lawn for a last diatribe before they settled down to another night in the snug foliage. I close my eyes and see the heavy bunches of jackfruit which every season bent the branches of the tree that peeped in at our bedroom window.

In particular, I remember 2010, a year of battering rains in Mumbai when, on occasional Sunday mornings, I would sneak downstairs and stretch out on the leather couch tucked into the semicircular alcove opposite the main staircase, ostensibly to do some serious reading. But the soothing strains of the interminable rain, the luxury of having someone else attend to the opening and closing of windows and doors as the deluge revived or abated, sent me into an almost comatose state far removed from the 'fever and fret' of real life. I must, however, confess that every such occasion was invariably vitiated by twinges of guilt at the thought of millions of Mumbai slum dwellers under leaky roofs for whom the rain meant the loss of daily earning, and hungry children.

On the Learning Curve

Needless to say, the 'Baptism by Fire' was a crash course for me in central banking, and a rewarding one too. What would have taken me months, if not years, to learn in 'peace time', I got to learn in a few weeks. The brainstorming sessions, extending over several hours and often stretching late into the evening, were an opportunity to learn, cutting across the standard departmental silos and vertical hierarchies. These sessions were also an opportunity to bond with my senior staff and build personal and professional relationships that would prove very valuable as I led the Reserve Bank in the months and years ahead.

I must add here that I was tremendously impressed by the agility, creativity and intelligence demonstrated by the staff of the Reserve Bank in addressing the surprises and uncertainties thrown up by these unusual circumstances. Every so often I would pick up some stray bit of information from a casual conversation with an outsider or from a newspaper I read or TV report I watched at home in the night, on which Reserve Bank action might be warranted. I would worry the whole night if our staff were aware of it and were preparing for it. In just a few weeks, I realized that I need not have worried. The Reserve Bank staff were almost always on top of most developments and quite clear about what developments required response and what did not. Deputy governors Rakesh Mohan, V. Leeladhar, Shyamala Gopinath and Usha Thorat, as well as their teams, were a tremendous source of support and reassurance to me during this critical period.

Sure, the crisis was a testing time for us in the Reserve Bank. There were tensions and apprehensions. There was anxiety about the known unknowns and fear of the unknown unknowns. But the crisis also brought out the best in the Reserve Bank.

~

Across large sections of the public, including among educated and informed people, there was dismay that the contagion of the global financial crisis had spread to India. One of my big challenges in that first year was not only to respond to the crisis at the policy level, but also to explain to the public why we were, in fact, hit by the crisis.

In order to understand the public dismay, it is necessary to throw our mind back to the heady days of 2008 before the Lehman collapse. Recall that India was on the verge of being christened the next miracle economy of the world. Growth was surging at more than 9 per cent; the fiscal deficit was on the mend; the rupee was appreciating and asset prices were rising. There were inflation pressures but the general perception was that our inflation was a problem of success, a sign of rising incomes and shared prosperity, rather than a symptom of failure. Most importantly, we thought we had 'decoupled'—that even if advanced economies went into a downturn, emerging-market economies would not be affected because of their improved macroeconomic management, robust external reserves and sound banking sectors. But there was no decoupling, after all.

So why did India get hit by the crisis? The reason we were hit was that, by 2008, India was more integrated into the global economy than we consciously recognized. India's two-way trade (merchandise exports plus imports), as a proportion to the gross domestic product (GDP), more than doubled over the past decade: from about 20 per cent in 1998–99, the year of the Asian crisis, to over 40 per cent in 2008–09, the year of the global crisis.

If our trade integration was deep, our financial integration was even deeper. A measure of financial integration is the ratio of external transactions (gross two-way current account plus gross capital account flows) to the GDP. This ratio had more than doubled, rising from 43 per cent in 1998–99 to 111 per cent in 2008–09, evidencing the depth of India's financial integration. What this integration meant was that if global financial and economic conditions went into turmoil, India could not expect to remain an oasis of calm.

I thought it was my responsibility to disseminate this message in the larger public domain. I did so at every possible opportunity, especially while speaking to students. But as I asserted this, I also had to be prepared for a logical follow-up question. If India had to suffer global convulsions because of integrating into the world economy, wouldn't we be better off withdrawing from globalization?

The important point is that globalization is a double-edged sword; it offers immense opportunities but also poses ruthless challenges. Nothing illustrated this more strikingly than the global financial crisis.

Recall that in the years before the crisis—during the Great Moderation spanning roughly twenty years till 2008—the world saw steady growth in advanced economies and accelerating growth in emerging and developing economies, and low and stable inflation all around. More than anything else, this was a consequence of globalization—in particular, a dramatic expansion in global trade coinciding with a period of tremendous boost to world production and productivity as a result of India and China joining the world labour markets.

If the Great Moderation was the positive side of globalization, the financial crisis of 2008–09 was its negative side. That a financial bubble in a quintessentially non-tradable sector like housing snowballed into a global financial crisis, taking a devastating toll on global growth and welfare, is a demonstration of the ferociousness of the forces of globalization.

It would be tempting, based on the experience of the crisis, to believe that India and also other emerging-market economies would be better off reverting to insularity. That would be like throwing away the baby with the bathwater, clearly a misguided response. Globalization comes with benefits and costs. Our response should be not to withdraw from the global economy but to learn to manage globalization in ways that will maximize its benefits and minimize its costs.

Lessons from the Crisis

As someone said, this crisis was too valuable to waste. I, for one, learnt many lessons on crisis management and leadership.

By far the most important lesson I learnt is that the primary focus of a central bank during a crisis has to be on restoring confidence in the markets, and what this requires is swift, bold and decisive action. This is not as obvious as it sounds because central banks are typically given to agonizing over every move they make out of anxiety that failure of their actions to deliver the intended impact will hurt their creditability and their policy effectiveness down the line. There is a lot to be said for such deliberative action in normal times. In crisis times though, it is important for them to take more chances without being too mindful of whether all of their actions are going to be fully effective or even mildly successful. After all, crisis management is a percentage game and you do what you think has the best chance of reversing the momentum. Oftentimes, it is the fact of the action rather than the precise nature of the action that bolsters confidence.

Take the Reserve Bank's measure I wrote about earlier of instituting exclusive lines of credit for augmenting the liquidity of NBFCs and mutual funds (MFs) which came under redemption pressure. It is simply unthinkable that the Reserve Bank would have done anything like this in normal times. In the event of a liquidity constraint in normal times, the standard response of the Reserve Bank would be to ease liquidity in the overall system and leave it to the banks to determine how to use that additional liquidity. But here, we were targeting monetary policy at a particular class of financial institutions—the MFs and NBFCs—a decidedly unconventional action.

This departure from standard protocol pushed some of our senior staff beyond their comfort zones. Their reservations ranged from: 'this is not how monetary policy is done' to 'this will make the Reserve Bank vulnerable to pressures to bail out other sectors'. After hearing them out, I made the call to go ahead. Market participants applauded the new facility and saw it as the Reserve Bank's willingness to embrace unorthodox measures to address specific areas of pressure in the system. In the event, these facilities were not significantly tapped. In normal times, that would have been seen as a failure of policy. From the crisis perspective though, it was a success inasmuch as the very existence of the central bank backstop restored confidence in the NBFCs and MFs, and smoothed pressures in the financial system.

Similarly, the cut in the repo rate of one full percentage point that I effected in October 2008 was a non-standard action from the perspective of a central bank used to cutting the interest rate by a maximum of half a percentage point (50 basis points in the jargon) when it wanted to signal strong action. Of course, we deliberated the advisability of going into uncharted waters and how it might set expectations for the future. For example, in the future, the market may discount a 50 basis-point cut as too tame. But considering the uncertain and unpredictable global environment and the imperative to improve the flow of credit in a stressed situation, I bit the bullet again and decided on a full percentage-point cut.

Managing the tension between short-term pay-offs and longer-term consequences is a constant struggle in all central bank policy choices as indeed it is in all public policy decisions. This balance between horizons shifts in crisis times, as dousing the fires becomes an overriding priority even if some of the actions taken to do that may have some longer-term costs. For

example, in 2008, we saw massive infusion of liquidity as the best
bet for preserving the financial stability of our markets. Indeed, in
uncharted waters, erring on the side of caution meant providing
the system with more liquidity than considered adequate. This
strategy was effective in the short-term, but with hindsight, we
know that excess liquidity may have reinforced inflation pressures
down the line. But remember, we were making a judgement call
in real time. Analysts who are criticizing us are doing so with the
benefit of hindsight.

The QE, launched by the US Federal Reserve, presents a
more high-profile example of the dilemma of balancing short-
term compulsions against potential longer-term threats. The
Fed's immediate concern was to repair broken financial markets
for which QE was seen as the best policy option. But there was
always the risk of the excess liquidity leading to the mispricing
of risk and threatening financial stability. And now that the fire
is out, QE is also being criticized for accentuating inequality and
for taxing prudent savers in order to bail out reckless borrowers.
It is unlikely that these concerns would have escaped the Fed
policymakers as they embraced QE. By taking the plunge though,
they presumably calculated that the immediate concerns of
stabilizing the markets and stimulating demand outweighed the
longer-term threats.

A second lesson to be drawn from the crisis pertains to
communication. Mere words can have a miraculous effect in a
crisis. For example, it is now widely held that the unconventional
monetary policy of the Fed would not have been effective if it
were not accompanied by the repeated assurance that the ultra-
easy monetary stance would be maintained over an 'extended
period of time'.

At home too, I realized that once I gave up my early reticence
and took to active communication, it did a lot to restoring
market confidence. I got feedback, for example, that even as

we took a host of measures all through October–December 2008, there was always a lingering anxiety in the market that the Reserve Bank had not come out of the inflation-control mindset, was clearly uncomfortable with all the monetary easing under way and would clamp down at the earliest. If those expectations got anchored, it would have undermined the effectiveness of all the unconventional measures we were instituting. I took the opportunity of the media conference on 6 December 2008 to emphasize that inflation had fallen sharply owing to a crash in oil prices as well as demand recession at home. My intent was to regain control of the narrative and credibly convey to the markets that inflation had receded as an immediate concern and that they were misguided in thinking that the rollback of the accommodative stance was around the corner. The reassurance comforted investors enough for them to make long-term plans.

Reassuring markets is half the battle but there is also a dilemma there for central banks. How much do they reveal and what do they hold back? There is typically an information asymmetry between central banks and the markets. Central banks, by virtue of being financial sector regulators, have inside information on evolving developments. If they level with the markets on all they know, they risk triggering avoidable anxiety which could turn into panic. On the other hand, if they hold back information, they risk denying the market participants valuable time to make the necessary adjustment to the expected market developments. This is a fine line that central banks have to tread carefully.

Let me illustrate this with an example. The Reserve Bank had maintained all through the crisis months that the Indian financial sector was safe and sound. This was certainly true and the intent behind this assertion was to send a message of reassurance. But there was a concern too about whether such an unequivocal message was also spreading an unwarranted sense of complacency in the market and leading financial sector institutions to relax their guard. Was it not the responsibility of the Reserve Bank to keep the markets prepared for any unexpected development by mixing reassurance with caution?

Similarly, in those early months of the crisis, as the rupee was falling consequent on capital flight, a frequent question to me was whether we had enough reserves to defend the exchange rate. Even as you reassure the market that you do indeed have enough reserves to stem excess volatility, you do not want your reassurance to be interpreted as a commitment to defend a specific level of the exchange rate. That would be a moral hazard; assured of a stable exchange rate, they would pile on too much risk. This was a fine line that I had to tread carefully.

Another lesson we learnt is that even in a global crisis, central banks have to adapt their responses to domestic conditions. I am saying this because all through the crisis months, whenever another central bank, especially an advanced economy central bank, announced any measure, there was immediate pressure that the Reserve Bank too should institute a similar measure. Such straightforward copying of measures of other central banks without first examining their appropriateness for the domestic situation can often do more harm than good. Let me illustrate.

During the depth of the crisis, fearing a run on their banks, the UK authorities had extended deposit insurance across board to all deposits in the UK banking system. Immediately, there were commentators asking that the Reserve Bank too must embrace such an all-out measure. If we had actually done that, the results would have been counterproductive if not outright harmful. First, the available premium would not have been able to support such a blanket insurance, and the markets were aware of that. If we had glossed over that and announced a blanket cover anyway, that action would have clearly lacked credibility. Besides, any such move would be at odds with what we had been asserting—that our banks and our financial systems were safe and sound. The inconsistency between our walk and talk would have confused the markets; instead of reassuring them, any blanket insurance of the UK type would have scared the public and sown seeds of doubt about the safety of their bank deposits, potentially triggering a run on some vulnerable banks.

Finally, an important lesson from the crisis relates to the imperative of the government and the regulators speaking and acting in unison. It is possible to argue that public disclosure of differences within closed doors of policymaking could actually be helpful in enhancing public understanding on how policy might evolve in the future. For example, a 6–6 vote conveys a different message from a 12–0 vote. During crisis times, though, sending mixed signals to fragile markets can do huge damage. On the other hand, the demonstration of unity of purpose would reassure markets and yield great synergies.

I recall one occasion when the government, the Reserve Bank and SEBI timed their policies to be released shortly before 11 a.m. when the prime minister was scheduled to make a statement on the crisis in the Lok Sabha. That coordinated move—which, for us, was a complicated piece of theatre—was criticized on two counts: first, that the government was trampling on the autonomy of the regulators, and second, on why the Reserve Bank had resorted to a market-moving policy announcement during market hours. This criticism was clearly ill-informed.

The experience of the crisis from around the world, and our own experience too, showed that coordination could be managed without compromising regulatory autonomy. Merely synchronizing policy announcements for exploiting the synergistic impact need not necessarily imply that regulators were being forced into actions that they did not own.

Regarding the criticism on the timing, the decision to release the statement during market hours was deliberate. It is true that the standard practice of the Reserve Bank is to release unscheduled policy announcements after market hours to prevent any knee-jerk reactions. There have been exceptions to this general rule but the effort generally is to minimize such exceptions. In this instance, we decided to deviate from the standard practice to time the announcement with the prime minister's Lok Sabha statement. In the event, I believe, the synchronization had a greater impact than if we had announced the measures at the close of business the previous evening.

Spring Shoots

By the time of the London G20 meeting in April 2009, there was much talk of spring shoots in the advanced world and credible recovery in emerging markets, and a growing view that maybe, with concerted and coordinated action, governments and central banks had managed to extinguish the embers sooner than we had originally thought. Alas, that turned out to be a false hope as the global financial crisis morphed into the eurozone sovereign debt crisis that would continue to agitate the global economy and financial markets for several years thereafter.

At home in India though, attention started turning to exit policies and strategies. However, given that the eurozone crisis was in full bloom, we could not take crisis management off our radar and out of our mind space.

At a personal level, the turning point in the crisis was also a turning point in my motive force, as a fear of failure had given way to a desire for success.

3

Baby Step Subbarao

Combating Inflation

India recovered from the crisis by the middle of 2009, sooner than most other emerging economies, but we barely had a chance to celebrate as inflation too caught up with us. The beginning of this episode of inflation, which would preoccupy my mind space for over two years, was actually quite dramatic because inflation, as measured by the wholesale price index (WPI), actually went negative for a few months in 2009. For us in India, conditioned to think of high inflation as evil, it is disorienting to view deflation as evil too. The reality, though, is that deflation can hurt growth and welfare as deeply as inflation, indeed oftentimes even more so. It was not surprising, therefore, that some analysts even started to talk about this deflation pushing India into a deeper recession.

That anxiety was clearly misplaced. This was by no means a bad deflation caused by falling output and jobs, but a good one caused by falling global input prices. In the event, the deflation also turned out to be transient as prices started rising rapidly thereafter and inflation remained in the 9–10 per cent range in 2009–11; it started declining only gradually in 2012.

To appreciate the severity of inflation during this period, you only need to note that the average WPI inflation during the three-year period 2010–12 was 8.7 per cent, significantly higher than the average inflation of 5.4 per cent during the entire previous decade (2001–10). Bringing inflation down by raising interest rates understandably became my foremost priority and remained so for much of my term. This anti-inflation policy stance, called 'monetary tightening' in technical jargon, invariably attracts criticism, often ill-informed, that the high-interest-rate policy of the Reserve Bank is choking growth by inhibiting consumption and investment. My concurrent challenge therefore was to evangelize that any growth obtained in an environment of high inflation would be transient and that low and steady inflation is a prerequisite for sustained growth.

Exit from Crisis-driven Easy Policy

Over much of the previous year, 2008–09, we had run an easy monetary policy—low interest rates and ample liquidity—to mitigate the impact of the crisis on the economy. Rolling back that accommodation was always on the cards but the rapid pick-up in inflation meant that we had to do so sooner than we had originally thought. We were also aware that in contrast to the policy path on our way into the crisis, when being swift, even radical, was more important than the precise contours of the measure, in reversing our way out of the crisis, meticulous calibration had to be a critical part of the strategy.

Our dilemma was similar to the one that confronted the US Federal Reserve as it agonized over reversing its ultra-easy monetary policy. To be sure, the Federal Reserve had invested a lot of thought into embarking on the extraordinary monetary accommodation needed to fight the collapse of confidence in the financial markets in the wake of the Lehman meltdown. Given the ferocity of the crisis and the urgency of dousing fires, the broader decision to bring the interest rate down to the zero lower bound and undertake QE became much more critical than the precise contours of the policy. Just contrast this with the feverish debate and high drama that surrounded the taper and the eventual halt to the asset-purchase programme in 2014 as well as the interest rate 'lift off' in 2015, when so much seemed to hang on whether the markets were, in fact, prepared for these most expected 'surprises'.

~

In the Reserve Bank, we started preparing the market for the so-called exit from the crisis-driven measures starting the second half of 2009. We had a rough road map too: we would begin with unwinding the unconventional policies, then move on to withdrawing the liquidity measures and finally, tighten the policy interest rate consistent with the inflation trend. Even as our plans were driven largely by our domestic developments, such as rising output and inflation, which were quite contrarian to the global trends, I was conscious that we had to keep an eye on external developments which continued to be uncertain and unpredictable. It was also clear to me that we had to navigate the reverse path very carefully; interest rates had gone to historically low levels during the crisis and an abrupt reversal would disrupt the recovery.

There was active media speculation on our exit path, and quite unsurprisingly it turned into an FAQ for me. The media would actively quiz me on the considerations that will go into the glide path of the exit. It so happened that I had just recently finished reading Gurcharan Das's much-acclaimed book, *The Difficulty of Being Good,* and the tales of Mahabharata were fresh in my mind.

So, in one media conference, without any prior contemplation, I found myself likening the Reserve Bank's situation with regard to 'exit' to that of Abhimanyu who knew how to break into the Chakravyuh, the battle formation of the Kauravas but, because of Krishna's cosmic design, never got to learn how to break out of it. This wasn't the answer to the question but the media was nevertheless happy writing stories about whether I would, like Abhimanyu, get trapped in the Chakravyuh, or, like Arjuna, make a successful exit.

We stayed with our road map by withdrawing the unconventional measures in October 2009, and while doing so, had explicitly signalled that this would constitute the first phase of our 'exit'. We followed up by raising the CRR in the January 2010 policy meeting. Thereafter, we had to deviate from the road map, not so much in sequencing but in timing, as inflation started rising rapidly because of supply-side pressures. It became clear that interest rates had to be raised soon and we thought it inadvisable to wait until the next policy meeting in April 2010. We raised the repo rate through an ad hoc policy announcement in mid-March 2010. Starting from that point up until October 2011, in a space of just eighteen months, I took the effective policy rate up from 3.25 per cent to 8.5 per cent, raising it a total of thirteen times, a record by a long stretch.

How rapidly and by how much we raised rates were critical to reining in inflation and inflation expectations. We raised rates by 50 basis points (0.5 per cent) on occasion, but much of the time the increase was in steps of 25 basis points, earning me the moniker of Baby Step Subbarao. Many analysts thought this baby-step approach to be too timid and too inadequate in the face of such stubborn inflation, and some of them started to ask whether the governor would ever grow up and take an adult step. But I am getting ahead of myself in telling that story.

Drivers of Inflation

The key to monetary policy calibration lies in understanding the drivers of inflation. We would talk about this a lot within the Reserve Bank and it would also be the focus of much of our dissemination effort during this admittedly difficult period. In the internal brainstorming sessions, the discussion would be more in-depth, analytical and multidimensional. My challenge was to absorb all of that technical analysis and communicate our understanding of the problem and our response to the public domain in simple language.

Several factors—some of them cyclical but many of them structural—stoked inflation and kept it elevated during this period. Every time I met him, the prime minister would ask me why inflation was so unrelenting. I would tell him that our inflation was, of course, a problem, but it was a problem of success. The government's affirmative action programmes led by the employment guarantee under the Mahatma Gandhi National Rural Employment Guarantee Act (MGNREGA) pushed up wages without raising the underlying productivity while the expanded subsidy schemes, combined with improved delivery systems, had contributed to raising rural incomes at a record pace. A result of this rapid growth in incomes was a spurt in demand for consumption goods which, in the absence of commensurate increase in production, put upward pressure on prices.

But as they say, there are no free lunches. The government's apparent success on one side was also its failure on another front. It was spending way beyond its means by borrowing in the market. Since the total pool of money available in the market for borrowing is limited, the more the government borrows, the less there is for the private sector. And if the private sector did not borrow and invest, we would not be able to expand the productive capacity of the economy to meet the growing demand for goods and services. It would have been some consolation if the government, even if it borrowed way too much, spent the borrowed money on building capital or infrastructure, which would then add to the productive capacity of the economy; but they were spending it on consumption which was only driving up inflation.

The reason for this rather long exposition is to say that in telling the inflation story to the prime minister, I would give him both the positive and negative sides of it. As an economist, he understood my arguments, but as a politician, he felt helpless. Most of the time, all I would get by way of a reply would be a wry smile.

Criticism of Baby Steps

There was criticism of my monetary policy stance, ironically from opposite directions—by the hawks for being too dovish and by the doves for being too hawkish. The hawks argued that we were too soft on inflation, that we were late in recognizing the inflation pressures, and even after recognizing the problem, we remained behind the curve. The baby-step tightening that defined my anti-inflation strategy, according to them, was a timid and hesitant response. The drip-drip effect of repeated baby steps, the argument went, did not give the sense of overwhelming power being directed to fight inflation head-on.

From the other side of the spectrum, the doves' charge was that raising interest rates as I was doing was a futile exercise since our inflation was fuelled largely by food and other supply shocks over which monetary policy has little impact. Our actions, they contended, would not tame inflation; they would only end up stifling growth. 'Is this man killing India's growth?' was the dramatic title of a feature in the *Economic Times* of 17 September 2011.

Let me respond to this criticism from both ends of the spectrum.

To those who say we were behind the curve and failed to close the monetary spigots in good time, my simple response is to recall the context of the years 2010 and 2011. The world economy was still in recession and the much-heralded spring shoots turned out to be a false dawn. The eurozone crisis was pounding global markets; confidence all around was fragile, and markets remained testy. And as we learnt from the experience of the post-Lehman developments, India remained vulnerable to adverse external developments, especially as the eurozone kept the global financial sector on tenterhooks by moving from one 'five minutes to midnight solution' to another. Our 'baby steps' were therefore a delicate balancing act between preserving stability on the one hand and restraining inflation on the other.

With the benefit of hindsight, of course, I must admit in all honesty that the economy would have been better served if our monetary tightening had started sooner and had been faster and stronger. Why do I say that? I say that because we now know that we had a classic V-shaped recovery from the crisis, that growth had not dipped in the Lehman crisis year to as low as had been feared, and that growth in the subsequent two years was stronger than earlier thought. But remember, all this is hindsight, whereas we were making policy in real time, operating within the universe of knowledge at that time.

Let me now respond to the doves—inclusive of senior officials and advisers in the government—who argued that the Reserve Bank was too hawkish in its inflation stance.

First, I do not agree with the argument that the Reserve Bank failed to control inflation and only ended up stifling growth. WPI inflation had come down from double digits to below 5 per cent (April–May 2013); core inflation had declined to around 2 per cent (June–July 2013). Yes, growth had moderated, but to attribute all of that moderation to tight monetary policy would be inaccurate, unfair and, more importantly, misleading, as a policy lesson. India's economic activity slowed owing to a host of supply-side constraints and governance failures which were clearly beyond the purview of the Reserve Bank. If the Reserve Bank's policy rate was the only factor inhibiting growth, growth should have responded to our rate cuts of 125 basis points between April 2012 and May 2013, CRR cuts of 200 basis points and open market operations (OMOs) of ₹1.5 trillion in 2012–13.

Admittedly, monetary tightening did have some negative impact on growth. But this was only to be expected. After all, the objective of monetary tightening is to compress aggregate demand, and some sacrifice of growth is programmed into it. But this sacrifice is only in the short-term; there need be no sacrifice in the medium term. Indeed, low and steady inflation is a necessary precondition for sustained growth. Any growth sacrifice in the short-term would be more than offset by sustained medium-term growth.

What about the criticism that monetary policy is an ineffective tool against supply shocks? This is an ageless and timeless issue. I was not the first governor to have had to respond to this, and I know I won't be the last. My response should come as no surprise. In a $1500 per capita economy—where food is a large fraction of the expenditure basket—food inflation quickly spills into wage inflation, and therefore into core inflation. Indeed, this transmission was institutionalized in the rural areas where MGNREGA wages were formally indexed to inflation. Besides, when food has such a dominant share in the expenditure basket, sustained food inflation is bound to ignite inflationary expectations.

As it turned out, both these phenomena did play out—wages and inflation expectations began to rise. More generally, this was all against a context of consumption-led growth, large fiscal deficits, and increased implementation bottlenecks. If ever there was a potent cocktail for core inflation to rise, this was it. And it did—rising from under 3 per cent at the start of 2010 to almost 8 per cent by the end of the next year. It is against this backdrop that our anti-inflationary stance in 2010 and 2011 needs to be evaluated.

Data Deficiencies and Monetary Policy

This may be an appropriate point to comment on how the Reserve Bank's monetary policy calibration goes astray because of data deficiencies. As I said before, the Reserve Bank operates within the universe of knowledge available in real time, and that universe is largely shaped by data. If the data are reliable and available in good time, policy response can be accurate and confident. But the Reserve Bank is oftentimes wrong-footed because of the questionable quality of data.

For example, our data on employment and wages, crucial to judging the health and dynamism of the economy, do not inspire confidence. Data on the index of industrial production (IIP), which gives an indication of the momentum of the industrial sector, are so volatile that no meaningful or reliable inference can be drawn. Data on the services sector activity, which has a share as high as 60 per cent in the GDP, are scanty.

The poor quality of data is compounded by frequent and significant revisions, especially in data relating to output and inflation which are at the heart of monetary policy. As governor Y.V. Reddy put it with his characteristic wit, everywhere around the world, the future is uncertain; in India, even the past is uncertain. It is this data uncertainty under which the Reserve Bank has to make policy; it does not have the luxury of waiting until the past becomes crystal clear.

I have already written about how our baby-step approach to fighting inflation was in part informed by data which were telling us that recovery was still fragile. In the event, subsequent revisions to output data showed that growth in 2009–10 was, in fact, more than a full percentage point higher than the original number. It is a fair conjecture that the tightening cycle to rein in inflation would have been steeper had we known that output growth was significantly better than we knew in real time. Another instance of data wrong-footing us was the indication of a significant drop in inflation which prompted me to cut the repo rate by 50 basis points in April 2012. But that inflation number was retrospectively revised upwards; it turned out that inflation had not declined as sharply as we were given to understand in real time.

Flawed data was also the culprit behind the 'stagflation' puzzle we had encountered in 2012 when growth moderated steeply from 8.9 per cent in 2010–11 to 6.9 per cent in 2011–12 even as inflation remained elevated. Many analysts had put me in the dock to explain why inflation had not softened even in the face of such a sharp decline in growth and whether the Reserve Bank's tight monetary policy was actually pushing India down the quagmire of stagflation—a frightening combination of low growth and high inflation similar to the US experience in the late 1970s.

The Reserve Bank denied suggestions of stagflation but that was more an assertion than a persuasive reply. The only conjecture we could offer was that potential growth, which is difficult to measure, had possibly declined more steeply during the crisis years; as a consequence, even at a very moderate rate of output expansion, we were experiencing fairly high inflation. And even as the issue of stagflation was important and needed to be probed, the whole debate remained ill-informed because of unreliable data.

It now turns out that there was no puzzle, after all. Subsequent data revisions tell us that growth had not slowed as sharply as indicated by real-time data, which explains both the presence of high inflation and absence of any stagflation. If, in fact, the Reserve Bank had fallen victim to the groupthink, acquiesced in the stagflation theory and responded accordingly, the macroeconomic implications of the policy error would have been very costly.

The Reserve Bank, under my leadership, had come under frequent criticism for consistently getting its forecasts of growth and inflation wrong. Could we have done better? One straightforward option would have been not to make any forecast at all. Someone, it was perhaps Groucho Marx, said, never make a forecast, especially about the future! Alas, not putting out forecasts is not an option available to the Reserve Bank.

I wish there was a single or a simple explanation for getting forecasts wrong. An important reason, of course, was data flaws that I have spoken about as also the large and unanticipated spikes in global oil and other commodity prices. These forecasts are based on time series models, and if the data in the series are inaccurate, the forecast could go wrong. Arguably, flawed data were not unique to my period. But what was unique to my period was the trend shifts in growth and inflation. The structural models that we use lose their predictive capability around these turning points. They tend to under-predict when the trend shifts upwards, as happened in the case of inflation, and over-predict when the opposite happens, as happened in the case of growth. It was these turning points in the perverse direction that led our forecasts astray.

The Reserve Bank's analysts and modellers are among the best in the business and are impressively innovative in scenario-building to forecast the future path of the economy. But there are some developments, global and domestic, that escape all analysts, not just the Reserve Bank economists. Take the global oil price scenario. Whoever could see the upward price spike in late 2010, and equally, who could see the reverse shock in 2014? The only difference is that the shock in 2010 was an ugly one that hurt our economy and the Reserve Bank got the rap; the shock in 2014 was a happy one, at any rate for a massive oil importer like India, and the forecast error went largely unnoticed!

Differences with the Government on Monetary Policy

There was constant and decidedly unhelpful friction between the ministry of finance, under both Pranab Mukherjee and later Chidambaram, and the Reserve Bank on what the government saw as the Reserve Bank's unduly hawkish stance on interest rates, totally unmindful of growth concerns. The distilled version of their argument went as follows. All the government's efforts to kick-start the supply response in the economy were being stymied by the high-interest regime of the Reserve Bank. If only the Reserve Bank relaxed on the interest rate, investment would take off and launch the economy into a virtuous cycle of increasing growth and declining inflation.

When Chidambaram was asked in a media interaction in July 2013 why he was frustrated with the Reserve Bank when all it was doing was pursuing its mandate of price stability, he admitted that the Reserve Bank's mandate was indeed price stability but that 'mandate must be understood as part of a larger mandate of promoting growth'. The clear implication was that the Reserve Bank was mistaken in interpreting its mandate.

I believe both Pranab Mukherjee and Chidambaram had erred in seeing the Reserve Bank as being fixated on inflation, unmindful of growth concerns. On the contrary, the Reserve Bank interprets its mandate exactly as Chidambaram had said, although not as he implied. The Reserve Bank was targeting price stability precisely because it is a necessary condition for sustained growth.

The argument is slightly technical but I will try to communicate this as simply as possible. Textbook economics tell us about the famous 'Phillips curve', put forward by the New Zealand economist William Phillips in 1958, which shows a historical inverse relationship between unemployment and inflation in every economy. Stated simply, lower unemployment in an economy correlates with higher inflation. Subsequent research led by Milton Friedman showed that the inverse relationship is true only in the short run; in the long run, you cannot reduce unemployment by simply tolerating higher inflation.

If we transpose the Phillips curve research to the Indian context, the inference that follows is that there could possibly be a trade-off between growth and inflation in the short-term. In other words, it might be possible to grease the wheels of growth by acquiescing in higher inflation; but such growth is bound to be fickle. In the long run though, higher inflation takes a heavy toll on growth. If we want sustained growth, low and steady inflation is a necessary prerequisite. It was this understanding based on historical evidence and empirical research that underpinned the Reserve Bank's interpretation of its mandate.

The burden of my argument both in the public domain as well as internally to the government was that the Reserve Bank was running a tight monetary policy not because it did not care for growth but because it *did* care for growth. But the government remained unpersuaded or chose to be unpersuaded.

In order to defend his position vis-à-vis the Reserve Bank and possibly to sound a conciliatory note, in a media conference in July 2013, Chidambaram had generalized this divide between governments and central banks by saying that 'governments are for growth and central banks are for price stability'. This stereotyping was misinformed not only with reference to India but even from a broader experience.

In fact, no central bank in the world, not even an inflation-targeting central bank is, or indeed can afford to be, insensitive to growth concerns. Take the case of the Bank of England which is statutorily mandated to target inflation. If the BoE fails to deliver on the inflation target, it is required by law to write to the chancellor of the exchequer explaining the reason for its failure. Given this strict discipline, you'd think that the BoE would prioritize inflation management over all else if only to avoid the stigma of having to explain its failure to the government. Not so. Even the BoE takes cognizance of growth and employment concerns in its policy calculus as evidenced by this excerpt from an explanatory letter dated January 2008 from the governor of the BoE to the chancellor: 'If the Bank rate was set to bring inflation back to the [2 per cent] target, there would be unnecessary volatility [that is fall] in output and employment.'

The issue is more straightforward in the case of the US Federal Reserve. It cannot focus exclusively on inflation as it has, by law, a twin mandate, requiring it to balance price stability with maximum employment. Take the case of Japan which went through a high-decibel debate on the mandate of the Bank of Japan in January 2013 shortly after Prime Minister Shinzō Abe had returned to office. Given the quagmire of deflation that Japan had sunk into, we would have thought that the government would mandate the BoJ to raise inflation to the target level to the exclusion of all other concerns. But even in the midst of such compelling circumstances, the BoJ was required, while pursuing its inflation target 'to ascertain risk to sustainable economic growth'. All these examples clearly demonstrate that central banks everywhere interpret their price stability objective in the context of growth, contrary to Chidambaram's stereotyping.

~

Although the high-interest-rate regime would be the main area of difference between the government and the Reserve Bank, there were other issues that stoked the friction even deeper.

One such issue which was almost always a point of contention in my pre-policy meeting with the finance minister was the estimate for growth that the Reserve Bank would be putting out in its policy document. The government's pet peeve was that the Reserve Bank was being too cynical in its forecasts. Either the secretary of economic affairs or the chief economic adviser (CEA) would contest our estimate with their assumptions and estimates which I thought was par for the course. What used to irritate me, though, was that almost seamlessly the discussion would move from objective arguments to subjective considerations, with one of the senior officers suggesting that the Reserve Bank must project a higher growth rate and a lower inflation rate in order to share responsibility with the government for 'shoring up sentiment'. Finance Secretary Arvind Mayaram went to the extent of saying in one meeting that 'whereas everywhere else in the world, governments and central banks are cooperating, here in India the Reserve Bank is being very recalcitrant'.

I was invariably discomfited and annoyed by these objections and insinuations. I was also often dismayed that the ministry of finance would seek a higher estimate for growth while simultaneously arguing for a softer stance on interest rate without seeing the obvious inconsistency between these two demands. I used to take a consistent and firm position that the Reserve Bank cannot deviate from its best professional judgement just to doctor public sentiment. Our projections have to be consistent with our policy stance, and tinkering with estimates for growth and inflation would erode the credibility of the Reserve Bank.

Another constant source of friction used to be the position taken by the Reserve Bank on the government's fiscal stance. The government's large fiscal deficit was one of the prime drivers of inflation, and its inability to roll back expenditure undermined the Reserve Bank's anti-inflation stance. There was no way the Reserve Bank could tell a credible inflation story without pointing this out. The finance ministry used to be irritated by the Reserve Bank making an issue out of its fiscal stance, and Pranab Mukherjee was always miffed about it; he clearly showed it even though he never said anything. But for me, skirting around this issue was neither appropriate nor advisable.

It was my standard practice to apprise the prime minister too of our statement on the government's fiscal stance. He understood the economic logic but always seemed uncomfortable with the Reserve Bank pointing it out. He never intervened directly with me, but in early 2012, he told Rangarajan, the chairman of his Economic Advisory Council and my former boss when I was secretary to the council, to convey to me that he did not expect Subbarao, 'who was finance secretary in the government and understood its political compulsions' to take such a strident stand on the fiscal stance. I certainly had sympathy for this point of view but was unwilling and unable to show any accommodation.

~

Curiously, the eurozone sovereign debt crisis and the debate it triggered on fiscal austerity provided fresh ammunition to the government to contend that fiscal deficits were not as bad as they were projected to be. Although this debate did not play out much in the public space, it turned out to be a contentious issue between the ministry of finance and the Reserve Bank, and warrants telling if only to illustrate the pitfalls of transposing arguments from one context to another without checking about applicability.

As the PIGS (Portugal, Ireland, Greece and Spain) in the eurozone were struggling with sovereign debt sustainability issues in 2010 and 2011, a common conditionality imposed on them by the IMF-led bailout programmes was fiscal austerity—drastic reduction in public spending in order to bring government's books of account into balance. There was recognition that this might hurt growth but the understanding was that the negative impact on growth would only be in the short-term. In the medium term, the argument went, growth would pick up since the austerity programme would enable more efficient private investment to replace the less efficient government spending.

Then, in 2012, the IMF came out with an influential and somewhat controversial study, showing that the fiscal multipliers in the eurozone countries were indeed higher than originally projected, implying that the negative growth impact of the fiscal austerity imposed on PIGS would be higher than the figures built into the bailout programmes. In plain English, this was a plea for softening the fiscal austerity conditionality so as to reduce the hardship on the public.

Some senior officials in the ministry of finance caught on to the new IMF research and argued that like in the eurozone, in India too, the adverse consequences of fiscal deficits were being exaggerated and that the Reserve Bank was being misguided in taking a negative view on the government's fiscal adjustment path.

I was dismayed by this effort to extend the eurozone arguments to India without reckoning with India's altogether different macro parameters. Our fiscal adjustment road map was by no means aggressive; besides, the IMF research applied to countries with a demand recession and a negative output gap, certainly not to a country like India where a cocktail of sizzling demand and strained capacity was stoking inflation pressures. My standard response to the ministry of finance was that whereas the debate in Europe could be *fiscal austerity versus growth*, for us in India, it has been and will continue to be *fiscal austerity for growth*.

My discussion of the differences with the government on fiscal issues will not be complete without a reference to the fiscal dominance of monetary policy—a situation in which a central bank's monetary policy is forced to accommodate its government's fiscal stance. In some sense, this has always been the case in India with the Reserve Bank's degrees of freedom in monetary policy curtailed by the government's expansionary fiscal stance.

The Reserve Bank's constant refrain was that it was left to do all the heavy lifting to manage the tension between growth and inflation while the government took the easy way out with its loose fiscal stance. Given this scenario, some analysts would quiz me, in informal discussions, on why the Reserve Bank just does not force the government into fiscal discipline by unilaterally easing on the monetary side. The resultant inflation pressures, the argument went, would force the government to restrain its 'borrow and spend' policy. That would make a good coffee-house argument but is highly impractical and strictly inadvisable in the real world. Public policy simply cannot be made through an adversarial stance.

The only redeeming feature in all of this is that fiscal dominance of monetary policy is neither new nor unique to India. It has a long history going back over seventy years and manifests in many countries and many situations, including in advanced economies. Let me cite some recent examples.

In the thick of the eurozone crisis, the European Central Bank had to stretch its mandate in order to buy treasury bonds of stressed countries to soften their debt pressures—a clear case of subordinating monetary policy to fiscal compulsions. In the United States, the Fed became hostage to the fiscal stance of the government when in the autumn of 2013, it was forced to defer the much-publicized taper of quantitative easing in view of the political impasse over debt sequestration. The tussle was even sharper and more public in Japan when Prime Minister Abe tried to push the Bank of Japan into quantitative easing, overruling Governor Masaaki Shirakawa's argument that monetary easing without support from fiscal consolidation would be ineffective, if also risky.

Equity Considerations in Monetary Policy

The narrative of our growth–inflation debate is also shaped by what I call the 'decibel capacity'. The trade and industry sector, typically a borrower of money, prioritizes growth over inflation, and lobbies for a softer interest-rate regime. I believe this is a legitimate lobby comprising constituencies which contribute to growth, and its demand deserves every consideration by the Reserve Bank.

At the same time, the Reserve Bank cannot afford to forget that there is a much larger group that prioritizes lower inflation over faster growth. This is the large majority of the public comprising several millions of low- and middle-income households who are hurt by rising prices and want the Reserve Bank to maintain stable prices. Inflation, we must note, is a regressive tax; the poorer you are, the more you are hurt by rising prices.

But here is the thing. The business sector is organized, has a platform for voicing its demand and even has an opportunity to present its point of view to the governor in the pre-policy consultation meeting. On the other hand, the large majority of the public that is hurting under inflation is scattered and unorganized, has no avenue to voice its concern and does not have the privilege of a pre-policy meeting with the governor. I always believed that this asymmetry placed an obligation on the Reserve Bank to bend over backwards to listen to the voices of silence.

One comforting factor is that this tension of balancing the interests of a vocal minority with those of a silent majority is not unique to the Reserve Bank—all central banks face this dilemma. Alan Greenspan, the former chairman of the US Federal Reserve, said in an interview following the publication of his latest book, *The Map and the Territory*: 'In the eighteen and a half years I was there, I got a huge number of letters or notes or whatever, urging us to lower interest rates. On the side of getting letters which say you've got to tighten [raise rates], it was a zero. So it is a huge political, regulatory asymmetry.' ('What Alan Greenspan Learned Till 2008': interview to Justin Fox)

This concern for the less privileged raises a larger debate about whether central banks should at all reckon with the distributional consequences of their monetary policy. In other words, should central banks worry about how their policy might affect the poor vis-à-vis the rich or remain strictly agnostic? I raise this issue because some analysts said that I was distorting the debate by looking at inflation from an equity perspective instead of treating it as any other macro variable.

This is not just a poor-country issue. Even in rich countries, there is a contentious debate under way, especially in the context of the heightened concern about growing inequalities, on whether central banks should concern themselves with how their policies affected the rich vis-à-vis how they affected the poor. Take QE by the Federal Reserve. A principal objective of QE is to raise the prices of assets so that the wealth effect would induce more spending, and thereby stimulate the economy. Some left-leaning economists have criticized the Fed for acting like a 'reverse Robin Hood' since it is the rich who hold a disproportionate share of the assets whose prices are being primed by QE. Bob Corker, a senator, accused Bernanke of 'throwing senior citizens under the bus' by keeping interest rates low.

This argument that QE has adverse distributional consequences has expectedly been countered on several grounds. Most importantly, it has been argued that the tools available to the Fed are best suited to raising the level of national prosperity which is generally neutral in its distributional consequence as much as a rising tide lifts all boats. If indeed there are any consequent equity issues, it is for the government to take corrective action. It will be costly for the central bank to deviate from an optimal policy course to accommodate equity concerns. Also, it is risky for an independent central bank to wade into politically sensitive issues like equity.

This is a debate that frowns on moderation; we are unlikely to see a consensus. But for me, the issue has always been clear. In a poor country like India, the Reserve Bank just cannot afford to be insensitive to the distributional consequences of its policies.

Public Debates on Monetary Policy

News and commentary on monetary policy would normally remain confined to the business pages of newspapers, and business TV channels. Occasionally, however, some issues spill over into the larger public space.

One such instance I recall centred on the changing dietary habits of low-income households. Reserve Bank research showed that one of the structural drivers of inflation in India has been the persistent rise in the prices of protein foods. This, in turn, was a consequence of rising rural incomes. We know from development economics that when low-income households experience an increase in their incomes, one of the first significant changes they effect is to shift their diet from carbohydrates to protein food, pushing up the prices of the latter. The Reserve Bank acknowledged this trend in its policy statements; and I also recall having made this point in a couple of speeches.

A member of Parliament took umbrage at the Reserve Bank pointing this out and charged me of looking upon the improvement in dietary habits of poor households as an unwelcome development which needed to be reversed to help contain inflation. It was a completely ill-informed and inappropriate value judgement. If anything, in the Reserve Bank we welcomed this development. Yes, it was a problem but, as I said before, a problem of success. What the situation warranted was a supply response by way of increased production of protein foods to meet the growing demand without stoking inflation. I refrained from joining issue on this for fear of giving currency to a debate that had no merit in the first instance.

~

Another debate that wrong-footed me centred around a new normal for inflation. As part of the silver jubilee celebrations of the Indira Gandhi Institute for Development Research (IGIDR) in December 2012, there was a panel discussion on the outlook for growth and inflation. I moderated the discussion, which comprised former governors: C. Rangarajan, Bimal Jalan and Y.V. Reddy. At some point during the discussion, Y.V. Reddy made the point that as the crisis abates, advanced economies would settle at a higher normal inflation as a consequence of the excesses of QE. He argued that if India's standard practice was to peg our inflation target a few percentage points above that of advanced economies, the Reserve Bank should consider raising its inflation target.

There was a brief discussion following this comment, with both Rangarajan and Jalan contesting Reddy's view. As I brought the discussion to a conclusion, in my capacity as the moderator, I said something to the effect that the Reserve Bank would certainly examine Reddy's argument, but made no comment on revising our strategy.

I was aware of the pitfalls of acknowledging a new normal for inflation, especially at a time when the Reserve Bank was involved in a two-year battle with inflation. I was also fully sensitive to the need to remain committed to the medium-term inflation goal of 4–5 per cent that the Reserve Bank had set for itself. But I thought Reddy's point deserved more than an outright dismissal. All I wanted to convey was that we had an open mind and would examine this argument with professional integrity.

I was dismayed by how my comment was completely misinterpreted by some analysts who said that RBI was admitting defeat in its fight against inflation. They said that by acknowledging a higher normal for inflation, the Reserve Bank was preparing the ground for monetary easing under pressure from the government for lower interest rates. I was amazed at how some analysts saw deep conspiracy in what was, by all accounts, an unrehearsed, free-flowing conversation at the panel discussion conducted in an academic setting.

Even though the debate was not picked up by the rest of the media and had indeed died down, I thought it advisable to unequivocally put across the Reserve Bank's position. At a speech to the Bankers' Club in Delhi shortly after this episode, I asserted that there was, in fact, no new normal for inflation.

Reforms to Monetary Policy Formulation

Even in the midst of fighting such fierce inflation, we introduced several innovations to the monetary policy framework

The system I inherited had two policy rates, the repo rate, the rate of interest charged on commercial banks when they borrow overnight from the Reserve Bank, and the reverse repo rate, the rate of interest paid to banks when they deposit money overnight with the Reserve Bank. Both these rates used to be varied independently to calibrate the monetary policy stance. This system of two independently varying policy rates afforded more degrees of freedom to the Reserve Bank, but at the cost of higher uncertainty in the money market about the precise monetary policy stance of the central bank.

We reformed the framework in May 2011 by increasing the degree of certainty to the market by voluntarily curtailing our own degrees of freedom. First, we said that the repo rate would be the only independently varying policy rate. The reverse repo rate would be made a dependent variable by pegging it at a fixed 100 basis points (1 per cent) below the repo rate. Banks borrow from the Reserve Bank's liquidity adjustment facility (LAF) window by giving government securities as collateral. But what happens if they do not have sufficient government securities to borrow? The second bit of reform was to provide for such a contingency by instituting a marginal standing facility (MSF), which is a window open to banks to borrow at a penal rate of interest.

Third, we indicated that the weighted average call money rate would be the operating target for the Reserve Bank, which is to say that the Reserve Bank would manage liquidity in such a way that the call money rate would remain within the 100 basis points band defined by the repo rate and the reverse repo rate. Finally, we indicated that we would manage liquidity in such a way that the commercial banks' access to the LAF window where they borrow overnight would be restricted to 1 per cent of the bank's total net demand and time liabilities.

The introduction of the corridor system and the explicit identification of the weighted average call rate as the operating target of monetary policy allowed banks to manage their daily liquidity more efficiently and reduced volatility in the money markets.

A related reform was my decision to replace the benchmark prime lending rate (BPLR) of banks by a base rate which was to be a floor for the interest rate charged to its borrowers. Again technicalities aside, the intention behind this decision was to discipline the banks into making the interest charged on the borrowers more transparent and contestable. We realized though that even as this reformed the system significantly, there still remained some lacunae which the Reserve Bank is fixing, and is a work in progress.

One reform that was widely understood even at a layman level and much appreciated was my decision in October 2010 to deregulate the interest on savings deposits. Not many may recall, but prior to 1991, the Reserve Bank regimented the entire structure of interest rates in the economy, both on the lending and the deposit sides. This elaborate and extensive regimen was gradually dismantled as part of the reform process starting 1991, but one rate that remained pegged at 4 per cent was the interest rate on savings deposits.

Many of my predecessor governors considered letting go of this as well but stopped short of making the final call, mainly because of uncertainty about how the interest rate structure might unfold consequent on deregulation. On the one hand, there was the attractive possibility that deregulation would spur competition among banks, leading to product innovation, improved customer service and an increased interest rate benefitting millions of low-income households in the country for whom a savings deposit account is the only saving option. But there was also the apprehension that competition among banks to capture this large segment of low-cost deposits would raise the overall costs for banks and distort the entire interest structure with potential financial stability concerns. The discussion paper that we put out elicited wide commentary but no consensus. Eventually, after much deliberation, I decided to bite the bullet.

This decision was widely applauded, with some people going as far as to say that this decision, more than anything else, would determine my legacy. In the event, the feared destabilization in the banking system did not materialize; but neither did fierce competition or innovation. My only reading is that the benefits of this move will take longer to manifest. My legacy hangs in the balance!

Another reform implemented on my watch was the introduction in mid-2010 a mid-quarter policy review essentially doubling the policy reviews from four to eight per year. The reason for this was that we found the prevailing gap of a full quarter between two policy meetings to be too long in what was turning out to be an uncertain macroeconomic situation. On several occasions, the fast-paced developments forced us into off-schedule policy actions which, although necessary, created market uncertainty. Besides, every data release triggered speculation about an off-schedule response from the Reserve Bank which compounded the already prevailing uncertainty. The mid-quarter reviews enabled the Reserve Bank to respond to the data flow in a more structured manner and helped manage expectations.

The introduction of the mid-quarter review reduced, but did not eliminate, the probability of an off-schedule policy adjustment. For example, in March 2012, we realized that systemic liquidity, already quite tight, might be further exacerbated because of advance tax payments due by the middle of the month. This happens because advance tax payments have the effect of transferring money from the open pool and locking it up in the government's account with the Reserve Bank. To ease the liquidity situation, we cut the CRR by 75 basis points just six days before the scheduled policy date, based on the judgement that waiting till the policy date would be too late.

Setting a Record despite Baby Steps

The global and domestic circumstances during my five-year tenure as governor were unique in many respects, and the Reserve Bank's policy responses too were unique. As a result, I acquired many distinctions, most notably in interest-rate setting. By calibrating the interest rate a total of twenty-three times, raising it thirteen times and cutting it ten times, I remain the most activist governor to date, no matter that some of the credit was earned in baby steps! Also, whereas previous governors moved interest rates only in one direction, either up or down, the macroeconomic circumstances during my tenure were so turbulent that I had to move the interest

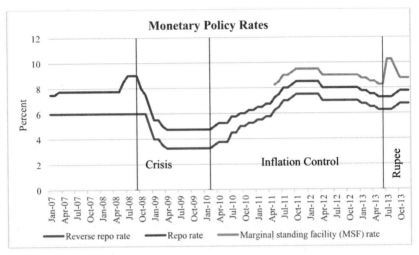

Source: Data on the policy interest rate of RBI.

rate both up and down. During the crisis in 2008–09, I cut the rate, raised it in the two years following that to fight inflation, started cutting it as inflation had come below the target level in 2012, but raised it again to defend the rupee in 2013.

This is a record I would like to preserve not so much because it makes me unique but because I hope no other governor has to face such a crisis all through his or her tenure.

4

'When the Facts Change, I Change My Mind'

Do You Endorse Inflation-targeting?

In 2015, the Reserve Bank, under Governor Raghuram Rajan, adopted 4 per cent consumer price index (CPI) inflation as the anchor for its monetary policy. As governor, I had expressed reservations on inflation targeting. Several people have asked me if I endorse Rajan's approach. I do, notwithstanding some reservations I continue to have. In order to explain my position, it's necessary to first understand the issue of inflation-targeting in a broader global context.

Inflation-targeting around the World

The years before the global financial crisis in 2008 saw a powerful intellectual consensus building around inflation-targeting. A growing number of central banks, starting with New Zealand in the late 1990s and thereafter numbering over thirty, embraced the principle of gearing monetary policy almost exclusively towards stabilizing inflation. This involved the central bank openly committing to a target for consumer price inflation and making the achievement of that target the overriding priority of monetary policy. This approach seemed successful, delivering as it did the Great Moderation—an extended period of price stability accompanied by stable growth and low unemployment. In the world that existed before the crisis, central bankers were a triumphant lot. They believed they had discovered the Holy Grail!

That sense of triumph was short-lived. The global financial crisis dented, if not dissolved, the consensus around the minimalist formula of inflation-targeting. Inflation-targeting was premised on the view that if policymakers took care of price stability, financial stability would be automatically assured. The crisis proved that wrong by actually demonstrating the opposite—that an exclusive focus on price stability can blindside central bankers to threats to financial instability. In light of this received wisdom, central bankers found themselves charged with neglecting financial stability in their single-minded pursuit of an inflation target, and thereby abetting, if not causing, the global financial crisis.

One of the big lessons of the crisis is that financial stability is neither automatic nor inevitable and that it has to be explicitly safeguarded. Central banks, in particular, cannot afford to keep financial stability off their radars.

Does this mean the inflation-targeting approach has to be abandoned altogether? Alternatively, can inflation-targeting be made more flexible to accommodate concerns about financial stability? Quite predictably, these questions were in constant play in international policy conferences as well as in the global media in the post-crisis period. The ensuing debate also raised a host of related questions on inflation-targeting, financial stability and the broader issue of the mandates of central banks. What exactly is financial stability? Is monetary policy an appropriate instrumentality for preserving financial stability? Is it sufficient? If not, what other policies are required and how should monetary policy dovetail with these other policies? Apart from financial stability, how should the inflation-targeting approach reckon with the imperatives of real-sector variables like growth and employment? Is inflation-targeting possible in a globalized economy where the prices of goods and services are set by global rather than domestic demand–supply balance? How effective is inflation-targeting in economies where wages are determined more by the government's immigration policy rather than the central bank's monetary policy? How should the mandates of central banks be redefined to reflect these fresh concerns?

By their very nature, these were open-ended questions, and the only broad consensus that emerged was that inflation-targeting was not the magic bullet it was once thought to be and that strict inflation-targeting should yield to more flexible inflation-targeting, meaning that monetary policy should shift from just stabilizing inflation alone to stabilizing both inflation around the inflation target and real activity in the economy at its potential level, while simultaneously keeping an eye on financial stability.

Inflation-targeting in India

Coincidentally, in India too, a debate about inflation-targeting started picking up momentum at around the same time, triggered, in part, by two high-profile committee reports, one by Percy Mistry, and the other by Raghuram Rajan. While Mistry strongly urged that the gold standard for stabilizing monetary policy is a transparent, independent inflation-targeting central bank, Rajan held that reorienting the Reserve Bank towards inflation-targeting will have to dovetail with the government's commitment to maintaining fiscal discipline and not hold the central bank accountable for either the level or the volatility of the nominal exchange rate.

The Rajan committee formally presented its report to the prime minister in September 2008, shortly after I assumed office as governor. I was invited to that meeting as were some Cabinet ministers and advisers to the government. I recall that although the committee recommendations straddled a wide range of issues in the financial sector, almost the entire discussion at the meeting was on inflation-targeting. Opinion was quite varied on whether it was advisable for the Reserve Bank to shift to an inflation target given our macroeconomic circumstances. In any case, reaching a firm decision on the issue was not on the agenda of the meeting, and we dispersed with the issue of inflation-targeting remaining open-ended.

In my first year as governor, even as we were fully preoccupied with the crisis, I had frequently encountered questions on inflation-targeting. Would the Reserve Bank adopt inflation-targeting as suggested by Percy Mistry? Have the preconditions indicated by the Rajan report been met? Is it advisable for the Reserve Bank to move to inflation-targeting at a time when, world over, there is a rethink on its advisability? My response to inflation-targeting got shaped in this context. I was, in particular, concerned that the Reserve Bank should not move towards inflation-targeting when the theory and practice on the subject were in such a flux. Instead, we should wait for the lessons of experience to become clearer and then adapt them to the Indian situation.

My reservations on inflation-targeting extended beyond the lessons of the crisis to India-specific circumstances and vulnerabilities. In an economy where short-term inflation is driven more by supply shocks, be they of food or energy, than by demand-side pressures, can the Reserve Bank deliver on an inflation target? Will the government support the Reserve Bank by remaining committed to fiscal responsibility or will inflation-targeting become hostage to fiscal dominance? How effective would inflation-targeting be in a situation where monetary policy transmission is impeded not just by large fiscal deficits but also by administered interest rates on small savings and illiquid bond markets? Wouldn't the Reserve Bank's policy of managing large and volatile capital flows compromise inflation-targeting?

My main concern was that inflation-targeting in the face of these compulsions might lock the Reserve Bank into a no-win situation. If it is fixated on fulfilling its inflation target, there may be occasions when the Reserve Bank may have to tighten the interest rate so much that growth and jobs will be hit. On the other hand, if it fails repeatedly to meet the target, it will risk losing credibility. Once people have lost confidence in an inflation target, it becomes very hard for the central bank to persuade them to trust the target again.

Besides these policy considerations, there was also a very practical issue that prevented a change in the policy regime. A necessary requirement for inflation-targeting is a single inflation index that is representative of the entire economy of 1.3 billion people, fragmented markets, diverse geography and heterogeneous economic conditions. We did not have one.

Notwithstanding my reservations on inflation-targeting, it is not as if I was fully satisfied with the 'multiple-indicator, multiple-target approach' that guided monetary policy during my tenure. Under multiple indicators, the Reserve Bank monitored a host of variables—reserve money, money supply, industrial output, bond yields and equity prices—and juxtaposed that data against output and prices. As for multiple targets, price stability, growth and financial stability were the joint and simultaneous targets of monetary policy, with the inter se priority among them shifting in accordance with the evolving macroeconomic situation. In theory, this was unexceptionable as it allowed monetary policy to respond flexibly to the changing macro situation. In practice though, the multiple-indicator approach, which allowed the Reserve Bank to shift from one priority to another virtually seamlessly, confused the markets and fumbled our communication. It also diluted the Reserve Bank's accountability since any policy mix could be explained away as being consistent with the multiple-objective approach. Internally, we were deeply conscious of the need for our policy calibration to be logical and consistent, but communicating that remained a challenge always, with the result that our policy actions were sometimes criticized in the media and by some analysts as being inconsistent and, occasionally, even arbitrary.

Given this mixed record of the multiple-indicator, multiple-target approach, the shift to an inflation-targeting regime under Governor Rajan's leadership was, I believe, a well-advised move. In saying so, I am following the example of no less a luminary than Keynes whose famous riposte to a critic when accused of being a flip-flopper was: 'When the facts change, I change my mind. What do you do, sir?'

I believe that at least some of the facts underlying my reservations on inflation-targeting have changed. At a very practical level, we have today a composite all-India consumer price index with long enough historical data points to provide a nominal anchor for the inflation target.[1] Even though the government deviated from the fiscal road map in 2015–16, it reaffirmed its commitment to fiscal responsibility in its budget for the fiscal year 2016–17. The administered interest rate regime is being dismantled, with the government indexing the interest rates on small savings to the yield on government securities. That should ease the impediments to monetary policy transmission and support inflation-targeting. The food distribution network is improving, thereby reducing the chance of food supply shocks

---

[1] As of now, this methodology is still the second best. I understand the Reserve Bank is still having to interpolate the new series into the past using the CPI for industrial workers.

undermining the achievement of the inflation target. With the softening of oil prices, the probability of supply shocks from oil has also become low.

Also, contrary to my initial apprehension, the Reserve Bank's inflation-targeting framework builds in significant flexibility. Importantly, the monetary policy framework agreement between the government and the Reserve Bank acknowledges that the objective of the monetary policy is to maintain price stability 'while keeping in mind the objectives of growth', thus discouraging the Reserve Bank from adopting a rigid approach to achieving the inflation target. The statement on the Reserve Bank's website 'that the relative emphasis assigned to price stability and growth objectives in the conduct of monetary policy varies from time to time depending on the evolving macroeconomic environment' reiterates the flexible inflation-targeting approach. Moreover, the wide tolerance band of ±2 per cent around the inflation target of 4 per cent reinforces this flexibility.

In the event of failure to meet the inflation target, the framework agreement enjoins the governor to report to the government the reasons for failure, as also the remedial action being taken to return inflation to the target range. This provision is comforting as it acknowledges the possibility that the target could be missed under extenuating circumstances, thus minimizing the probability of the Reserve Bank pursing the inflation target 'at any cost'.

Going forward, the success of the Reserve Bank's inflation-targeting approach will depend on two factors: first, how intelligently the flexibility of the framework will be used, and second, the autonomy the government will allow the bank in pursuing the target. Let me comment on both of these.

Global experience shows that an inflation-targeting framework is neither necessary nor sufficient to maintain price stability. Just to cite one example, the US Federal Reserve had adopted, as recently as 2011, a numerical target for its inflation objective but as stated on its website, the Federal Reserve 'is firmly committed to fulfilling its statutory mandate from the Congress of promoting maximum employment, stable prices and moderate long-term interest rates'. Even with this multiple mandate, the Federal Reserve has a better track record on managing inflation expectations, and thus inflation, than economies with an explicit inflation target.

For sure, openly committing to an inflation target helps a central bank guide expectations, and thereby maintain stability in the economy. But that very stability can be impaired by a single-minded pursuit of the inflation target to the exclusion of other macroeconomic concerns. The challenge in inflation-targeting is maintaining credibility even while flexibly deviating from the target when the circumstances so warrant.

The second condition for the long-term success of inflation-targeting is that the government will have to steadfastly respect the autonomy of the Reserve Bank notwithstanding its compulsions to accelerate growth in the short-term. Growth and inflation are not independent variables, which is to say that you cannot simultaneously set targets for growth and inflation. If one is fixed, the other is automatically determined. In practical terms, this means that if the Reserve Bank is enjoined to deliver an inflation rate, the government will have to acquiesce in the growth rate that results. If the government imposes a growth target on top of the inflation target, inflation-targeting will lose credibility. The resultant macroeconomic implications will be costly.

In this context, the following provision in the draft Indian Financial Code (IFC) is perplexing: 'The objective monetary policy is to achieve price stability while striking a balance with *the objective of the central government to accelerate growth.*' Is the government implying that accelerating growth is its exclusive objective and the Reserve Bank does not share that objective? Will the government therefore set a growth target and require the Reserve Bank to balance its inflation target with the government's growth target? Perhaps I am overreacting, but it is important that the wording in the IFC is unambiguous and the intent behind that wording is honoured. The point to recognize is that monetary policy can only provide a conducive environment for growth to reach its potential; it cannot raise the potential. That remains the government's responsibility and the task of its supply-side responses.

Needless to say, the Reserve Bank's inflation-targeting framework is yet to be fully tested. The test will come in a macroeconomic situation when growth is trending down and inflation is trending up, not an unlikely possibility. The test will come if and when commodity prices move back up, pressuring both inflation and fiscal rectitude. The test will also come when the new framework is called upon to address threats to financial stability arising, in particular, from surges and stops of capital. The Reserve Bank will have to tread the fine line of being flexible on inflation-targeting without compromising its credibility. That will be a difficult—but not an impossible—challenge.

5

Inside the Chakravyuh

The Process behind Monetary Policy Formulation

The Reserve Bank is a 'full service' central bank with a wide mandate; setting monetary policy is only one of its many responsibilities. Nevertheless, it is monetary policy that is the most glamorous—it gets the maximum public attention and media coverage. With growth in numbers of people shifting from the informal to the formal sector of the economy, has also come a growth in the number of people interested in the Reserve Bank's monetary policy. Millions of households which have taken housing loans have a stake in how the Reserve Bank sets interest rates. This interest is no longer restricted to the English-language media; the vernacular media too has joined in, thus extending the outreach to hundreds of millions.

This increasing awareness of the Reserve Bank's monetary policy is certainly a force for the good. But there is still quite some way to go. My experience from speaking to ordinary people during my travels across the country was that while most people were aware that the Reserve Bank's setting of the interest rate made a difference to their finances, they did not understand how exactly that happened.

Quite early in my tenure, I realized that explaining to the larger public how the Reserve Bank's monetary policy influences their finances and, therefore, their daily lives, has to be an important part of my job chart. It is only when there is wider awareness of what the Reserve Bank does can the larger public hold it accountable for its performance. In my efforts at outreach, I did not confine myself to a uniform format or any specific forum. I spoke about the impact of the Reserve Bank's policies on people's everyday lives whenever the opportunity presented itself; I would, of course, tailor the messaging to suit the type of audience.

On the Learning Curve

I was familiar with the theory of monetary policy before I entered the Reserve Bank. I also learnt a bit of the practice from the sidelines during my tenure as finance secretary. But doing monetary policy hands-on was an altogether different proposition—a fascinating, if also a challenging, learning experience.

For example, the open market operations by the Reserve Bank—buying and selling government securities in the open market so as to increase or reduce the money supply in the system—is an easy enough concept to understand at a theoretical level. But doing it in practice—determining the amount, the timing, the tenor of bonds to trade and indeed a host of intangible variables—is a complex decision that requires you to superimpose your judgement on the numbers thrown up by the models.

Central banks, as we know, set the policy interest rate in the expectation that this very short-term interest rate will influence the entire interest rate structure in the economy, which, in turn, impacts output and prices, through a process, technically termed 'monetary policy transmission'. But monetary policy transmission does not happen automatically; central banks have to work at it by managing the amount of money in the system—what they refer to as liquidity management. OMOs are an important instrumentality for this.

At the heart of a decision on OMOs is an estimate of the money supply for the period ahead consistent with the Reserve Bank's growth and inflation objectives, and an assessment of the short-term liquidity position of banks. In making these projections, the Reserve Bank has to contend with a host of variables, some predictable and some not. For example, money supply abruptly expands when the government pays out salaries and pensions at the end of each month because this entails money in the government's bank account maintained with the Reserve Bank being released into circulation; in a reverse process, money supply contracts and banks' liquidity position tightens after the quarterly advance tax payments. Currency in circulation also goes up during festival times and election times, tightening in the process the banks' liquidity position.

These jump shifts in money supply and liquidity position of banks are largely predictable, and the Reserve Bank can build them into its models. But there are one-off events that can affect money supply too. For example, recall the auction of telecom licences by the government in 2010 which yielded bids much higher than expected. When the winning bidders deposited the bid amounts, the transactions involved shifting money from the commercial banking system into the government's account with the Reserve Bank, in the process sharply draining liquidity in the system and pressuring money market rates.

Pre-policy Consultations

There is a well-set process leading to each monetary policy review which works to clockwork precision. The drill for a mid-quarter review is slightly less intensive as it is not accompanied by an extensive consultation and dissemination exercise like in the case of a quarterly review. With eight policy reviews coming roughly at six-week intervals and the end of one round marking the countdown for the next, life felt like a relentless continuum of monetary policy. There was never any respite.

Early on in the policy calendar, the governor and his top management team hold a series of pre-policy consultation meetings with stakeholder groups, typically with banks, non-banking financial companies, including microfinance institutions, urban cooperative banks, and representatives of financial markets and chambers of business. As finance secretary, I had participated in the finance minister's pre-budget meetings in Delhi. The Reserve Bank's pre-policy meetings are different from the government's pre-budget meetings in the sense that they are smaller, about twenty invitees on average, and are less formal and more interactive. I found these meetings very useful not only to get stakeholder views on the monetary policy stance, but also to give them an opportunity to raise issues that they believe warrant the Reserve Bank's attention. In fact, many reforms initiated by the Reserve Bank beyond the monetary policy domain have their origins in these consultations.

Of all the pre-policy meetings, the meeting with the chambers of commerce would be the most predictable since the business and industry representatives would invariably 'talk their book', pleading for a rate cut, no matter the macroeconomic situation. This argument that a rate cut by the Reserve Bank would improve the investment sentiment never cut much ice in the situation prevailing during much of my tenure as governor. All through the policy-tightening cycle, our staff appraisal was that there were many factors, most importantly implementation bottlenecks and governance concerns, which were holding back investment. Certainly, the interest rate was an important variable in an investment decision, but at that juncture it was far from being a binding constraint.

Just to check if our understanding of the ground situation was right, in one such meeting, where some of India's largest corporates were present, I asked how many of them would make an investment commitment in the following month if we did actually cut the rate. They all looked at each other sheepishly but not one hand went up! There was some collective embarrassment on both sides. I felt guilty too because they may have thought I was putting them on the mat. That certainly was not my intention.

I added to the list of pre-policy consultation meetings by introducing a meeting with economists drawn from the financial sector, the academia and the media. These meetings were always very lively, invariably brought fresh perspectives on familiar issues and certainly deepened my understanding of the macroeconomic situation. In all the pre-policy meetings, and even more so in the meeting with the economists, the effort from our side was to engage them in active communication, but without betraying any bias towards any one point of view. I went into these meetings with an open mind although I was aware that at least some participants felt that we suffered from what psychologists call 'confirmation bias'— filtering out all ideas and views that did not accord with ours.

I can't recall any meeting with economists where there was a consensus or even a near-consensus on the policy advice to the RBI. This may be no surprise given the cliché of two economists and three opinions, but for me it was also comforting since no matter how I decided, there would be someone agreeing with me!

Needless to say, we were spoilt for choice by way of the large talent pool of economists we could draw from. But that very luxury of choice posed a problem for drawing up the list of invitees for the meeting. Our experience told us that the optimal size for meaningful and effective consultation was fifteen which meant we had to make ruthless choices. The grapevine had it that being invited to these meetings was seen as a badge of honour in professional and media circles, which only increased our obligation to ensure that the process of selecting invitees for each round of meetings was objective and also was seen to be objective. We developed a roster but there would inevitably be complaints and grievances after each meeting from some of those left out.

Internal Strategy Meetings

There are two reports accompanying each policy review. The report on macroeconomic and monetary developments, abbreviated for convenience as the money macro report, containing an analysis by the Reserve Bank staff of the macroeconomic situation, financial conditions and market developments, is released a day prior to the policy review, while the governor's monetary policy statement is released on the day of the policy.[1] These two reports would be works in progress, constantly being updated and edited, till they went to print a day before their scheduled release. The two reports are prepared by two different departments of the Reserve Bank on the logic that the money macro report should be a stand-alone, objective document uninfluenced by the proposed policy action which will be contained in the governor's statement.

One of the critical inputs into the monetary policy is the internal monetary policy strategic group which meets at least twice before every quarterly policy review—the first meeting about three weeks before the policy review and the second just a week before. This group brings together economists and analysts from three different departments of the Reserve Bank—the monetary policy

---

[1] This report has since been restructured as Monetary Policy Report on Governor Rajan's watch, and is released simultaneously with the governor's policy statement.

department, the department of economic policy and research, and the department of statistics and information management. From the management side, the governor, all the deputy governors, executive directors and several heads of departments, altogether about fifty staff members, assemble to think through the strategy for the forthcoming policy.

At the heart of these meetings are presentations by each of the departments of its outlook on the macroeconomic situation and estimates for growth and inflation. These, in turn, would be based on all available data as well as on several surveys conducted by the Reserve Bank covering household inflation expectations, consumer confidence, industrial outlook, corporate performance, order book, inventory position and capacity utilization in the industry, and credit conditions. The three departments are enjoined to work independently. This has been a long established and deliberate arrangement instituted to mitigate the hazard of groupthink at the institutional level. In practice, the dividends this process yielded have been much richer; it gives the top management the benefit of a diversity of analytical insights and viewpoints. I also used to notice an undercurrent of competition between the teams to be more incisive in their analysis and more accurate in their projections which I found very charming.

The list of issues we would discuss at these meetings would actually make for a rich and interesting collection of box items in a standard economics textbook. At one meeting, the discussion veered to the impact, if any, of the government's decision to terminate minting of the 25 paise coin. The issue really was whether all prices would be rounded *up* to the next 25 paise limit or some might be rounded *down* too, and how consumers might respond. Our staff ran some statistical models and concluded that the net impact on inflation might be neutral.

There would be a lively debate following the presentations that was invariably very rewarding. I used to make an active effort to engage everyone in a free-flowing conversation around the analytical issues and found it very endearing that some of the younger staff would challenge my views. In fact, this culture of speaking freely without any fear of consequences, rare in India's hierarchical traditions and even rarer in its bureaucracy, is one of the institutional strengths of the Reserve Bank, a legacy from which I benefitted immensely.

At the end of each strategy meeting, I used to take a poll of all the staff present, mostly mid-level professionals, on three options—cut the rate, pause or raise the rate. Although this was an oversimplification of the policy matrix, it used to give me a sense of 'the wisdom of crowds' within the Reserve Bank—a crowd that I deeply valued.

Technical Advisory Committee

Under the RBI Act, it is the governor who decides on monetary policy. As I write this, there is an initiative under way to introduce the system of a Monetary Policy Committee so as to make monetary policy-setting the collective decision of a committee rather than that of an individual. Even though there was no MPC during my time, the Reserve Bank has had, since 2005, a Technical Advisory Committee (TAC) to advise the governor on the policy stance. The committee is chaired by the governor and comprises all the four deputy governors and seven external members, all nominated by the governor. Two of the external members are drawn from the board of the Reserve Bank while the other five are chosen from a wider pool of economists from the academia and think tanks.

The meeting of the TAC is convened typically a week before the policy date. The TAC members receive, in confidence, a draft of the money macro document, which forms the basis for the discussion.

Chairing a meeting, big or small, formal or informal, is always a challenge. Through my long civil service career, I learnt that there is no one-size-fits-all strategy for an effective meeting. It depends on the subject matter, the format, nature of participants and the expected outcomes of the meeting. In some meetings, you have to loosen hold so as to allow a free flow of ideas; in others, you have to hold a tight leash to prevent the discussion going off track. But one norm that almost always helped was to maintain discipline about the start and end times of a meeting. Rakesh Mohan, who evidently was aware of this time-discipline syndrome of mine, advised me before my first TAC meeting that I relax my tight leash and allow these meetings to be open-ended and free-flowing. I followed Rakesh's advice and benefitted immensely from doing so.

The TAC meetings would typically run for four to five hours, and on occasion even longer. There is an extensive presentation by the Reserve Bank staff of their analysis which is freely interspersed by several interventions, clarifications and comments by the members. After the presentation and discussion, and several rounds of samosas, pastries and tea giving ample food for thought, each external member would be invited to give his or her perspective on the macroeconomic situation, estimates for growth and inflation, and specific advice on the policy parameters.

The evolved best practice in central banks has been to release the minutes of their monetary policy committee meetings after a gap of three to four weeks. This transparency is aimed at guiding market participants on the different points of view and nuances that informed the final decision of the committee. Although the TAC is strictly not a monetary policy committee, we decided, in consultation with the external members, to adopt the global best practice, and in 2011, began the practice of putting out the minutes of the TAC meeting in the public domain four weeks after the meeting date. The recommendations of the members would be recorded in the minutes without attribution so that the market could get a sense of the TAC advice that informed the governor's decision.

More often than not, I differed with the advice of the TAC, especially during the tightening cycle when the TAC typically advised a softer approach relative to my final decision. Quite unsurprisingly, the media would play this up with catchy headlines like 'Subbarao differs again with his advisers', or 'Governor overrules his committee'. Even if there was a bit of sensationalism in the headlines, I welcomed this publicity since generating a discussion, hopefully an informed one, on the deliberations of the TAC was indeed the intent behind the release of the minutes.

Given how often I differed with the majority view of the committee, I began to get uncomfortable about whether the members of the TAC would misunderstand the committee process. What if they thought that the whole TAC process was a charade, that the Reserve Bank had no respect for the views of the members but was simply going through the motions just so as to earn brownie points for its consultative approach?

But then this begs the question why I differed so often with the majority view of the TAC. It was clear was that this divergence arose from differences in the way we saw the growth–inflation balance. When the external members advised a softer approach, their motivation was the slowing growth and the recognition that the government was not doing anything about it, leaving an interest-rate cut as the only possible stimulus. On the other hand, from within the Reserve Bank, we saw inflation control as a prerequisite for sustainable growth and believed that interest rate was not a binding constraint for investment in the prevailing situation.

I was conscious that this differing judgement of the growth–inflation balance was not a sufficient explanation for the internal–external divide within the TAC since it would raise the logical follow-up question of why indeed did the two sides see the balance differently. Both sides draw their analytical foundations from the draft money macro report and the presentations at the meeting. It is in interpreting that analysis based on their experience and expertise that differences arise. I believe on both sides there was realization that inflation was being driven by demand-side pressures as well as supply shocks. Perhaps the external members assigned a higher weight to supply shocks and thought that monetary policy was an inappropriate instrument for tackling such an inflation, whereas we, from within the Reserve Bank, thought that no matter what the driver of inflation, monetary policy has to be the first line of defence as persistent high inflation can harden inflation expectations and accentuate the pressure. All this, of course, is in the realm of conjecture.

Even as a clear explanation remained elusive, I levelled with the members of the TAC in one of the meetings to tell them that we respected their advice and that the TAC discussion added enormous value to our final judgement. I pointed out that during the entire tightening cycle, the TAC advice was never unanimous, suggesting that my decision was always finely poised. If I agreed with the minority view, it was just incidental.

The external members of the TAC are typically big names with impressive track records in the academia and economic policy. Some of them are respected columnists; and even others used to write or comment in the media sporadically. Unsurprisingly, their views would often address monetary policy issues. Both their pre- and post-policy commentary had potential market ramifications. The pre-policy view would be seen, quite logically, as the advice the member would give in the TAC, thereby setting off speculation on how it might influence the governor's decision. Similarly, any criticism by them of the policy after the release risked being misinterpreted as a note of dissent. On occasion, this became quite contentious. But we also believed that forcing an obligation of total silence on the TAC members would be unfair and unwarranted since their expression of views decidedly added value to the public discourse. To resolve this, in consultation with the TAC, we imposed a code of conduct for the external members—a voluntary 'shut period', beginning two weeks before the policy and ending a day after the policy, during which time they would not express any opinion in the media on monetary policy issues.

I made it a standard practice to follow up the full TAC meeting with a meeting with all the deputy governors. They too were members of the TAC and I believed it was only fair that I sought their views as explicitly as I did with the external members. There was seldom consensus even within this smaller, internal group; in fact, I can't recall even a single occasion when we were all agreed on a single policy mix.

You should have got the big picture by now. Opinion and advice from the wider world of analysts is all over the map, and neither the TAC nor even the core insider group of the TAC, produces a consensus. It is in this complex situation that the governor has to make a judgment call. More than ever before, I could relate to the phrase, 'the buck stops here'.

Pre-policy Interaction with the Government

There is a standard practice of the governor meeting the finance minister a few days before the scheduled policy review to apprise him of the Reserve Bank's assessment of the macroeconomic situation and the policy stance.

In the aftermath of the terrorist attacks in Mumbai, Chidambaram moved from the finance ministry to the home ministry in November 2008, two months after I took over as governor, and returned to the finance ministry in August 2012 after Pranab Mukherjee became the President of India, roughly a year before I stepped down. So, during much of my tenure as governor, Pranab Mukherjee was the finance minister, with Chidambaram returning for the last thirteen months. The prime minister held the finance portfolio for brief periods during the transitions.

The meetings with Chidambaram and Pranab Mukherjee were different in their setting. Chidambaram would always meet me alone, although occasionally he would invite the finance secretary and the chief economic adviser to join for the last ten minutes or so. He would typically hear me out and give his point of view, or 'advice' as he called it, unequivocally and firmly.

The meetings with Pranab Mukherjee, on the other hand, were more formal and larger in setting with all the secretaries of the finance ministry and all his advisers being present and actively participating.[2] All the talking at these pre-policy meetings would be done by his team while he himself mostly stayed quiet. I could never figure out if they had a strategy session in preparation for this meeting or if all of the presentations of the 'finance minister's view' by his staff were spontaneous.

There was also a difference, at a substantive level, in the meetings with Pranab Mukherjee and Chidambaram. Mukherjee's stance was straightforward—that the Reserve Bank should ease on the interest rate to support growth. Chidambaram, on the other hand, was more nuanced; he believed that I should cut rates in acknowledgement of his efforts at fiscal consolidation, and would assert his arguments more firmly and forcefully.

---

[2] Incidentally, I don't recall having a one-on-one meeting with Pranab Mukherjee except on two occasions—the first when I had expressly requested an exclusive meeting with him to discuss Usha Thorat's reappointment as deputy governor, and the second time when he invited me to his office to explain the amendment to the RBI Act in the context of the ULIP (Unit Linked Insurance Plans) controversy, both of which I will write about later.

I have been asked both while in office, and even more so after I stepped down, if there was pressure from the government to not tighten interest rates. I will write about this in a little more detail in a later chapter devoted to the autonomy and accountability of the Reserve Bank but the short answer is that there indeed was pressure.

Despite these pressures and disagreements, the meetings were always cordial; both Chidambaram and Pranab Mukherjee were invariably courteous. I know many people think that Chidambaram has an abrasive streak but I never experienced it. Even when I was his direct subordinate as finance secretary, he always treated me with courtesy and respect. Sure, he would, on occasion, show some irritation, but certainly no more irritation than I did with my own colleagues in the office. Chidambaram's behaviour towards me after I became governor was even more meticulous. For example, if there was going to be any delay in making it at the appointed time, his office would invariably call my office to let us know of that so as 'not to keep the governor waiting'.

There was some old-world charm to the way Pranab Mukherjee held both the institution of the Reserve Bank and the office of the governor in high esteem. As finance minister, he was criticized for being locked into the '70s mindset, not realizing that the world of finance had undergone a sea change in the three decades since. There were some positive dimensions to this so-called 'lock-in' though; one of them was that he looked upon the Reserve Bank with the respect that he developed for the institution in the '70s when as a younger and aspirational politician, he looked up to the stalwart governors of the Reserve Bank.

~

I have already written about how, when I went to call on him after my appointment as governor, the prime minister encouraged me to see him whenever I felt the need to. In deference to this suggestion, I made a meeting with the prime minister a standard task in the pre-policy drill. These meetings were always one-on-one. One of Dr Manmohan Singh's strong qualities is that he is a good listener and I always found him eager to get the Reserve Bank's perspective on every macroeconomic issue. The fiscal situation would, of course, figure in our conversation and my tale of woe about how the fiscal stance of the government was undermining the Reserve Bank's anti-inflation position was standard fare. To his enormous credit, he never interfered in the policy action. 'I hope you've settled this with the finance minister' was all he'd say. I never felt comfortable about this bit of the conversation but I would nevertheless tell him of the finance minister's reservations, and the matter would rest there.

This quarterly conversation with the prime minister typically extended beyond macroeconomic issues. He once asked me, from out of the blue, if banks were functioning normally in extremist-affected areas. I was deeply embarrassed because it never occurred to me to probe this question. He was also given to seeking my views on political economy issues weighing on his mind such as, for example, allowing foreign direct investment in multi-brand retail, the land acquisition bill or expanding the employment guarantee scheme and even on issues that do not directly fall within the domain of the Reserve Bank such as the goods and services tax. My expertise on these issues was modest; but that did not stop me from masquerading as an expert and pontificating! He also looked upon me as an Andhra expert and would inquire about issues like agricultural distress, farmer suicides and the agitation for a separate Telangana. I had left Andhra Pradesh over fifteen years ago and could not keep abreast of all the developments there because of job pressures. Almost always, I felt inadequate in giving him any fresh insights.

On one occasion, sometime in mid-2010, the prime minister surprised me by asking why so many people in the government were airing views in the public on the Reserve Bank's monetary policy. This was at a time when virtually every Delhi policy mandarin, major or minor, was commenting on what the Reserve Bank ought to be doing. I had no answer for his question but I told him that this was certainly vitiating the already fraught relationship between the government and the Reserve Bank. The Reserve Bank is a respected institution and people should not play with it, was all he said. He surprised me again by calling me a few days later to tell me that he had issued instructions that government functionaries should refrain from commenting on the Reserve Bank's policy. The Delhi decibels remained subdued after that, at any rate in the public domain.

~

The importance of keeping the policy decision strictly confidential is quite obvious. Any leakage would cause market turmoil, potentially embroil the Reserve Bank in legal action for unduly benefitting some individual or group and inflict serious damage to the bank's credibility. Within the Reserve Bank, there is a firm protocol on confidentiality, and disclosure is entirely on a need-to-know basis. Outside of it, only the prime minister and the finance minister, and on occasion a few top ministry officials, are in the loop. That there never has been a policy leak is a tribute to the diligence and professional integrity of the Reserve Bank staff.

I had one unpleasant surprise though—on the day of the policy review in April 2012, when, after thirteen rate hikes, I cut the rate by 50 basis points. Finance Minister Mukherjee was scheduled to address a business chamber in Delhi an hour before the policy release time. As he was entering the meeting hall, he commented informally to the corporates and the media that surrounded and greeted him—a doorstop interview as it were—that 'the governor will shortly give you good news'. This was most inappropriate and indiscreet. I am positive the finance minister did not intend any mischief; nor did he want to undermine the Reserve Bank. I think he was just being naive, overanxious to be the bearer of good news to the corporates in the midst of widespread criticism of policy paralysis in the government, hoping that some of the credit for this would rub off on him.

Agonizing over Language

The policy documents, as I said before, remain work in progress for a couple of weeks up until the final print order. Typically, on the weekend before the policy review, a small group of us—the deputy governor and the executive director in charge of monetary policy, the head of the monetary policy department and I—would sit over an extended session, going through the policy statement in great detail, discussing every turn of phrase and nuance. Let me give an illustration of how we used to agonize over how every adjective and adverb might be interpreted.

In the mid-quarter review of September 2010, as part of the forward guidance, we had said: 'The Reserve Bank believes that the tightening that has been carried out over this period has taken the monetary situation *close* [emphasis mine] to normal.'

There were two communication dilemmas here. The first was whether we should say '*close to*' or '*closer to*'. After much deliberation, we determined that saying *closer to* had no additional information content; it would be restating the obvious. On the other hand, saying '*close to*' would convey that there was some, albeit a small, room for further rate action.

The second dilemma was about whether 'normal' would be interpreted as 'neutral'. This dilemma arose in the context of the question frequently asked of us as to 'whether the policy rate had become neutral'. As per textbook economics, the neutral policy rate is the policy rate consistent with potential growth and low and stable inflation. But we also know from textbook economics that it is not possible to precisely determine the neutral rate, especially for a rapidly growing and structurally transforming economy like that of India. On the other hand, the 'normal' rate is the sweet spot which balances demand and supply, and can be broadly inferred from the crest and trough of the policy rate over the growth-inflation cycle. Obviously, such an elaborate explanation in the statement would be out of place. Realizing though the importance of this message, I made an extra effort to communicate our intent in the post-policy dissemination exercise.

Agonizing over language, I realize, is a standard item on the job chart of a central bank governor. In his memoirs, *The Courage to Act*, Bernanke writes: 'We sweated every word. Should I say that additional rate cuts "may be necessary" or "may *well* be necessary"? Should I say that we stood ready to take "*substantive* additional action" or "*meaningful* additional action"? The absurdity of our discussion did not escape us, but we had learned through bitter experience that a single word often mattered.'

Policy Dissemination

The pre-policy drill also includes a briefing session for the governor by the senior management on probable questions in the media conference following the policy. Even though the media conference is scheduled in the context of the policy, the engagement is not restricted to monetary policy. There has for long been a tacit agreement between the Reserve Bank and its media interlocutors that the entire domain of the central bank's functions would be par for the course. Our preparation too would accordingly cover a wide canvas, with senior staff stretching their imagination to think of possible questions and tips on how responses might be nuanced. These prep meetings would be conversational and free-flowing, far from the 'murder boards' of the American political and corporate scene where the staff pose as the media and the CEO practises his answers.

The media build-up on the policy starts a week before and reaches fever pitch by the announcement date. What with proliferation of business channels, there would be dozens of commentators on air talking about what the Reserve Bank *should* do and what it *would* do. As a matter of habit, I am not much of a TV person; I usually got my inputs from the print media but there would be enough speculation there as well, although less dramatic than that on TV. Polls of economists and analysts on the Reserve Bank's policy stance are now common fare. Some friends would ask me if all the speculation in the media prior to the policy review influenced my decision. I don't believe it has, but of course, by definition, I cannot speak for any unconscious osmosis of ideas.

As early as 8 a.m. on the policy day, OB vans park outside the Reserve Bank central office with reporters from TV channels and wire agencies milling around and sending live feeds from the scene of action. There is understandably competition among TV channels to 'be the first with the policy' which entails the risk of the first outburst of comment being incoherent or even ill-informed. To mitigate this risk, the Reserve Bank provides privileged access of the policy statement to reporters in advance with a strictly enforced embargo protocol.

At 9 a.m., these privileged reporters are conducted into the 'embargo room' where they surrender their cell phones and data cards and settle down in front of their systems sans any communication tools. A Reserve Bank official reads out the embargo rules, including a clause that once the policy document is given to them, they cannot leave the room even to use the loo! As soon as the statement is handed over, the room turns into an examination hall. All one can hear is the shuffle of papers and the click of keyboards as they prepare their headlines and stories while a hawk-eyed Reserve Bank staffer keeps a close watch on them.

Moments before 11 a.m., the Reserve Bank staffer gets an alert and the countdown begins: '5-4-3-2-1-Go.' The policy is announced—simultaneously on the Reserve Bank website and on TV screens and wire agency channels. But there is time enough only to give quick headlines before they rush for the governor's media conference.

A few minutes before the release time, the deputy governors, the monetary policy team and I would gather in my office on the eighteenth floor, watching the TV of course, and much like actors in a play, wait for the cue to enter the stage. When the alert comes, we would troop down three floors in the express elevator, go through the photo op with cameras clicking and bulbs flashing, and then enter the conference room for the media interaction.

Early on in my tenure, I used to start the media conference by reading a short, prepared statement but found that pattern to be too stilted. After a few meetings, I abandoned the practice in favour of an informal opening briefing after which we would get into conversation. Even as I thought I was well tutored by my staff for this 'inquisition', there would invariably be questions, or at any rate nuances on questions, which we had not thought of. I valued the opportunity of the media interaction as it was a useful platform for us to disseminate the rationale and expected outcomes of the policy in spoken and simpler language. It was a space where we could put out clear messages and oftentimes even explain some of the dilemmas we went through. In one interaction, I volunteered that opinion among my advisers too was divided on the policy action. Some of the media personnel were surprised that I would be so transparent but I thought communicating that the policy decision was finely balanced had its own signalling impact.

In an effort to improve the quality of our dissemination of the policy, we introduced a teleconference of analysts targeting a range of non-media stakeholders predominantly from the financial sector, but also drawing from the corporate world and academia. Deputy Governor Subir Gokarn was the inspiration behind this. The idea was to allow a day for the analysts to absorb the policy as also for an initial reaction by the media so that the questions would be more thought through. At the same time, the analysts' teleconference allowed those of us within the Reserve Bank an opportunity, through our responses, to reinforce some of the messages or correct any overt misinterpretation. I was pleased to see the teleconference rapidly gaining in popularity with not only the numbers signing up from both within the country and outside increasing, but also the depth and quality of questions improving.

Monetary Policy Outreach

The monetary policy process is anchored in the monetary policy department of the Reserve Bank, and even there only a handful of senior officers are in the loop about the entire process and on the final decision. On the other hand, the Reserve Bank is so quintessentially identified with monetary policy that the larger public sees every staff member of the Reserve Bank as having had a say in making the policy. Imagine a situation where a middle-level officer, say in the non-bank supervision department of the Reserve Bank, runs into a friend in the aisle of a supermarket and is accosted: 'Why did you people raise the interest so much yesterday? My EMI has shot up by 800 rupees.' I could relate to the embarrassment of my colleague who would have to say sheepishly that she works in a different part of the Reserve Bank, is not in the loop on interest rates and, in fact, knows as little as her friend! Embarrassment aside, this was also a foregone opportunity to demystify the Reserve Bank.

I believed that every staff member of the Reserve Bank should be broadly aware of the policy perspectives of the bank across its broad remit, irrespective of the narrow domain of his or her job chart in order to be an effective ambassador for the bank to the outside world. To operationalize this, we introduced a monthly thematic video conference, anchored in rotation by a specific central office department. The conference would link all the regional offices of the Reserve Bank, and the central office staff would run the agenda explaining the current policy perspectives. I also asked that the deputy governor and the executive director in charge of monetary policy do such a thematic video conference after each quarterly policy review so that all our officers could communicate the Reserve Bank's policy rationale to the larger public with greater knowledge and confidence.

Recall what I said earlier about my effort to increase awareness about what the Reserve Bank does so that it can be held to account for its performance. I, therefore, attached a lot of value to a more decentralized dissemination of the monetary policy. My idea was that universities and think tanks across the country, especially in non-metro and second-tier cities, should hold special sessions to discuss and debate policy. I realized that this would not happen by mere exhortation, and at least in the early stages, the Reserve Bank had to act as the catalyst. I used to urge our staff, both in the central office in Mumbai and our regional offices across the country, to take the lead in this. Given the limited staff resources, our reach was modest; so we prepared a roster for balanced geographical coverage.

I got a call one late evening in May 2013 from a senior citizen in Nagaland profusely thanking me, in halting English, for sending someone out there to explain what the Reserve Bank does. Just like my ninety-three-year-old mother-in-law, he gave me a detailed account of the pension he got, his growing monthly expenses and how it was becoming increasingly difficult to make ends meet. 'Do something about the prices, sir, especially the price of cooking oil,' he pleaded with me. It didn't miss me that in his own innocent and polite way, he was seeking accountability from the Reserve Bank.

He made my day.

6

Demystifying the Reserve Bank

How Does the Reserve Bank Make a Difference?

As I've already written, almost the entire first year of my tenure as governor was focused on crisis management—cutting interest rates, pumping in liquidity and stabilizing the markets. Everywhere I went, people seemed to be interested in knowing only one thing: when would I next cut the interest rate? Within weeks, I became quite an expert at giving a standardized, if also a sterile, reply to this FAQ. I also used to joke with my media interlocutors that contrary to my fears, the governor's job was, in fact, quite easy since all it required was cutting interest rates and what's more, the whole country cheered you as you went about the job with abandon!

Then in August 2009 when I was in London for a conference, an interviewer from Reuters asked me: 'You're soon going to complete one year as governor of the RBI. What goals have you set for yourself for your term?' You'd guess, and rightly so, that I was unprepared for this. Any question beyond cutting the interest rate was clearly outside the syllabus, as our students would say, and I was quite flustered. As I thought on my feet, I blurted out something to the effect: 'First, I'd like to position the RBI as a knowledge institution; second, I would want to make the RBI the best practice model among emerging-market central banks for expertise in making policies in a globalizing world; and third, I want to demystify the Reserve Bank.'

The last bit of my reply was playing in my mind through the rest of the day. Why indeed had the need to demystify the Reserve Bank come to me at such a pressured moment? Sure enough, I was quizzed quite a bit in subsequent interviews about what I meant by demystifying the Reserve Bank which forced me to give a concrete structure to my unconscious thought process.

Demystification—a Priority

There were two reasons why demystifying the Reserve Bank seemed such a high priority. The first was my strong feeling that the Reserve Bank has to render accountability for the outcomes of its actions. The Reserve Bank has, in fact, embarked on a number of voluntary initiatives to render accountability. But these measures are all in the nature of 'supplying' accountability; of what use are they unless they are matched by 'demand' for accountability from the larger public? And how can the larger public demand accountability unless they have at least a basic understanding of the role and responsibilities of the Reserve Bank.

It struck me that the large majority of people, even educated people, do not know very much about what the Reserve Bank does. Many know it prints currency but beyond that, the Reserve Bank is a black box, a mysterious institution, a sort of monolith, doing obscure things that have no real relevance for the everyday lives of people.

The reality is, in fact, very different. The Reserve Bank prints and distributes currency, of course, but it does a lot of other things besides. It is the monetary authority of the country, which means its main job is to keep inflation under control while also supporting growth. It is the gatekeeper of the external sector which entails monitoring and regulating capital inflows and outflows, and keeping the exchange rate steady. It regulates and supervises banks to ensure that the money which people save in banks is safe and is productively deployed towards generating economic activity; similarly, it regulates non-banking financial companies and segments of financial markets, again with the aim of channelling savings into productive investment. The Reserve Bank's regulation extends also to the payment and settlement systems with the objective of making financial transactions safe, robust and efficient. The Reserve Bank is the central bank—that is, it is the bank of banks, and the bank for the Central government as well as state governments. On top of all this, and importantly, the Reserve Bank has a key role in the economic development of the country and drives an impressive social development agenda.

That, in a nutshell, is the range and diversity of responsibilities of the Reserve Bank. And what it does affects the everyday lives of people across the country—from the prices they pay in the market, the interest they earn on their bank deposits, the interest they pay when they borrow from a bank, like, say the size of the EMI (equated monthly instalment) they pay on a house loan. It affects how much foreign exchange they can take out to spend or invest outside the country, say, for medical treatment or to educate a child abroad, and how the government pays for new roads, schools and hospitals.

My view was that if the Reserve Bank had to be held to account, we needed to demystify the institution so that the larger public understood what it did and how that connected to their lives.

There was another equally important motivation for my wanting to demystify the Reserve Bank. Not only do people not know what the Reserve Bank does, but they also have negative perceptions of the institution. A widely held stereotypical view of the Reserve Bank is of a rigid, wooden-headed monolith, making rules and regulations with little understanding of the realities of India.

I have personal experience of this negative stereotypical view of the Reserve Bank and how it becomes the scapegoat for virtually all maladies in the financial sector.

My first posting in the IAS after I completed training was as subcollector of Parvathipuram division in Srikakulam district of Andhra Pradesh. Those with long enough memory will recall that the tribal belt of north coastal Andhra Pradesh, particularly the tribal belt of Srikakulam district, was the first region outside of Naxalbari in West Bengal to come under the hold of the Naxalite movement in the late 1960s. By the time I went to Parvathipuram in the mid-1970s, the Naxalite influence in Srikakulam was tapering off; they had moved on into neighbouring Chhattisgarh.

The tribal people had historically suffered ruthless exploitation by the non-tribals—the 'plains people', as they were called—which pushed them into debt and even bondage. The ground-level administration was seen as not only being indifferent to but even complicit in this exploitation. It was this alienation of the tribal households which made them vulnerable to the Naxalite doctrine of begetting social justice though violence. Our priority in the district administration, therefore, was clear—improve the livelihoods of tribal households so as to wean them away from extremist influence.

Tribal livelihood typically depended on *podu* (shifting cultivation on hill slopes) which consisted of spraying the seed after the first rains and returning to the field thereafter only to collect what grew without tending to the crop in between.

Between sowing and harvesting, they were engaged in collecting minor forest produce and selling it in the 'plains area' village markets. Not only was the income from these activities scanty, but it was also seasonal. To smooth their incomes, tribal households typically borrowed from the moneylenders in the plains, and since default was quite common, they lost what land or animals they had to the moneylender and then ended up being bonded labour.

One of our tribal welfare tasks, therefore, was to reduce their dependence on moneylenders by designing and implementing income-generating schemes supported by bank credit. It was quite common for me as subcollector to visit banks to canvass loans for these tribal welfare schemes. Banks, however, used to be quite wary of lending to the tribals for fear of default. They would come up with one excuse after another, and when their imagination ran out, they would invoke their *brahmastra*—they can't give more loans because of 'RBI restriction'.[1] I remember one MLA who, while campaigning for re-election, had gone to the extent of saying that if the government was really interested in tribal welfare, the first thing they should do was to abolish the Reserve Bank!

This is just one example, perhaps an extreme one, of the common misperception about the Reserve Bank. As I moved on in my civil service career, I realized that there was much exaggeration in this negative stereotype. But I was never fully convinced that there was not some justification behind it.

Not until I became governor and got to see the Reserve Bank from within. In the one year that I spent in the bank by the time of the Reuters interview, all my misperceptions about the Reserve Bank had completely melted away. Not only is the Reserve Bank not closed and negative, but on the contrary, it is a remarkably

---

[1] I would learn only much later that 'RBI restriction' is a popular excuse that banks invoke when they don't want to do something.

open- and positive-minded institution. Its staff are caring and sensitive, and they always act in the larger public interest.

So, what explains the negative image? I figured that the reasons are inadequate information and even misinformation. Let me illustrate with an example.

The Reserve Bank, among other things, is also a financial sector regulator with the responsibility of ensuring that financial activity in the economy serves the larger collective good. For example, the Reserve Bank has decided to restrain the growth of deposit-taking NBFCs. A narrow evaluation might make this seem like a negative measure depriving the public of an opportunity of a high-risk, high-reward investment option. But if you factor in how millions of poor households are lured by these high rewards, not knowing the risk involved and end up in financial ruin, the wisdom behind this regulation becomes clear. The culprit here is inadequate information about the rationale for this regulatory restriction.

What Needs to be Done to Demystify the Bank?

What needed to be done to demystify the Reserve Bank, therefore, was quite clear. I must spread understanding about the role and responsibilities of the Reserve Bank widely and deeply, and also correct information flaws. The answer certainly was not to carve out a Department for Demystification of the Reserve Bank nor was it to entrust the task to a few people. The answer was to make demystification a part of everything we do every time and all the time. We must be more open, transparent, communicative and engaging—disseminating the right information deeply, which in itself should check the spread of misinformation.

I spoke many times at several places on the role and responsibilities of the Reserve Bank and on how all our actions and decisions are guided by the larger public good. The topic of my convocation address at Sambalpur University in February 2011 was, in fact, 'The Reserve Bank of India: Making a Difference to Everyday Lives'. The focus of my comments at all village outreach events was to explain the activities of the Reserve Bank in a manner and at a level that semi-literate village folk could understand and relate to. I took the opportunity of my formal speeches and informal comments to explain the rationale behind some of the decisions of the Reserve Bank which were topical at that time. For example, I explained the pros and cons of deregulation of the savings deposit rate, at a town hall meeting in Bhopal as part of the extensive campaign we had launched to get public opinion on this issue in which everyone who had a bank account had an interest.

Let me illustrate with some more specific examples. I've already written about how we tried to simplify the language and streamline the messaging of our quarterly monetary policy statements. But even after all this reinvention, they are still too technical to be understood by people beyond the world of economics and finance. The media and the analysts do some job of interpreting and explaining our language and our message, but much of that too is beyond the reach of most people. Besides, it is no substitute for the Reserve Bank itself doing more towards disseminating its reports, explaining in non-technical language what the report says and how the expected outcomes would impact everyday lives. I used to urge the Reserve Bank's economists to go to different parts of the country and hold seminars in collaboration with the economics departments of local universities on the Reserve Bank publications. The rule, of course, was that they should step out of the metros and go to tier-2 cities. My hope and expectation is that in the course of time, the Reserve bank itself would bring out a non-technical companion to all its technical reports.

Financial Literacy

By far the most systemic and sustainable way to demystify the Reserve Bank is through spreading financial literacy. Financial literacy is a large programme with several dimensions and the Reserve Bank is only one of the many players in the space. The Reserve Bank runs a huge financial literacy programme and also encourages banks to do so.

The one initiative in financial literacy that was dear to me was the introduction of a curriculum on finance in school textbooks so that the next generation of children would pass out of schools financially literate and in the process also develop an understanding of the role and responsibilities of the Reserve Bank. In fact, canvassing this would be part of the standard agenda of my meetings with chief ministers across the country. The Reserve Bank has prepared standard introductory material on finance at various class levels through the schooling period. I used to offer to the chief ministers that the Reserve Bank staff would work with the state school boards to adapt the standard material to the state context and even translate the material into the local language and idiom.

This is, by its very nature, a work in progress and my success has been partial. But I do count this effort of mine at financial literacy as one of the flagship initiatives to demystify the Reserve Bank in a robust and sustainable way.

7

Rupee Tantrums

The Challenge of Exchange Rate Management

Remember I began this book with the old Chinese saying: 'May you live in interesting times'. In the five years I was at the Reserve Bank, I had more than my share of 'interesting times', managing the once-in-a-generation global crisis in 2008–09 and combating a decade-high inflation in 2010–11 which segued into a battle against the slide of the rupee starting mid-2012 up until the close of my tenure in September 2013. Many people ask me about my most difficult challenge in the Reserve Bank, almost invariably expecting me to reply that managing the impact of the global financial crisis in 2008–09 as a greenhorn governor was my most testing time. There is surprise, therefore, when I say that battling the sharp depreciation of the rupee in 2013 was by far my toughest challenge.

Most Formidable Challenge

Why was the rupee problem my most formidable challenge? For several reasons. First and foremost, exchange rate battles are typically of the 'here and now' variety. In deciding on monetary policy to rein in inflation, for example, there is time—time to deliberate, time to analyse, consult, weigh the alternatives, time even to agonize. I felt the same way while managing the global financial crisis. Notwithstanding all the anxiety and uncertainty of that time, there was enough time to reflect and deliberate before deciding on any action. In responding to sharp exchange rate movements, however, there is no such luxury of time; you are oftentimes forced to decide and act 'on the go', as it were.

Of course, we had a time-tested policy and a big-picture strategy in place for exchange rate management. The Reserve Bank also has a well-established process for operationalizing the strategy in the form of a financial markets committee which meets every morning, and in crisis times, several times during the day to review the tactical plans. Even so, market developments are often so volatile, and twist and turn in such unforeseen ways that we are forced to swiftly tweak our tactics in real time.

The second factor that makes exchange rate management an especially daunting task is the challenge of managing expectations. Managing expectations to alter behaviour is critical to the success of several aspects of Reserve Bank policy, such as, for example, preserving financial stability and controlling inflation. What is different in managing expectations about the exchange rate is that in times of pressure, market behaviour becomes susceptible to even stray bits of news, leading to speculative self-fulfilling prophecies. When expectations about the exchange rate become as volatile as the exchange rate itself, spiralling one-way bets on the currency become a distinct risk.

Why do I specifically pick on the 2013 exchange rate pressure as a particularly difficult challenge? For sure, we had exchange rate episodes earlier in my tenure too, most notably in the midst of the global financial crisis towards the end of 2008. But in 2008, we were not alone; many countries, both advanced and emerging, had exchange rate pressures, giving us the comfort of numbers. Also, in 2008, our macroeconomic situation was more supportive; inflation had suddenly fallen—in large part because of the crash in the global oil price; output growth was still rapid, the fiscal deficit was on the mend, and most importantly, our forex reserves were relatively robust. In 2013, in contrast, we were one of a small group of emerging economies, the 'fragile five', which came under severe pressure. Our reserves were low, inflation was high, commodity prices were firming up, fiscal consolidation lacked credibility, and growth prospects were at their bleakest in nearly a decade.

Taper Tantrums

The 'taper tantrums' that reverberated across the world, setting off capital flight from emerging markets and plunging their currencies to new lows, were triggered by a statement in May 2013 by Ben Bernanke, the then chairman of the US Federal Reserve, that they were considering gradually tapering their asset purchase programme, popularly known as 'quantitative easing'.

I would have thought that any news like this, implying that the American economy, the epicentre of the global financial crisis, was showing signs of a robust recovery, would have been cheered by the financial markets; instead, the panic sell-off showed that investors, used to the ease of abundant liquidity, were unprepared for the 'punchbowl' being snatched away. The transition from the comfort of making investment decisions in a world of ample liquidity to the challenge of making investment decisions based on economic fundamentals was always going to be a difficult one; the reaction to Bernanke's statement showed that it could even cause panic.

As capital fled in the tidal wave of taper tantrums, the rupee tumbled steeply from ₹55.52 to a dollar on 22 May 2013, the day after the Bernanke statement, to ₹67.03 on 4 September 2013 when I stepped down from office, recording a depreciation of 17 per cent in just a little over three months.[1]

Changing Perspectives on the Exchange Rate

I have often been asked if there were differences between the government and the Reserve Bank on exchange rate management. The short answer is, not very much. There was a time, even after the regime-changing economic reforms of 1991, when the political class in India looked upon a strong exchange rate as a sign of economic might and a depreciation of the currency as an erosion of that might. However, with India's rapid integration into the global economy, and two-way movements of capital as well as exchange rate, that emotional perception has yielded to a more agnostic view. We no longer attach any political economy significance to the exchange rate and have grown to look upon it as a pure macro variable. We understand that not just a weak rupee, but even a strong rupee can cause pain. This was clearly in evidence going by the broad political support for the exporters' agitation—when the rupee appreciated sharply in the pre-crisis years of 2006–08—that the Reserve Bank should check the rise of the rupee.

---

[1] The exchange rate, or more appropriately the nominal exchange rate, defines the number of units of domestic currency that is needed to buy one unit of foreign currency; for example, ₹60 is needed to buy one dollar. A decrease in this number denotes nominal appreciation of the domestic currency while an increase in the number denotes nominal depreciation. Thus, if the rupee moves from ₹60 to a dollar to ₹50 to a dollar, it is said to have appreciated in nominal terms and vice versa.

Shared Responsibility but Differing Messages

Unlike monetary and regulatory policies where the Reserve Bank is, or at any rate, should be autonomous, management of the exchange rate is a shared responsibility of the government and the bank. In normal times, the Reserve Bank typically acts on its own and keeps the government in the loop, but in times of crisis, there is invariably consultation, coordination and, where necessary, synchronized action. During these 'tantrum months', Chidambaram and I met several times; deputy governors Harun Khan and Urjit Patel were in constant touch with Finance Secretary Arvind Mayaram and Chief Economic Adviser Raghuram Rajan. We were largely agreed on the overall strategy for managing the exchange rate although there were the inevitable differences on tactics and timing. Quite obviously, on neither side did we have an idea of how much bleeding would take place and when it would stop.

Even as we were engaged in a fierce exchange rate defence, one issue that troubled me all through was the narrative that was taking shape about the origin of the problem. The government, in particular, was attempting to paint the rupee problem as caused entirely by external factors. Sure, the timing and pace of depreciation were a response to the impending 'taper' of the ultra-easy monetary policy by the Fed. But global factors were just the proximate cause for our exchange rate turmoil; the root cause lay in our domestic economy where, for years, we had been heaping pressure on the rupee, an issue that the Reserve Bank consistently raised in its monetary policy statements. An implosion was inevitable; it was incidental that the trigger came by way of the taper tantrums.

My concern was that we would go astray in both the diagnosis and remedy if we did not acknowledge that at the heart of our external economy problem were domestic vulnerabilities. I had several conversations with Chidambaram on this, but found him reluctant to face up to this inconvenient truth. He is too intelligent not to have seen the point; I suspect he found it politically convenient to point to an external scapegoat rather than call attention to domestic structural factors.

What were these domestic structural factors? At its root, the problem was the huge current account deficit (CAD) we had been running for three years in a row and possibly for the fourth year in 2013–14. In other words, at the economy level, our total import bill was far higher than our total export earnings, making us dependent on external financing for filling the gap. The CAD was 4.2 per cent of GDP in 2011–12, 4.8 per cent in 2012–13, and most forecasts put the CAD for 2013–14 at over 4.0 per cent[2]—well above 3.0 percent of GDP, the sustainable limit as estimated by the Reserve Bank.

Why indeed did the CAD widen so much? A potent cocktail of factors was at play. First, recall that we had a classic V-shaped recovery from the crisis even while much of the world was still struggling with recession. This meant that our imports grew rapidly even as our export prospects remained bleak because of subdued global demand. The pressure was exacerbated by some real appreciation of the rupee, a consequence of our higher inflation relative to that of our trading partners, which made importing more attractive and exporting more difficult.[3] Second,

---

[2] The actual CAD in 2013–14 was 1.7 per cent of GDP.

[3] The real exchange rate defines the purchasing power of two currencies relative to each other. While two currencies may have a nominal exchange rate in the forex market, it does not mean that the goods and services purchased in one currency cost an equivalent amount in the other currency converted at the nominal exchange rate. This straightforward calculation will change if the two jurisdictions have different inflation rates. The real exchange rate is thus the nominal exchange rate adjusted for the differing rates of inflation. For example, if India has higher inflation than the US, the rupee can get 'strong' relative to the dollar in real terms even if the nominal exchange rate does not move.

the global crude price had spiked which added to our import bill, and thereby to the CAD. Third, gold imports surged, more than doubling from 1.3 per cent of GDP in 2007–08 to 3.0 per cent in 2012–13 due to larger import volumes and higher global prices. Finally, judicial orders unwittingly added to the pressure. The Supreme Court struck down the coal block allocation made by the government to private parties which resulted in a sharp decline in domestic production and forced power producers to turn to imports to meet the shortage. The Supreme Court also banned iron ore mining, on environmental grounds, which affected ore exports.

Reserve Bank's Exchange Rate Defence

There were two dimensions to our exchange rate management strategy. The first was to smooth the trajectory of the exchange rate adjustment path by tactically selling foreign exchange from our reserves. The second was to manage expectations and contain potential herd behaviour in the market by implementing measures to augment inflows and stem outflows.

We regularly intervened in the forex market all through this period by selling dollars from our forex reserves. The standard operating procedure I followed was to approve the quantum of intervention for a limited period, say for a week, but leave the operational details to the staff. Consistent with global practice across central banks, the Reserve Bank does not disclose its interventions on a daily basis but markets, by and large, manage to get a sense of that by analysing the volumes of forex coming into the market.[4] They then speculate about the coded message that the bank might be sending through the size and timing of

---

[4] The Reserve Bank does, however, disclose its monthly total interventions with a lag of a month.

its interventions. Managing this messaging is part of the Reserve Bank intervention strategy which requires an understanding of the markets, intelligence, tact and quick thinking, all of which the forex dealers of the Reserve Bank have in abundance. This is a quiet but enormously talented bunch of professionals.

The other dimension of our exchange rate management, as I said, was capital-flow management measures. We increased the quota for foreign buying into the rupee-denominated debts issued by both the government and the corporates. This was consistent with our road map for the gradual opening up of the capital account although the timing was admittedly influenced by the taper tantrums.

If an Indian corporate defaults on its domestic borrowing, it hurts its credit rating. If an Indian corporate defaults on its foreign borrowing, it hurts the credit rating not just of the corporate but of the entire economy. Because of this spillover impact, the Reserve Bank disciplines external borrowing by corporates by imposing an upper bound on the total debt servicing cost, technically called 'all-in-cost'. Considering the need to augment inflows, we relaxed the upper bound of the all-in-cost for external commercial borrowing so as to make it easier for corporates to negotiate external loans.

For a long time, Reserve Bank regulations allowed corporates to contract foreign borrowing only to meet forex expenditure, but over time, we relaxed this requirement, making it possible for them to use foreign loans even to meet rupee expenditure. Corporates were also allowed to keep their forex borrowing meant for rupee expenditure outside the country until they actually needed to spend it at home. To relieve the pressure on the rupee, we now mandated that all ECB raised for rupee expenditure should be brought into the country immediately even if their project was not yet ready to absorb the loan proceeds.

India provides two main facilities for NRIs to invest their savings in the country: non-resident external (NRE) rupee accounts where the exchange rate risk is borne by the NRI depositor; and foreign currency non-resident (FCNR) accounts where the exchange rate risk is borne by the deposit-accepting bank. The Reserve Bank regulated the maximum interest rate that banks can offer on NRI deposits mainly out of a concern that if there was no such restraint, banks would race to the bottom by offering ever higher interest rates to NRIs which would aggravate our collective vulnerability. Given the pressure to augment capital inflows, we withdrew this ceiling on the interest rate on rupee-denominated NRI accounts, thereby allowing freedom to banks to set the interest rate themselves; we continued, however, with an interest rate cap on FCNR accounts but raised the cap.

One of the big problems to contend with in exchange rate defence is speculative pressures as they can be both self-fulfilling and self-reinforcing. For example, in a scenario where the rupee is sliding continuously, exporters would defer bringing in the export receipts, and importers would buy forward, and both those actions, what markets call 'leads and lags', would exacerbate the run on the currency. One of our aims, therefore, was to restrict the options open to the market participants, including banks, to take undue advantage of the market volatility. Towards this end, we restricted the flexibility available to both exporters and importers to maintain open foreign exchange positions and reduced the limits available to banks to trade on the rupee.

We have two separate markets for taking a position on the future of the rupee—the over the counter (OTC) 'forwards' market which is restricted only to those having an underlying foreign exchange exposure—for example, importers and exporters—and the exchange-traded 'futures' market which is open to all. In normal times, the two markets would be roughly synchronized, and together they help efficient price discovery; in crisis times though, there is oftentimes a disconnect between the two markets which opens up opportunities for speculators to exploit the arbitrage and reinforce the one-way pressure on the exchange rate. To limit such opportunities, we proscribed proprietary trading by banks in the currency futures market; in other words, banks could transact in this market only on behalf of their clients.

Restraints on Gold Imports

As I wrote earlier, gold was a big source of import pressure. The Indian appetite for gold is part of folklore, but why indeed did the demand for gold spurt so suddenly? Clearly, some idiosyncratic factors were at play. Our gold demand comprises three segments. The largest segment is the 'folklore' demand, especially from middle- and low-income households, who find investing in gold to be an attractive option as it provides a hedge against inflation while also providing liquidity, as gold can be sold or offered as collateral for emergency borrowing. The second demand segment comprises jewellers who import raw gold and convert it into jewellery for re-export. Finally, there is speculative demand from people taking positions on the global price of gold, which itself is a consequence of the global macro outlook. Between 2009 and 2012, the folklore demand for gold had shot up, as our inflation remained elevated and the real returns on bank deposits turned negative. The speculative demand spiked too as average gold price zoomed from $867 per troy oz (₹12,890 per 10 grams) in 2008–09 to $1654 per troy oz (₹30,164 per 10 grams) in 2012–13, making investment in gold look like a one-way bet.

The need for imposing restrictions on gold import to help reduce the CAD was obvious. The direct, blunt, and possibly the most effective in the short-term, way of doing this was to raise the customs duty on gold so as to raise the import cost of gold. This, however, entailed big risks. As part of the reform process in the

1990s, India had liberalized the import of gold, which put an end to smuggling and to the crime and mafia activity that came with it. Raising customs duty would mean undoing those gains and the need for treading cautiously was clear.

Between May and August 2013, the government raised the customs duty on gold imports from 6 per cent to 10 per cent, clearly wary of crossing the tipping point beyond which smuggling would become an attractive option. From the Reserve Bank side, we imposed restrictions on the import of gold as well as on its use as a collateral for loans. We banned the import of gold coins and medallions, prohibited non-banking financial companies from lending against the security of gold in any form, restrained loans against gold by banks, and restricted import of gold on consignment basis by both banks and other agencies.

One constant vexation in the middle of this rupee turmoil was that many large corporates had not hedged their foreign exchange exposures and had set themselves up for huge losses as the rupee rapidly lost value. Notwithstanding past experiences where several of them had lost heavily because of unhedged exposures, they still calculated that the costs of hedging outweighed the benefits. This is clearly a miscalculation as one 'black swan' episode can wipe out all the past gains. Our investigations revealed that banks too were quite negligent about educating their corporate borrowers on the prudence of hedging their forex exposures.

We were concerned about this nonchalance—bordering on indifference—as corporate defaults on external borrowing can complicate what is already a complex problem. For a long time, the Reserve Bank had been cautioning banks on the importance of encouraging their corporate borrowers to hedge their forex exposures. As persuasion did not work, we had to eventually issue a regulatory mandate that every bank should have a board-approved policy regarding hedging of forex risks by its corporate borrowers, including small and medium enterprises, and that they should take into account the risk of unhedged foreign exposures in pricing the credit risk premium.

~

The currency turmoil in emerging markets continued all through May and June 2013. It did not help that Bernanke reiterated his message about the taper with a follow-up statement in a press conference in June 2013 that if the US economy continued to improve, they could start winding down the asset purchase programme in 2013 and wrap it up in 2014. Markets around the world sold off aggressively on the news, with major indices dropping more than 1 per cent.

At home, because the exchange rate adjustment was not yet complete, the rupee continued to slide with no obvious reversal in sight even as the calendar turned to July 2013. The rupee problem required my undivided attention which meant that I had to pare down most other commitments. I felt guilty though, as there were only two more months to go of my tenure and I had piled up a huge number of commitments. Most of all, I wanted to complete visiting all the regional offices of the Reserve Bank. There are altogether twenty-nine of them across the country and I had visited twenty-seven; I wanted to go to the remaining two—in Kanpur and Shillong—before I stepped down, but that remained an unfulfilled wish. I had attended the BIS bimonthly meetings of governors fairly regularly and I was looking forward to attending the June-end meeting which would be my last, but I decided to skip that. All through my tenure, I tried to honour all speaking commitments, as I was conscious that postponing at the last minute would be very disruptive to the hosts, but with my schedule going haywire, I had to opt out of them as well.

Both Chidambaram and I were to travel to Moscow for a G20 meeting scheduled on 19–20 July. On 15 July, I met Chidambaram in Delhi and told him of my decision to deploy monetary policy to sharply tighten market liquidity as a measure of exchange rate defence. The specific measures consisted of raising the marginal standing facility rate by a whopping 2 per cent, imposing a quantitative restriction on banks' access to the repo window and open market sales of government securities.

This decision to use monetary policy to defend the exchange rate was by far one of the toughest decisions I had to make as governor. It is not lightly that a central bank, particularly the Reserve Bank, would use its monetary policy weaponry for exchange rate defence. For sure, the Reserve Bank's regular monetary policy decisions, calibrated with other objectives such as inflation and growth in view, would have an impact on the exchange rate, but that is an incidental, albeit considered, by-product. Directly deploying monetary policy to manage the exchange rate itself is an altogether different ball game. But as one central bank colleague told me: 'Sometimes, it is time to think the unthinkable.' I thought the time had come for me then.

The motivation for this bazooka action, as some analysts called it, was to curb speculative activity which was exacerbating the one-way pressure on the rupee. We had market intelligence to believe that the relatively comfortable liquidity in the system and the relentless one-way movement of the rupee were together fuelling speculation, especially in the overseas non-deliverable forwards (NDF) market. Tightening domestic liquidity was imperative to make it more expensive to borrow in rupees to take dollar positions. Furthermore, we believed that this extraordinary action would signal our resolve to stem the rupee volatility. Incidentally, given that the rupee depreciation was inflationary, these measures to arrest its slide were consistent with our inflation management objective, both in terms of their potential impact on the exchange rate itself and through the more conventional monetary policy channel.

Over the years, the Reserve Bank had liberalized the capital account by not only making it easier for non-residents to bring in capital and take it out, but also allowing options for resident Indians to convert their rupee holdings into foreign currency for investment abroad under the Liberalized Remittance Scheme (LRS). On 14 August, we reduced the maximum amount that individuals and corporates could take out under LRS. The market reaction was swift and brutal; the rupee fell from ₹61.43 to a dollar on 13 August to ₹68.36 on 28 August, while the bellwether stock index Sensex fell from 19,230 on 16 August to 17,996 on 28 August.

Why was the market so unforgiving? After all, deploying price or quantity controls to calibrate capital flows in order to manage pressures on the exchange rate had been standard practice for the Reserve Bank. For example, in 2007–08, the year before the crisis, when there were large inflows that put the rupee under severe appreciation pressure, governor Y.V. Reddy, in an effort to throw sand in the wheels of inflows, had tightened the ECB policy, making the conditions under which corporates could borrow abroad more exacting. During the financial crisis in the months after I took over, when the rupee came under depreciation pressure, I did the opposite— reversed the restrictions on ECB to increase inflows. Similarly, interest rates on NRI deposits were adjusted in the past both up and down to neutralize the impact of large capital flows in either direction.

If, as described above, the market is used to the Reserve Bank using controls to calibrate capital flows, what was different about the restrictions on LRS that they triggered such a sharp reaction? Evidently, the market saw the LRS restrictions not as a usual, temporary capital-flow management measure but as an unusual and regressive move. My calculation was that this decision would be interpreted as the Reserve Bank's resolve to contain expectations about the rupee's fall. Instead, the market saw this perceived willingness to deviate from the broad thrust towards increasing rupee convertibility as an extreme action triggered by panic which reinforced the negative perceptions on the currency.

Did I make a costly misjudgement of the market reaction? That's a question that I agonized over all through the next couple of weeks till I left the Reserve Bank and indeed several times even afterwards. My only comfort is that I was not alone. Virtually every central bank governor has experienced market reaction contrary to expectation at some time or other. Bernanke, I am sure, must have been surprised by the panic set off by his advance warning of 'the taper' in May 2013, and Xiaochuan, governor of the People's Bank of China, must have been surprised by the sense of shock in the global financial markets when China adjusted the exchange rate peg of the yuan in August 2015, ostensibly as a prelude to making the exchange rate more market determined.

Is it presumptuous then on the part of central banks to believe that they can accurately judge market psychology? An analogy from physics comes to mind. We all know that the two great theories of twentieth century physics—Relativity and Quantum Mechanics—are inconsistent with each other. All through his life, Albert Einstein could not reconcile to the probabilistic nature of the universe implied by the quantum theory and famously declared: 'God does not play dice.' To this, his friend and pioneering quantum physicist Neils Bohr replied, 'Albert, stop telling God what he can or cannot do.' Similarly, central bankers can hardly presume to tell markets how to behave no matter the intentions behind their policy moves. If the crisis has taught us anything, it is that central banks have to be more humble about their ability to predict market behaviour.

Challenges in Exchange Rate Management

Let me now turn to some challenges we confronted in exchange rate management during this period. By far the most formidable challenge was to manage expectations. Fears were stoked by a number of factors. Some commentators, for example, wondered whether India was once again heading into a twin deficit problem—a combination of a large fiscal deficit with a large current-account deficit that can derail growth, fuel inflation and threaten macroeconomic stability. The origins for this apprehension trace back to our balance of payments crisis of 1991 which, it is now widely agreed, was a direct consequence of the fiscal profligacy—the government borrowing way beyond its means—of the 1980s. We were once again experiencing a potent mix of twin deficits, in 2012. Might we be setting ourselves up for another balance of payments implosion?

I thought these fears were overdone and I did my best to emphasize why an implosion had been imminent in 1991 and how 2012 was different from 1991.

Between 1991 and 2012, the structure of the Indian economy had changed in fundamental ways. Our exchange rate was now largely market determined. Our financial markets had become more mature, more diverse and much deeper, and were capable of absorbing most shocks. Our regulatory systems and our crisis response mechanism were more robust and sophisticated. Our forex reserves, both in absolute and relative terms, were much larger, and our external debt, as a proportion of GDP, much lower than in 1991. Importantly, the share of services in the GDP was significantly lower in 1991 than in 2012 which is a source of resilience, as service activity is less vulnerable to shocks than agriculture and industry.

I was, of course, conscious of the risk of sounding too complacent or even upbeat. So, every time I gave this reassuring message, I used to take care to balance it with the warning that we had, by no means, insulated ourselves against all future crises. There were several fissures in the macroeconomy which needed to be fixed to keep the economy from derailing.

The feedback I got was that this message went down well with the markets. The prime minister had seen media reports of my public comments and on more than one occasion commended me in private for sending out such a measured message, combining reassurance with a firm call to action to fix the growing vulnerabilities.

Preserving credibility is the other big challenge in exchange rate management. Loss of credibility can be costly for any institution, public or private, but the stakes are much higher for central banks. If a central bank is credible, its actions deliver the intended outcomes effectively; and if its credibility is low or impaired, even good decisions fail to deliver results, which explains why central banks attach so much value to maintaining their credibility. Nowhere is the credibility issue more evident than in exchange rate management where, as accumulated experience from central banks around the world demonstrates, a failed defence can be worse than no defence at all.

Resisting currency appreciation and currency depreciation are both complex challenges that test a central bank's credibility, but between the two, the former is arguably a better problem to have because of an important asymmetry that goes largely unrecognized.

When a central bank is trying to prevent appreciation of its currency, it intervenes in the market, buying forex by paying for it in the domestic currency, thus increasing the supply of domestic currency and reducing its value. A central bank's war chest of domestic currency is, at least in theory, unlimited as it can print any amount of the stuff it wants. There are, of course, negative side effects to such an action. The domestic currency that the central bank unleashes into the system in payment for the forex can fuel inflation, trigger asset bubbles and threaten financial stability. These are admittedly costly to deal with, but to the limited extent of exchange rate defence, the market can be in no doubt about the virtually unlimited firepower of the central bank.

Fighting depreciation of the currency, on the other hand, requires the central bank to sell forex from its finite reserves. If the central bank is seen to be losing reserves even as capital continues to exit and the domestic currency continues to fall, the nervousness in the markets can pull the currency down in a vicious spiral. This is a bigger risk.

The possibility of a putative tipping point is another challenge in exchange rate management. What is a tipping point? It is the point at which the floor caves in, foreigners lose confidence in the currency and pull out 'to cut losses', setting the exchange rate into a free fall. After May 2013 when the rupee slid sharply with no reversal in sight, some commentators started speculating on what the tipping point for the exchange rate might be—₹65 to a dollar? Or ₹70?

I was not persuaded by this tipping point argument. It is, in fact, possible to turn the argument around. The tipping point could actually act as a floor, the level below which the exchange rate will not go, because that will be a point at which it becomes more costly for foreign investors to pull out than to stay in and ride out the currency adjustment!

Criticism of Exchange Rate Management

The Reserve Bank's action and inaction on the exchange rate front attracted plenty of criticism which intensified as the rupee continued on its relentless slide. This criticism was all over the map and straddled virtually every dimension—policy, strategy, tactics and communication. Abstracting from all the details, I can crystallize the criticism into two distinct strands. First, that I was too hands-off, did not build forex reserves when there were copious capital inflows in 2010 and 2011, and that failure had cost us dearly in managing the exchange rate when it came under pressure in 2013. The second strand of criticism was that the Reserve Bank's defence of the rupee was too hesitant and tentative, and lacked credibility. That, as governor, instead of projecting confidence and resolve, I betrayed diffidence and ambiguity which, according to this school of thought, undermined our efforts to arrest the slide.

As I look back on those anxious months from this distance of time, I see that at least some of the criticism was valid. Perhaps this is an appropriate point to explain where I was coming from, not so much to defend my record, but to communicate some of the dilemmas I confronted as governor.

Take the first criticism that I did not intervene in the market when there were capital inflows in 2010 and 2011, thereby failing to build a defensive buffer of reserves for a future fight against exchange rate depreciation. What was worse, by allowing the rupee to appreciate through my hands-off approach, I had dented India's export competitiveness.

This alleged inaction on my part has to be evaluated in the context of the Reserve Bank's stated exchange rate policy, which is not to keep the rupee at a certain level but only to tamp down volatility in the exchange rate. In other words, during an episode of depreciation, for example, the attempt is not to prevent the fall of the rupee but only to engineer the trajectory of the fall.

Admittedly, we had large inflows in 2010 and 2011, but there was no volatility in the exchange rate; it was gradually moving up on the strength of the inflows. Intervention under these circumstances, I believed, would not be consistent with our stated policy. I felt obliged to walk the talk.

Besides, intervention under these circumstances would also involve a moral hazard. As we were gradually opening up the external sector, it was important that all market participants, in particular the corporates, learnt to manage exchange rate risks. If the Reserve Bank were to step in every time the exchange rate moved, they would never learn to cope with exchange rate movements and would happily outsource their exchange rate risk management to the Reserve Bank. Exchange rate panics are never pretty, but their virtue is that they restore fear and humility to the market players.

My relative hands-off stance also arose from the view that intervention in the absence of any evident volatility would be interpreted by the market as targeting a specific exchange rate, notwithstanding assertions to the contrary by the Reserve Bank. Believing that they are insured against exchange rate losses, speculators will then make the rupee a one-way bet and we would become vulnerable to being gamed.

I must admit that on the policy spectrum, my bias was towards non-intervention; in other words, the weight of evidence had to be higher than normal for me to approve intervention in the forex market. My staff as well as senior officials in the government would sense this. All too often they would persuade me to act, and the argument would be that in times of volatility, exchange rates overshoot and intervention is important to correct the overshoot and bring the rupee back to its equilibrium level.

The logical next question then is: what is the equilibrium exchange rate? It is that level of the nominal exchange rate which corresponds to a neutral real effective exchange rate (REER = 100). I did not find this argument persuasive. First, it is difficult to detect overshoot in real time. Second, the neutral real effective exchange rate has never been an anchor for the nominal rate. In other words, when the rupee had been relatively stable, the nominal exchange rate did not correspond to the neutral real exchange rate. Also, if indeed there was an overshoot of the exchange rate, it would correct itself, and intervention would be an avoidable waste of scarce forex resources.

There are, of course, counterarguments on all these counts, but the bottom line is that targeting the real exchange rate can be as complex and futile as targeting the nominal exchange rate.

Many times during this period of turmoil, I had wondered about the gap between the Reserve Bank's stated exchange rate policy and its actions in the forex market. For one, 'volatility' is the crucial word in the policy statement, but we have never defined what we meant by that, or more specifically, what level of volatility would trigger interventionist action. Analysts who track the Reserve Bank's behaviour would note that we had intervened in the market even when there was a sharp one-way movement in the exchange rate. How does this square with any definition of volatility in the policy statement? Is building reserves an acceptable justification for intervention? If so, what according to the Reserve Bank is the optimal level of reserves?

These questions would be standard fare in the countless situation room meetings we had during those tumultuous months. My staff would concede that the market could be bewildered by the Reserve Bank's actions but would not acquiesce in the idea that we should make our policy more explicit. Their main argument was that the exchange rate is a sensitive and critical macro variable, that the Reserve Bank should retain all flexibility to act swiftly and decisively, and should not voluntarily become hostage to a more explicit and restrictive policy statement. Besides, no central bank, they would contend, is transparent about its exchange rate policy and it does not pay for any one country to be an outlier, especially in a world of 'currency wars'.

Notwithstanding the global acrimony over the currency wars, I believe there is a case for the Reserve Bank to review and restate its exchange rate policy. I can hardly attempt to outline a full policy statement here, but the revised policy should be based on the following premises. First, the Reserve Bank should be less interventionist than it has traditionally tended to be; in other words, it should minimize the moral hazard by shifting more of the burden of adjustment to exchange rate movements to market participants. Second, reflecting the less interventionist stance, it should indicate more clearly what would be considered 'excess volatility' that would trigger intervention. Admittedly, the more precisely 'excess volatility' is defined, the less flexibility it will leave for the Reserve Bank. But I think more rules and less discretion will, in the long run, yield sustainable benefits by better managing expectations and minimizing opportunities for self-fulfilling, speculative behaviour. Finally, the Reserve Bank should admit what is now evident to everyone, that building forex reserves is an objective of exchange rate management, and in order to be credible, should indicate the norms that will determine 'adequate' level of reserves.

A logical question would be: what prevented me from reshaping the policy as above? The only explanation I can offer is that I was fully persuaded about the imperative of reviewing the policy only after my experience with rupee tantrums in 2013. But a change of policy when the exchange rate was on the boil would have been absolutely the wrong thing to do. The exchange rate cooled only after I left the Reserve Bank, not giving me a window of opportunity for any policy re-engineering.

Let me turn to the second strand of the criticism, that during the entire rupee episode, communication by the Reserve Bank, particularly by me as the governor, lacked credibility and, therefore, what we were saying was shaking rather than bolstering market confidence.

How indeed should the governor have spoken about the rupee? There were some suggestions that the Reserve Bank should have been much more assertive, more 'alpha male', as some commentators put it, like the Swiss National Bank (SNB). Recall that the Swiss franc came under massive and sustained appreciation pressure when the European Central Bank unleashed huge liquidity into the markets to fight the sovereign debt crisis. The euros so released were flooding the safe haven of Switzerland and putting upward pressure on the Swiss franc. In the face of this, the SNB declared that it would not allow the franc to appreciate beyond 1.20 francs to a euro.

The 'alpha male' imagery was striking but the parallel with the SNB was misplaced. The SNB was seeking to prevent a potential appreciation of the franc unrelated to their economic fundamentals; whereas we, in the Reserve Bank, were engaged in preventing a sharp depreciation of the rupee driven largely by economic fundamentals. There is, as I said before, an asymmetry between the two battles. The SNB was in the fray from a position of strength, whereas we were battling from a position of weakness. More importantly, given the external and internal pressures ranged against the rupee—elevated inflation, declining growth, large fiscal deficits and the large and unsustainable current-account deficit—it would have been very unrealistic, if also enormously costly, to draw a line in the sand on the rupee exchange rate. We had necessarily to cross the river by feeling the stones.

What or who exactly is an alpha male? I googled and was baffled by the variation and confusion in the meaning and description of an alpha male. At this point, it is not even clear to me whether I should take not being an alpha male as a badge of honour or as a certificate of weakness. I have decided to let the matter rest. But could I have been more confident, consistent and, importantly, more tactful? With the benefit of hindsight, I can see that I could have done better on all these criteria. Let me illustrate with some examples.

In the post-policy media conference in late July 2013, at the height of the rupee crisis, I had said that the Reserve Bank's actions were not aimed at defending any specific exchange rate, but aimed only at facilitating an orderly adjustment of the exchange rate to its market-determined level. As far as I was concerned, this was just an unequivocal reiteration of the Reserve Bank's standard policy and should not have stirred any reaction. But the markets decided that I had announced an immediate end to all intervention in the market, and reacted sharply. My statement was seen as too dovish, maybe even as too indifferent, and the rupee plunged to a three-week low within hours.

Needless to say, I was quite perturbed by the unsparing market reaction. Was I guilty of fraying market nerves when I should actually have been soothing them? I reflected on this overnight and used the opportunity of the post-policy conference with analysts the following day to get the communication back on track. I asserted that the Reserve Bank would use all the instruments at its command to defend the rupee; I was careful not to make any reference to a 'target rate' or 'volatility', and added that we had enough firepower to stem the rupee's fall. The strategy worked. The statement helped assuage the concerns raised by my previous day's 'hands-off' approach, and within hours, the rupee recorded its biggest intra-day gain of 2013.

I had another chastening experience in the context of the savage market reaction to the capital controls imposed by us on corporates and individuals in mid-August 2013 that I wrote about earlier. Note that these restrictions applied only to the capital that residents could take out; we did not curb the freedom of non-residents in any way. Besides, at the level these facilities were being used, they would not have been binding except in a very few cases. So these capital controls triggered fear not so much because they were limiting on a stand-alone basis, but because they were seen as prelude to more draconian controls down the line.

I took the opportunity of the Palkhivala Memorial Lecture in late August 2013 to allay the fears on capital controls by reiterating that it was not the policy of the Reserve Bank to resort to capital controls or reverse the direction of capital account liberalization and that these measures were temporary and would be withdrawn when the rupee stabilized.

Structural Causes of the Rupee Turmoil

The thrust of my communication effort all through this period was to drive home a more basic message: India was running an unsustainable current-account deficit by spending more on imports than we were earning from our exports. What was worse, we were importing not capital goods that would add to production capacity and help resolve our massive supply constraints, but were importing unproductive goods like gold.

Just as a household cannot spend more than it earns unless someone is willing to lend it money, even an economy cannot run a current-account deficit unless an external party is willing to lend it foreign currency to finance the deficit. And the more we depend on external financing—kindness of strangers, as it were—the more vulnerable we become to 'sudden stop and exit', a phrase that has become popular to describe a situation when external finance not only stops but even the investment already made is withdrawn. In normal times, there are checks against pressures building up to such unsustainable levels, as external financiers would raise the price of funding and alert us to the impending implosion. The system would self-correct through an exchange rate depreciation to limit the deficit to the available external financing.

Such an adjustment did not take place in our case because these were not normal times. Advanced economies were running historically easy monetary policies to stimulate their economies and all the 'quantitatively eased' money they were unleashing was flooding the global markets. This money was looking for quick returns, and short-term investments in emerging markets like India looked like an attractive option. These investments financed our deficits, and in the absence of the usual alert signals, we were lulled into complacency even as pressure was building on the rupee. By not addressing our structural imbalances and bringing the current account down to its sustainable level, we had set ourselves up for an abrupt and painful adjustment. Finding a scapegoat in Bernanke's statement was politically convenient but, from an economic management perspective, clearly misleading.

My view was that the government and the Reserve Bank could not, and indeed should not, stand in the way of this adjustment as any such effort would be futile and costly. On the other hand, the sooner the exchange rate correction was over and done with, the sooner we would be able to make a fresh start. The effort of the government and the Reserve Bank, I thought, should be focused only on navigating the adjustment and guiding the exchange rate to its market-determined level.

I had genuinely believed that acknowledging that a massive correction in the rupee was unavoidable would not only manage expectations but also act as a lesson for the future. In the event, this did not go down well and was interpreted as being defensive and hapless.

After stepping down from the Reserve Bank, I reflected on my efforts at communication during this crisis period. Some people have told me that I was right on the message but wrong on the timing. In other words, I should have deferred the message till after the pressure had subsided, and focused, during the crisis, only on building confidence. I am not persuaded that this would have been the right strategy. My message was clearly situated in the context of the crisis and aimed at managing expectations. If that message had to be effective, it had to be given during the crisis.

The Endgame

Notwithstanding the exchange rate defence launched by the Reserve Bank, the bloodletting continued into August 2013.

Adding to the domestic and external economic factors, political economy developments too came into play. The most significant was the threat of armed intervention in Syria in mid-August 2013 which caused crude oil prices to spike, and renewed the stampede of capital out of emerging markets. These developments sent the rupee to its trough on 28 August when it sank 21 per cent below its 1 May level.

Several factors helped the recovery of the rupee starting early September. By far the most important was that the adjustment had run its course; second, the risk of a flare-up in Syria abated; third, the Fed announced that it was postponing the taper indefinitely.

Finally, the scheduled leadership change at the Reserve Bank and the formidable reputation of my successor, Raghuram Rajan, helped restore confidence in the Indian markets. In fact, as chief economic adviser to the government, Raghu was on board all through the exchange rate turmoil and was more actively involved in all the decisions after he was named in early August as my successor.

As we approached the close of my term in the first week of September, Raghu and I had both agreed that the next steps should be to open a special forex window for oil companies and incentivize our commercial banks to raise tier-2 capital through their branches and subsidiaries abroad, and swap the dollars for rupees with the Reserve Bank at a premium. Raghu was kind enough to offer that I announce these measures before signing off. But I thought that the measures would be more effective if he announced them as the incoming governor. At least on this issue, my judgement worked!

Do Nothing in Defence of the Exchange Rate?

Let me conclude my experiences of steering the rupee in turbulent waters by reiterating a standard dilemma. Given my position that a sharp correction of the exchange rate was programmed and forex intervention by the Reserve Bank would only postpone the inevitable, wouldn't it have been more rational to just stay put till the adjustment had been complete?

Albert Edwards of Société Générale had an interesting analogy from football. 'When there are problems, our instinct is not just to stand there but to do something. When a goalkeeper tries to save a penalty, he almost invariably dives either to the right or the left. He stays in the centre only 6.3 per cent of the time. However, the penalty taker is just as likely (28.7 per cent of the time) to blast the ball straight in front of him as to hit it to the right or left. Thus, to play the percentages, goalkeepers will be better off staying where they are about a third of the time. They would make more saves.'

But goalkeepers rarely do that. Because it is more embarrassing to stand there and watch the ball hit the back of the net than do something (such as dive to the right or left) and watch the ball hit the back of the net.

The Reserve Bank is like a football goalkeeper. It knows that 'do nothing' is the best course. But it can't just stand pat.[5, 6]

---

[5] Drawn from an article by Vivek Kaul in the *DNA* of 7 August 2013.

[6] Indeed, the public expects policymakers to respond to every situation even though there are situations when the most sensible thing, from a long-term perspective, for policymakers to do is not to do anything at all. This dilemma was illustrated very lucidly in a creative video presentation on the differing ideologies of Keynesian and Austrian prescriptions for the global crisis. In the video, featuring a boxing match between Keynes and Hayek, Keynes asks Hayek about what he would do when unemployment is rising. Hayek trots out a few long-term prescriptions. But in the short-term, he would like the government to be a standstill goalkeeper. Sensible maybe, but virtually impossible in the shrill democracies of today.

8

The Signal and the Noise

The Challenge and Opportunity
of Communication

One of the nice things about being a central bank governor is that the markets hang on every word you say, treating every syllable, nuance and twitch of the face as a market cue. One of the stressful things about being a central bank governor is that the markets hang on every word you say, treating every syllable, nuance and twitch of the face as a market cue. That about sums up both the opportunity and challenge of central bank communication.

I believe there would be virtually no central bank governor who has not taken an ego trip on the magic of his spoken word or rued the fallout of some miscommunication. Experience helps, but is no guarantee against markets deciding that you said something different from what you believe you've said. I learnt along the way; and maybe, even the hard way. Before I write about my own experiences with communication, some broader context maybe useful.

The Power of Central Bank Communication

There are powerful examples from around the world of how central banks have exploited the power of their communication to enhance their policy effectiveness. Hours after the 9/11 terrorist attacks in the United States in 2001, the Federal Reserve put out a simple statement: 'The Federal Reserve System is open and operating. The discount window is open to meet liquidity needs.'

These two seemingly banal sentences, coming so soon after the attacks, had a remarkable calming effect on the US financial markets, and by extension, on the global financial markets. The 'announcement effect' was striking.

Similarly, in the midst of the eurozone crisis when the collapse of the euro seemed imminent, it was the European Central Bank President Mario Draghi's famous words in April 2012 that the ECB will do 'whatever it takes' that did more to save the euro than all the exhausting summits, emergency conclaves and emphatic communiqués of the eurozone leaders. Or take the case of the unconventional monetary policy (UMP) of the US Federal Reserve in the wake of the financial crisis of 2008. Analysts are now widely agreed that the UMP would have been futile had it not been accompanied by unconventional communication aimed at reassuring the markets that the exceptionally easy money regime will be maintained over an 'extended period of time'.

The positive impact of communication is not limited to crisis times, however. The received wisdom today is that greater transparency, active outreach and more open communication are always positive for central banks; the impact, of course, is more dramatic during crisis times.

Central Bank Communication—Old and New Orthodoxies

Given the potency of their communication, one would have thought central banks would have actively embraced communication as a valuable policy tool. The reality has, in fact, been quite the opposite. Until quite recently, the conventional role model prescribed for central banks has been that they should remain strictly in the background, and if their policies are credible, they would speak for themselves. Governors themselves should be backroom boys, speak as little as possible and when they do speak, they should do so with extreme circumspection.

A telling illustration of this old-school model comes from what Greenspan, then chairman of the Federal Reserve, said in 1987: 'Since becoming a central banker, I've learnt to mumble with great incoherence. If I seem unduly clear to you, you must have misunderstood what I said.'

The caution to central banks on communicating during crisis times was even more dire. In his bestselling book, *Lords of Finance*, a detailed and compelling account of the role played by four central bank governors (of France, Germany, the US and the UK) during the Great Depression of the 1930s, Liaquat Ahamed says that in times of crisis, the advice to central banks used to be to follow what mothers, cutting across cultures, tell their children when guests are expected: 'If you can't say anything nice, don't say anything at all.' This followed from the fine line that central banks have to tread between being reassuring without being dishonest.

So, what explains this remarkable shift in the theology of central bank communication from deliberate obscurity and caution to active engagement and transparency? There were three broad factors behind this. The first was the growing notion that in a democratic society, a central bank that prizes its independence has also to be conscious of its obligation to render accountability. An important way of doing this is for the central bank to explain its policies, the thinking underlying these policies and the expected outcomes so that the larger public can hold it to account for results.

The second factor that drove this shift towards more open communication was the realization that successful monetary policy is not just a matter of effective calibration of overnight interest rates, but also about shaping expectations on how those policies influence real-sector variables like growth and employment.

As citizens, we are all consumers of information put out by government departments and public agencies. But the information put out by a central bank is different from all the rest, and in an important way. Assume, for example, that we are talking not about the central bank's monetary policy, but about, say, the government's rural development policy—in particular, a decision by the government to connect every village with an all-weather road. It does not matter, except of course for reasons of electoral politics, whether the government announces this decision through a high-profile press conference on the TV or through a low-key press release or even if there is no prior announcement. When the road is built, people will benefit from it whether or not they knew about it in advance. It is different with monetary policy. If people know in advance how inflation and unemployment will unfold on the way forward, they will change their behaviour in ways that will be supportive of these outcomes. For example, if workers expect lower inflation, they will demand lower wage rises that will keep costs low and prices subdued, thereby actually delivering the low inflation outcome that the central bank wants. This type of behavioural response reinforces the need for central bank communication to shape expectations for the way forward.

The third factor that chipped away at the restraint of central banks towards more open communication was that the conventional wisdom about being reticent during crisis times turned on its head. Contrary to the notion of the 1930s depicted by Liaquat Ahamed, modern central bankers have found that in an atmosphere of anxiety and uncertainty, levelling with the markets—far from stoking fears—had actually helped to allay concerns and bolstered confidence. The difference arises from the vast changes between the 1930s and today by way of global integration and communication technology. Market participants today attach enormous value to knowing the true state of the economy and of the financial sector, no matter that it might be bad, as it allows them to make the necessary adjustment.

This is best illustrated by the dilemma that Bernanke talks about in his book, *The Courage to Act*, on the issue of releasing the results of the bank stress tests that the US regulators had conducted in the aftermath of the crisis. On one side, he writes, there were apprehensions that disclosing banks' weakness could further erode confidence, possibly leading to new runs and even sharper decline in bank stock prices. On the other hand, there was the prospect that releasing as much information as possible would reduce the 'paralyzing uncertainty' about banks' financial health. In the event, releasing the results in full had a salutary impact on confidence in the US banking system, a clear reinforcement of the new orthodoxy about central bank communication during stress times.

Communication Practices at RBI

As an institution, the Reserve Bank is deeply sensitive to its responsibility to communicate with the public, not just on monetary policy but on the entire range of its broad mandate—financial market developments, external sector management, regulatory issues, printing and distribution of currency and development issues. The Reserve Bank uses a variety of communication tools— governor's post-policy media conferences, interviews with the governor and deputy governors, speeches of the top management, press releases and lately, increasing dissemination through its website. In many respects, the Reserve Bank I inherited was ahead of even its advanced country peers in terms of communication. When Fed Chairman Bernanke held a media conference in 2011, it was reportedly the first in over thirty years, whereas the governor's post-policy media conference has been a regular feature in the Reserve Bank for at least a decade.

Even as the Reserve Bank set best practices in several dimensions of communication, I felt that we were still falling short, especially on two dimensions. First, our communication, except for the media conferences, was largely one way. We spoke but did not listen enough, much less engage in an active conversation. Second, we were not making sufficient effort to reach out to the larger public by communicating at a level and in a language accessible to them. Early on, I resolved that I should put a lot of effort into 'demystifying' the Reserve Bank, a topic I've addressed separately.

Forward Guidance on Monetary Policy

Giving forward guidance on monetary policy was a big, if also challenging, institutional innovation introduced during my time. At the heart of forward guidance is an indication by the central bank of how it would react to the evolving macroeconomic developments so as to shape market expectations and allow market participants to make the necessary adjustments.

In central bank circles, forward guidance on monetary policy has been a contentious issue and indeed remains so. It would figure frequently in the formal discussions and informal conversations at the BIS bimonthly meetings of governors in Basel, Switzerland. Even as central banks, as I've written earlier, embraced more open communication, there remained a view that giving forward guidance was taking openness too far. Some central bankers took a strong position, holding that surprise was an essential element of monetary policy and it would be foolhardy for central banks to voluntarily give up that weapon. There were others who were less robustly opposed; they were circumspect about making a policy commitment that they may not be able to honour.

The crisis tilted the cost-benefit calculus of forward guidance. Central banks discovered, to their pleasant surprise and I may add, enormous relief, that in a time of unprecedented uncertainty and anxiety, a carefully crafted forward guidance can yield rich dividends by way of calming the markets and nudging market behaviour in the desired direction. By far the most high-profile example of forward guidance was the one given by the Fed that the federal funds rate would be maintained at an exceptionally low level 'for an extended period'.

At the Reserve Bank, we deliberated internally on whether to adopt the practice of forward guidance. We recognized that it would not be a totally benign option but decided to go ahead nevertheless, because we felt that the benefits outweighed the costs, especially in a situation of continuing global uncertainty and India's contrarian macroeconomic developments.

The forward guidance is typically one short paragraph in a six-to-eight-page policy document, but we realized that crafting it can be a test of communication skills. Aware that there is a minor industry that sustains itself by parsing these few sentences in great depth and probing for coded messages behind plain English, we spent a disproportionate amount of time debating the exact choice of words, the precise turn of phrase and alternative ways of nuancing. Such agonizing might seem absurd to the uninitiated, but it always proved to be efficient use of time.

Along the way, we discovered several inherent challenges in giving forward guidance. For one, a central bank's indication of how it would act in the future is typically contingent on economic developments. But markets tend to ignore the caveats, and interpret the guidance as an irrevocable commitment, with the result that they find themselves wrong-footed when the actual outcomes do not turn out as expected. For example, in our policy reviews both in October and December 2011, we said that 'the cycle of rate increases had peaked and further actions are likely to reverse the cycle'. This generated a widely shared expectation of a rate cut in the January 2012 policy meeting, an expectation that did not materialize because inflation had not trended down as earlier thought. Even though our 'inaction' was consistent with the guidance, the market was unforgiving and believed we had reneged on our commitment.

Moreover, it is when financial conditions are uncertain that markets want greater and more specific guidance, but paradoxically it is precisely when financial conditions are uncertain that central banks are least able to deliver. Let me cite an example to illustrate this dilemma. In our November 2010 policy statement, we said: 'Based purely on current growth and inflation trends, the Reserve Bank believes that the likelihood of further rate action in the immediate future is relatively low. However, in an uncertain world, we need to be prepared to respond appropriately to shocks that may emanate from either the global or the domestic environment.'

Our guidance was situated in the context of domestic uncertainty about agricultural prospects and their impact on growth and inflation, as well as external uncertainty arising from the eurozone sovereign debt crisis. Many analysts thought the guidance, especially alerting markets to possible rate action, should actual outcomes deviate from the expected ones, was helpful; a few, however, thought that it was too vague to be of any use.

Mixed experience with forward guidance has not been unique to India. Many advanced economy central banks, too, had come under criticism for what they said, how they said it and for their inability to honour the guidance. The Bank of England had said in 2013 that interest rates would not be raised until unemployment came down to below 7 per cent and added for good measure that that was not likely to happen until 2016. But unemployment in the UK dropped below 7 per cent as early as in 2014 even as the BoE was not ready to raise rates. Technically, the

BoE had not strayed from its commitment, since the unemployment rate was only a necessary, but not a sufficient, condition for rate raise. Regardless, some analysts criticized the bank for reneging on its guidance.

The experience of the Bank of Japan with its quantitative and qualitative easing (QQE) is a more recent illustration of the challenge of managing forward guidance. Under the much-acclaimed QQE launched in April 2013, the BoJ set an inflation target of 2 per cent to be achieved in two years. Successive policy statements of BoJ kept asserting how the bond-buying programme under the QQE was consistent with the 2 per cent inflation target, even as other numbers put out by the BoJ seemed to be acquiescing in the timetable for the inflation target slipping away.

At RBI, as we moved on, I realized that markets demand not just guidance but also 'guidance on guidance'—in other words, an explanation of what the guidance means. This can be tricky because, as I said, a lot of thought goes into crafting the guidance and attempts to further explain risk distorting the message.

For instance, in the post-policy media conference following the November 2010 guidance I cited above, I was pushed to elaborate on what we meant by 'immediate future'. I could have stonewalled the question but that was not my practice. I replied that what we implied by 'immediate' was around three months, thereby implying, although not saying so explicitly, that we would stay away from a policy rate hike in the December 2010 mid-quarter review which was six weeks away and consider a hike only at the next quarterly policy review, three months away. This elaboration triggered criticism that a three-month pause implied by the guidance was too dovish and did not sit tidily with our statement on risks to inflation. We could have avoided all this by refraining from giving any guidance at all, but we persisted with it as we believed that we owed this obligation to the markets.

There are parallels from advanced economies on 'guidance on guidance' too. The Fed, for instance, had said in 2014 that it would be 'patient' in increasing interest rates, a comment which set off a flurry of speculation on what 'patient' meant. Rarely had investors lavished so much attention on a single word. When pushed to explain what 'patient' meant in Fedspeak, Janet Yellen, the chairperson of the Federal Reserve, interpreted that as 'not raising rates for at least two meetings'. In the event, the Fed honoured this commitment but it is quite possible that macroeconomic developments could have pushed it to renege on this.

Monetary Policy Documents

Another significant improvement in monetary policy communication that came on my watch was the streamlining of the policy documents. This initiative owes to Subir Gokarn who joined us as deputy governor in charge of economic and monetary policy, in November 2009. Subir told me shortly after coming on board that while the Reserve Bank's policy documents were rich in analytical content, they needed to be streamlined by way of cutting out overlap and repetition, making the language more direct and simple, and most of all, significantly trimming the length of the documents.

In his prior career as a leading analyst and commentator on India's macroeconomic policy, Subir was an avid consumer of the Reserve Bank's policy documents and he spoke from rich personal experience. I wholeheartedly supported the initiative as it was consistent with my goal of extending the outreach of RBI policies. My yardstick was that chief executives in the finance and corporate sectors, who are put off by the language and length of our policy documents and depend instead on summaries prepared by their staff, should now feel encouraged to read the original documents themselves. In addition to changing the style and presentation, we agreed on new standards in terms of length—a maximum of sixty pages for the money macro document and twelve pages for the governor's policy statement.

My Experiments with Communication

I have already written about my several communication missteps as I traversed a steep learning curve as governor. During the early part of my tenure, while battling the global financial crisis in 2008, I underestimated the importance of the governor frequently reassuring the market; instead, I yielded the stage to others, thereby letting all the noise distort the message. While combating inflation during 2010–11 when growth was also seen to be stalling, I had openly mused about the nuances of the growth–inflation trade-off instead of showing undivided commitment to inflation control. It was in managing the exchange rate during 2012–13 though that my communication faculties were put to the most gruelling test. I realized that what you said, or didn't say, was important, but how you said it and when was even more important. Let me illustrate.

Recall that on 15 July 2013, in the midst of the taper tantrums, I took the extraordinary step of raising interest rates to manage the exchange rate. Quite understandably, the decision attracted a lot of commentary and the usual share of compliments and criticism. We had a regularly scheduled quarterly policy review on 30 July, just two weeks after the above unscheduled policy tweaking. In the scheduled review, I saw no case for any further policy adjustment; we just reiterated our concern about the need for correcting the domestic structural imbalances to bring stability to the external sector.

The post-policy media conference that afternoon was to be my last as governor. For a long time I had been looking forward to this conference, expecting that it would be along the lines of a farewell engagement. Instead of a serious question-and-answer session on substantive issues, we would spend much of the time reminiscing about my five years as governor. That wasn't to be.

That the exchange rate issue would dominate the media conference was also a no-brainer. Sure enough, the first question was whether and when the monetary-tightening measures instituted to manage the exchange rate would be withdrawn. As I wrote earlier, the intent behind this unusual action was to squeeze systemic liquidity in order to curb speculation on the rupee, and thereby send a strong signal to the market about the Reserve Bank's resolve to defend the currency. I replied that these measures were temporary and would be rolled back once the exchange rate regained stability. On the timing of the rollback, I said that the Reserve Bank was sensitive to the short-term economic costs of tight liquidity but that I was in no position to get locked into a time frame for the rollback. My intention was to allay market fears that the tight liquidity policy of the Reserve Bank would choke the incipient growth impulses in the economy in the midst of growing concerns about rapidly declining economic activity.

The market reaction to my response was unsparing; the rupee fell from ₹59.63 to a dollar to ₹60.48 by market closing that day. According to media analysts and commentators, I sounded apologetic about my decision to use monetary policy for exchange rate defence and that my concern for growth was misplaced in a context when the market expected the Reserve Bank to be focusing on the exchange rate to the exclusion of all other concerns. Here is how the *Financial Times* of 1 August 2013 reported my statement: 'The Governor insisted he was not trying to defend the battered rupee but only stopping a vicious spiral of one way bets that could lead the currency to overshoot its fair value.'

As I look back, I realize that I may have been guilty of a communication misstep. I should have known that at a time when the rupee was under such pressure, being firm and assertive on the exchange rate was way more important than holding out reassurance on growth. Moreover, I muffled the message by openly deliberating on other concerns when I should have shown undivided focus on the exchange rate.

At the same time, I was also puzzled by the market reaction since my reply was almost exactly along the lines we had stated in the printed document. I checked with Harun Khan, deputy governor, Alpana Killawala, the communications chief, and a few other colleagues. The consensus view was that the criticism of 'apologetic tone' stemmed not so much from the precise content of the reply rather than from the nuance and perhaps the body language.

Even as I was close to finishing my job as governor, I had yet to learn a rookie lesson in communication: markets don't take what the governor says at face value. At least, I had learnt to be opportunistic! I used the analysts' teleconference the following day to correct this misinterpretation. While replying to a related question, I asserted the 'Reserve Bank's single-minded commitment' to stabilizing the rupee, and added that in the given context, the benefits of rupee stability outweighed any short-term sacrifice of growth. This was entirely consistent with what I had said at the media conference the previous day, but rephrasing it this way conveyed the message in the form that the market wanted to hear. I corrected for the nuance too. The previous day, I had said that *these measures will be withdrawn when* the rupee became stable. Now I turned around the nuancing to affirm that that *these measures will not be withdrawn until* the Reserve Bank had firm evidence that the rupee had stabilized. Perhaps that sounded alpha male enough. The market reacted positively and the rupee swiftly reversed the losses of the previous day.

It was fortuitous that there was an analysts' conference the following day offering me an opportunity to regain control of the narrative. What would we have done in the absence of such coincidence? Very rarely do central banks issue rejoinders on the statements by their governors or the senior management, and when they do, it is mostly to correct a misquotation rather than a misinterpretation. I found that the best way to correct a misinterpretation is to be opportunistic and slip in the 'guidance' slyly in a doorstop interview or in a speech.

For example, in early December 2011, we noticed that the daily aggregate borrowing by the commercial banks from the Reserve Bank's LAF window had suddenly spiked, breaching the indicative norm (1 per cent of NDTL) for several days in a row. This tightness arose from a combination of circumstances, including advance tax payments which have the effect of shifting money from open circulation to the government's account with the Reserve Bank. This was also a time when the rupee was under pressure and we were intervening in the forex market fairly regularly. Since we were selling dollars for rupees, our intervention was squeezing out rupee liquidity and adding to the liquidity tightness.

In a media interview in Kolkata later in December, following the Reserve Bank board meeting there, I had acknowledged that systemic liquidity was tight and said that we would be taking action to ease the situation. There were many options open to the Reserve Bank to ease liquidity, and withdrawing from the forex market was by no means the sole option. However, the market decided that I had declared my intent to stop forex intervention with immediate effect! I was frustrated by this tendency of the market to look for coded messages behind plain English, a clear example of what psychologists call 'confirmation bias', the market hearing not what was said, but what it wanted to hear.

Since this misinterpretation would distort market expectations, it was important for us to correct it. At the same time, it would have been uncharacteristic—and perhaps not expected—of the Reserve Bank to issue an explicit clarification. I was looking for an early and unobtrusive opportunity to correct it and it came a few days later when I was scheduled to speak at the annual convention of the Institute of Chartered Accountants of India (ICAI) in Mumbai.

By this time, over three years into my job, I was quite familiar with the standard drill of the governor's public-speaking engagements. As soon as the inaugural session where I would typically be featured draws to a close, when the delegates are breaking for coffee and I would be getting off the stage, the media attending the conference would mob me for a question-and-answer session. TV cameras would start rolling, still cameras would be clicking and flashing, and dozens of mikes would jostle for space in front of my face. I had routinely discouraged such impromptu media interviews for a number of reasons, including my realization that the media would flash what I said on the sidelines rather than what I had just said in the scheduled speech. I always felt that this was unfair to the hosts of the conference who are entitled to media coverage of their event.

Occasionally, I would break my discipline though, if only to use the opportunity to slip in a message that I wanted to. This time around, for example, after the inaugural session of the ICAI convention, when I was mobbed by the media for a 'quick sound bite', I had said that we would use all the instruments available to us, including intervention in the market, to check the rupee volatility, thereby delinking exchange rate action from liquidity management action.

Through the five years I was at the Reserve Bank, I had accumulated my share of mistakes, both on policy and the communication of that policy—more than my share maybe, according to some critics. Viewed from a cosmic perspective, communication mistakes are, in general, less egregious than policy mistakes, as their impact on the markets would typically be transient and the long-term economic damage quite minimal.

Even so, ironically, it was my communication mistakes that weighed me down more than my policy mistakes. Might it be that I thought they were avoidable or that they damaged my personal credibility much more, at any rate in the short-term? As I write this two years after I have left the Reserve Bank, I am still unable to be objective about this assessment.

It is some comfort though that virtually every central bank governor has his or her share of communication mistakes or gaffes. Some are more publicized than others. The most recent example, as I write this, comes from Mario Draghi, the president of the ECB who, despite a formidable reputation for his savvy communication skills, seems to have fallen short in anticipating the market reaction to what he said in a post-policy media conference in December 2015. In the backdrop of the stalling eurozone economy at that time, the market expectation was that the ECB would top up its ongoing quantitative easing by a weighty stimulus. The ECB did come up with some easing but the market shrugged it off as too feeble. What riled the markets even more was the statement by Draghi in the press conference that what was done was 'adequate'. The markets reacted sharply to these dashed hopes of stronger monetary stimulus with a wave of selling that rippled from Frankfurt to Paris, to Madrid and Milan. Draghi corrected for this by asserting just a few days later that 'there is no particular limit to how we can deploy all our tools'. The *Wall Street Journal* wrote: 'Mr. Draghi's comments were an attempt to fight the market's reaction to the policy meeting. The content of the speech is not enough to reverse yesterday's "own goal" but it does represent something of a pushback against tightening monetary conditions.'

In his book, *The Courage to Act*, Bernanke admits to some communication mistakes as he was traversing up the learning curve. He writes that in April 2006, when he was at a social event, he vented his frustration on a well-known TV anchor about the markets misinterpreting his recent testimony to the Congress. He thought this conversation with the anchor was off the record, but she didn't think so and reported the remark which played up in the media as Bernanke 'reversing himself' and suggesting that interest rates could actually go up at a time when he actually wanted to convey the opposite message.

Lessons from the Communication Experience

Learning is an unending task and my education in communication continued all the way to the close of my tenure.

I learnt, for example, that being too direct or explicit is sometimes inadvisable. In the post-policy conference on 30 October 2011, I was asked whether the Reserve Bank would intervene in the forex market to build up forex reserves, and I gave an 'in the face' answer: 'No, we would not.' My answer should not have surprised anyone or caused anxiety since I was just stating the obvious: that the only condition, under the Reserve Bank's declared policy which would trigger forex intervention was exchange rate volatility. However, the rupee came under heavy pressure the next day and some analysts faulted me for being too explicit and suggested that no matter what the intent, I should not be such a 'straight bat'.

I had also learnt, indeed several times over, that nothing the governor says is off the record no matter when and in what context you are saying it. For example, in mid-January 2013, I was speaking at IIM Lucknow and explaining to the students how the tension between growth and inflation is overplayed and why low and steady inflation was a necessary condition for sustained growth. This was just a couple of weeks before our scheduled policy conference on 29 January and there was more than the usual media buzz about what we might do with the interest rate, especially since Chidambaram had openly criticized the Reserve

Bank after our previous policy meeting in October for abandoning him to 'walk alone'.

My remarks to the IIM students were not situated in the 'here and now' context; my intent was to convey to them the broader dilemma of making a judgement call on a complex policy issue. The media would have none of it. They interpreted my comments as further policy tightening in the upcoming end-January policy review, and the news was on the wire agency tickers even before I finished speaking. Several of our usual interlocutors chided me for not realizing that that there was no question of the governor ever speaking 'in an academic context'.

And finally, I learnt of the need to shape my message better to ensure fuller and accurate coverage. For example, at the BANCON 2010, an annual bankers' conference, I focused my comments on the efficiency of the Indian banking system, while covering a host of issues, including the relative efficiency of public and private banks, their asset-liability management, credit standards and customer service, as well as the use of technology. In passing, I made a comment on the salary structure of public sector bank chiefs and said that it needs to be reviewed in order to attract talent.

I was perplexed by how the media reporting made it look like I had devoted the entire speech to bemoaning the salary structure of public sector bank CEOs and how, in my view, fixing it was critical to improving the efficiency of the Indian banking system. The *Mint*, in its edition of 8 September 2010, reported on my speech with the bold headline: 'Subbarao favours higher salaries for chiefs of state-run banks'. In follow-up articles and opinion pieces, there was extensive comparative analysis of the salary structure of public, private and foreign bank CEOs. Some lateral-thinking media analysts even put the measly salary of the Reserve Bank governor in their comparative charts. In an analytical piece titled 'RBI Governor earns less than 5 percent of top paid bankers', the *Economic Times* of 5 September 2010 wrote: 'In an irony of sorts, RBI gets to approve the salaries of all top level bankers in the country but the central bank's top officials themselves get less than 5 percent of what is paid to bank chiefs.' Admittedly, much of this reporting was constructive, but I still felt that the larger issues of banking system efficiency should have made it to the commentary.

Metaphors and Humour

I quickly learnt a few other things. The use of metaphors and humour often helped in making a point or evading a tricky question. In the summer of 2010, we were all in Thiruvananthapuram for the RBI Board meeting. Because of the drought in the previous year, there was nationwide anxiety about how the monsoon might turn out that year. This was also the time when we, in the Reserve Bank, were engaged in exiting from the accommodative policies of the crisis period which acquired additional urgency in view of inflation picking up momentum. Adjusting interest rates to subdue inflation and stimulate growth can be a tough job at the best of times but can get much tougher when the monsoon— some 60 per cent of India's farms are rain-fed—fails.

In the media interaction following the board meeting, there was the inevitable question about whether the Reserve Bank would tweak its 'exit path' in view of the monsoon prospects. Instinctively, what came to my mind was a book I had read several years ago— *Chasing the Monsoon* by Alexander Frater—a fascinating account of the New Zealander's journey across the Indian subcontinent in pursuit of the monsoon. Frater's romantic adventure, quite expectedly, starts in Thiruvananthapuram, where we then were. In answer to the question on the monetary policy stance, I replied that like millions of farmers across the country, we in the Reserve Bank too were chasing the monsoon. The media decided that I had answered their question. Perhaps they liked the imagery of the RBI governor sitting alongside farmers under a village tree, looking skywards for guidance on the interest rate policy. Here is a citation from a feature story, 'RBI's Subbarao Chases Monsoon', in the online edition of the *Wall Street Journal*:

> All RBI governors face this problem [of inflation caused by rising food prices on account of weak rainfall]. But it has a special resonance for Mr. Subbarao, as he discussed with reporters last week . . .
>
> . . . District collectors and sub-collectors play an important role when it comes to rains and water. They assess the ground situation to decide whether to declare a drought or to declare a flood—two events often generated by the monsoon rains, or lack of them.
>
> It was during that time that Mr. Subbarao realized 'my emotional well-being, my career prospects depended on rains,' he said at the RBI function.
>
> Nearly four decades later, he remains hostage to the monsoon.
>
> Now at the end of my career as the Governor of Reserve Bank, I realize that (my) entire performance will depend on the monsoon and not what I do about interest rates,' Mr. Subbarao quipped. 'If there is good monsoon, it is ok. Otherwise the Governor of the Reserve Bank is to be blamed.'

Humour also helps in making a point. I was asked once if I consult the finance minister on monetary policy decisions. I replied, no, I mostly decide by the toss of a coin: heads I raise rates; tails I cut rates, and if the coin lands on the edge, I consult the finance minister.

Humour also aided me in responding to criticism on the confusion about which measure of inflation the Reserve Bank was using. During my time, we were using wholesale price index inflation as the fulcrum of monetary policy instead of Consumer Price Index inflation which is, in fact, what people experience in the marketplace. This was clearly a second-best option but we were handicapped by the fact that there was no single CPI representative of the whole country. In fact, the Reserve Bank, on my watch worked with the government to develop two all-India CPIs—one for rural and the other for urban. Even as the new indices were brought into force starting January 2011, we could not shift immediately to CPI inflation-targeting for want of long enough historical data series. To facilitate the transition though, our monetary policy documents contained analysis of both CPI and WPI inflation. Some confusion was inevitable in this transition, but the analysts understood what we were trying to communicate. Nevertheless, there was criticism about this confusion.

I used my inaugural speech at the Annual Statistics Day celebrations in 2012 to respond to this criticism by deploying one of my hair jokes. I said: 'Most analysts think that I am unable to interpret inflation. There must be some truth to that because even at a personal level, I am failing on that count. Twenty years ago, when I had a thick mop of hair, I used to pay ₹25 for a haircut. Ten years ago, after my hair started thinning, I was paying ₹50. Now, when I have virtually no hair left, I pay ₹150 for a haircut. I struggle to determine how much of that is inflation and how much is the premium I pay the barber for the privilege of cutting the governor's non-existent hair.'

Humour, of course, is not always benign and can land you in tricky situations as I realized once while talking about financial stability. During the crisis, financial stability was an 'elephant in the room' type of issue with extensive dissection of the topic by policymakers, media analysts and academic scholars. What vexed everyone though was that a clear definition of financial stability proved to be elusive.

I was at a panel discussion in Hyderabad in August 2009 as part of the Reserve Bank's platinum jubilee celebrations where the topic of financial stability, in particular its definition, came up. I said: 'Financial instability is like pornography; you know it when you see it.' Most people thought that I had conveyed the message to great effect although some said that this was not dignified *centralbankese*.

Of all my experiments in humour, the one that got the most play was what I said about constituting a committee to advise me on whether the Reserve Bank should pay interest on the cash reserve ratio. As I wrote earlier, the Reserve Bank locks up a prescribed portion of each bank's deposits as a monetary as well as a prudential measure—to be released to the bank if ever it gets into liquidity pressure. Banks don't like this. Their grievance is that not only does the Reserve Bank lock up their money, but it doesn't even condescend to pay any interest on that! In the summer of 2012, the CRR issue heated up, with the staid but mature Pratip Chaudhuri, chairman of State Bank of India, arguing for payment of interest, locking horns with the gutsy and irascible Reserve Bank Deputy Governor K.C. Chakrabarty, himself a former commercial banker, who was totally dismissive of the idea.

The annual FICCI-IBA banking conference, usually held in September, is a premier event that brings together corporate and banking sector leaders to deliberate on issues of mutual concern. The hosts extend the courtesy of inaugurating the conference to the governor and I had the privilege of doing so for five years on the trot.

In the September 2012 conference, I was going to speak about the challenges of implementing Basel III banking regulations in India. As I got up to speak, I told the audience, with a grim face, that I had an important announcement to make before moving on to my prepared speech. I continued: 'Before coming to this event, I just signed off a paper constituting a committee to advise the Reserve Bank on payment of interest on CRR.'

Some reporters present at the event texted my remarks to their anchors and editors even before I finished, and very shortly the news was on some wire agency tickers and TV scrolls. Obviously, oblivious to the stir that I had unwittingly created, I went on: 'The members of the committee will be Deputy Governor Chakrabarty and SBI Chairman Pratip Chaudhuri. They will both be locked up in a room, and will not be let out until they have reached an agreement. Also they are mandated not to reach an agreement until my tenure is over.' The audience broke into laughter. And as the reporters got the joke, they rushed to withdraw their earlier messages so as to cut losses.

Following the event, there was the usual complement of bouquets and brickbats. Some thought that I had used humour effectively to extinguish the CRR interest debate by indicating openly where I stood, while others thought that I didn't show enough discretion by joking about such a market-moving issue.

Editors' Conference

The media is a bridge between the Reserve Bank and the larger public. It disseminates our news and our messages, and critiques our policies and actions through opinion pieces and analyses. All of this enhances public understanding and gives us, within the bank, valuable feedback. This process is enhanced if the senior management of the Reserve Bank and the senior editors in the media meet occasionally to exchange views and understand each other's perspectives.

This was, of course, not an original idea or a new initiative. Every governor before me had his own way of engaging with the editors—some met them casually and individually, others met them in small, informal groups. My strategy was to have an annual editors' conference with about fifteen–twenty editors for an in-depth discussion—'background' in media parlance.

Since the format was untested, the first time we organized the conference, in August 2010, we prepared an agenda indicating the topics for discussion. The objective behind the preselecting of topics was only to keep the discussion focused and prevent it from going all over the map. Some editors did not like this idea and thought that my 'control freak' disciplining of the format inhibited a free-flowing discussion. On the other hand, I was not comfortable with a total 'stream of consciousness' style of discussion as it might muffle our understanding and even distort the messages. We agreed on a compromise. Ahead of the conference, the Reserve Bank would provide the participants with a long menu which we would narrow down to three or four topics in consultation with the invitees. We will devote one half of the meeting to discuss the preselected topics, while the remaining half will be spent on a free-flowing conversation.

A host of issues figured on the agenda of these conferences. They ranged from hot-button issues like the monetary policy stance and exchange rate management to regulation of microfinance institutions and deregulation of the interest on savings deposits, allowing corporates into the banking space and the FSLRC (Financial Sector Legislative Reforms Commission) and the FSDC (Financial Stability and Development Council). The meetings were held under the Chatham House Rule—the editors could use the discussion at the conference to write their commentary or opinion without any attribution to the Reserve Bank. Needless to say, I found these meetings not only enjoyable but immensely rewarding.

Over the years I spent at the Reserve Bank, I developed an enormous respect for the media not only for the role they play in enhancing the effectiveness of Reserve Bank policies, but even more importantly for the role they play in making the Reserve Bank accountable. I was also impressed by the depth of media analyses and the insightful editorial and opinion pieces. Needless to say, I grew fond of the reporters on the Reserve Bank beat who would follow me on all public events within the country even if they put me in a tight spot more often than I liked. What I found most endearing of all was that they too loved the Reserve Bank as much as those of us inside it did, cared about the institution's reputation and credibility, and rejoiced in its successes and lamented over its setbacks.

Mixed Record

Like on other dimensions, on the communication dimension too my record at the Reserve Bank was a mixed bag. I was largely commended for bringing a culture of openness to a conservative and inward-looking institution, and was complimented for making the bank more transparent, responsive and consultative, for listening as well as speaking, for streamlining our written documents and simplifying our spoken language. In its assessment of my term as governor, titled 'Subbarao—End of a turbulent tenure', the *Hindu BusinessLine* of 3 September 2103 wrote: 'Without providing "sound bites", he still increased the tempo of communication from the central bank and tried to inculcate a culture of transparency. In particular, his attempt to provide "forward guidance" to markets while making it clear that he was retaining his options to act differently, were notable innovations.'

I was both praised for speaking up and derided for not speaking enough when the occasion demanded. I was criticized for showing self-doubt and reticence instead of conveying certainty and confidence, for not staying consistent with the message and for too much straight talk and too little tact. In an article defending my record in the *Business Standard* of 1 June 2011, Abheek Barua's concluding sentences were: 'Markets tend to like uber-confident alpha male central bank governors. Dr. Subbarao was not one. In retrospect, that may turn out to be his biggest flaw.' On the contrary, many others wrote that it was, in fact, my low-key demeanour and low-profile personality that commanded respect and aided effective communication. I will let it rest there.

There are many things I miss about being the governor. One of them is that I can no longer move the markets by my spoken word. Equally, there are many things I enjoy about not being the governor. One of them is that I can speak freely without any fear of moving the markets.

The Reserve Bank of India's first central board of directors at the time of its establishment. Standing (left to right): Sundar Singh Majithia, U. Bah Oh, Shri Ram, Badridas Goenka, Edward Benthall, F.E. Dinshaw, J.W. Kelly, A.A. Bruce, M. Ramachandra Rao. Sitting (left to right): Adam Hajee Mohammad Sait, Purshotamdas Thakurdas, James B. Taylor, Osborne A. Smith, Sikander Hyat-Khan, Homi Mehta, Muzammilullah Khan.

The central board of directors at the end of my term as governor, in Mumbai in August 2013. Standing (left to right): Damodar Acharya, G.M. Rao, Nachiket Mor, Rajeev Gowda, Kiran Karnik, Azim Premji, Dipankar Gupta, Y.C. Deveshwar, Bazil Sheikh. Sitting (left to right): Ela Bhatt, Urjit Patel, Anand Sinha, K.C. Chakrabarty, Raghuram Rajan, Duvvuri Subbarao, Arvind Mayaram, Rajeev Takru, H.R. Khan, Y.H. Malegam, Indira Rajaraman.

Taking over as governor from Y.V. Reddy in September 2008.

Accompanied by the four deputy governors, going into the conference
hall to announce the quarterly monetary policy in July 2010.

Post-policy media conference in February 2011.

The central board of directors meets seven to eight times a year.
This meeting was in Chennai in July 2011.

Over a quarter century of the RBI leadership packed into this picture. Along
with my three immediate predecessors (Bimal Jalan, Rangarajan and Y.V. Reddy)
in front of a portrait of another former governor, Manmohan Singh, during
the Reserve Bank's platinum jubilee celebrations in February 2010.

Prime Minister Manmohan Singh releasing a book on the Reserve Bank's
history at his official residence in New Delhi in August 2013.

It is customary for the governor to call on chief ministers while visiting state capitals. Here, with Chief Minister Nitish Kumar of Bihar when I went to Patna for the Reserve Bank board meeting in February 2010.

I delighted in visiting rural primary schools during my outreach visits. Here, at the primary school in Doba village at Lohardaga district of Jharkhand in December 2010.

US Treasury Secretary Tim Geithner and Federal Reserve Chairman
Ben Bernanke visited the Reserve Bank office in October 2012.

Speeches are a regular part of the governor's job chart.
Here, speaking at the Asia Society in New York in August 2012.

The governor's bungalow on M.L. Dahanukar Marg
(erstwhile Carmichael Road) in Mumbai is a heritage building.

In the lounge where the governor meets visitors against the backdrop of the governors' gallery on the wall. There were twenty-one governors before me.

Handing over to Raghuram Rajan in September 2013.

9

Walking Alone

Autonomy and Accountability of the Reserve Bank

Is the Reserve Bank independent? I don't have a binary answer to this question. The best I can do is offer a long and nuanced response.

A widely shared view is that the Reserve Bank has no independence and that the government pressures the Bank to act as per its bidding. This view is largely impressionistic, shaped more by perception than hard evidence. It is also an urban legend that has gained currency by sheer repetition. I have also often been struck that foreign media, whenever they write about the Reserve Bank, routinely qualify it as 'one of world's least independent central banks'. I believe this too is an uninformed bias rather than the result of any rigorous research on the relative independence of central banks around the world.

In my five years at the Reserve Bank, I was asked repeatedly about the independence of the Reserve Bank. I was not the first governor to confront this question and I know I won't be the last. It is an issue that keeps coming up in public discourse, in part aided by our energetic and enthusiastic media.

My predecessor, Y.V. Reddy, had a stock response to this question: 'The Reserve Bank is totally free within the limits set by the government.' This answer is clever, even technically correct, but still ambiguous. What indeed are the limits set by the government? Are they well defined and is there a shared understanding on both sides of their respective obligations and code of conduct? What are the remedies if there is a transgression?

Why Do Central Banks Need Autonomy?

Perhaps we should establish some basics here before getting into specifics. The issue of central bank autonomy typically arises in the context of its monetary policy function. Why is it important that a central bank have autonomy in setting the monetary policy? The principal aim of monetary policy is to preserve price stability by maintaining low and steady inflation consistent with the economy's potential growth rate. This requires taking a long-term view even if the path to price stability might entail some short-term pain. But political regimes, especially democracies, have little tolerance for such pain; electoral politics push them into compromising long-term sustainability for short-term expediency. This is where an autonomous central bank comes in. The hope and expectation is that an autonomous central bank, insulated from political pressures, will ensure that long-term macroeconomic stability is not held hostage to short-term compulsions.

In addition to being the monetary authority, the Reserve Bank is also a regulator. It regulates banks, non-banking financial companies, segments of the financial markets, and the payment and settlement systems. The theory of regulatory autonomy is now well established and I will not go into details here except to say that regulatory autonomy is critical to inspiring entrepreneurial impulses and investor confidence in the economy.

The Reserve Bank has other responsibilities too beyond monetary policy and regulation. It manages the external sector, prints and distributes currency, is the banker to the Central and state governments and to commercial banks, and has important responsibilities in furthering financial inclusion and economic development. There is no issue of autonomy on these other functions; the Reserve Bank works in consultation and coordination with the government.

Autonomy of the Reserve Bank in Theory and Practice

Under law, the Reserve Bank is not fully autonomous. The RBI Act lays down that: 'The Central Government may give directions to the Reserve Bank where considered necessary in public interest to do so, but after consultation with the Governor.' It is possibly this legal provision that is at least partly behind the perception that the Reserve Bank is not independent. But two points are to be noted here. First, the authority of the government to 'direct' the Reserve Bank is not absolute; it is circumscribed by the need to consult the governor beforehand, as well as the requirement that the direction be in the public interest. Second and more importantly, in the eighty years that the Reserve Bank has been in existence, the government has not invoked this provision even once. In some sense, this is a tribute to the sense of responsibility of both the government and the Reserve Bank.

But that is on the formal side. What about informal interference behind the scenes? Let me first talk about monetary policy. I have been asked several times if there was pressure from the government on setting interest rates. There certainly was, although the precise psychological mechanics of pressure would vary depending on the context, setting and the personalities.

I have already written about how I would schedule a meeting with the finance minister before every policy review to apprise him of the macroeconomic situation and of my proposed policy decision. For much of the time during my tenure, although not always, there were differences of view on the anti-inflation stance of the Reserve Bank. Both Chidambaram and Pranab Mukherjee were piqued by the Reserve Bank's tight interest rate policy on the ground that high interest rates were inhibiting investment and hurting growth.

As a columnist for the *Indian Express* after demitting office, Chidambaram wrote on 2 August 2015 ('Across the Aisle—Monetary Policy Committee: Vote or Veto?'): 'There is a view among commentators that finance ministers and central bank governors are always at loggerheads. That view may make interesting copy but it is far from the truth. On 8 out of 10 monetary policy statements or actions, the Government and the RBI will be, and in the past have been, on the same page.'

Chidambaram was finance minister for far longer than I was governor. The ballpark average that he cites—agreement eight out of ten times—may be his experience, but it certainly does not accord with mine. I found that all through my tenure, the government was distinctly uncomfortable with the Reserve Bank raising interest rates and seemed convinced that monetary policy was choking growth.

I invariably pushed back against the government's suggestions for softer interest rates. My standard counterargument to the finance ministry used to be that it was not high interest rates that were standing in the way of investments. What matters in investment decisions is not the nominal interest rate but the real interest rate, which is the interest rate after knocking out the impact of inflation. Even though the Reserve Bank was raising the policy interest rate to control inflation, real interest rates remained lower than in the pre-crisis period when we clocked record investment levels and sizzling growth. If interest rates were the only constraint, there should have been a similar investment boom now. The fact that there wasn't shows that it was not interest rates but other policy and implementation bottlenecks that were inhibiting investment.

Obviously discomfited by the ball being thrown back into their court, the government would rebut—argued in different ways by different people—that investors are influenced not by real interest rates but by nominal interest rates, an argument that I always found unpersuasive. The other argument that the government would routinely trot out is that a policy rate cut was necessary to buoy investor sentiment. The logic of why the Reserve Bank should compromise its judgement so as to become a cheerleader for the economy never appealed to me.

A tacit agreement between the government and the Reserve Bank was that we should keep our differences behind closed doors. That did not, of course, stop the media from speculating about internal squabbles—stories that would gather a momentum of their own. Notwithstanding these so-called squabbles, it is standard practice for the finance minister to issue a statement endorsing the Reserve Bank's monetary policy decision in the media shortly after it is announced.

There was a high-profile deviation from this standard practice in October 2012 when Chidambaram went public with his displeasure at the Reserve Bank's decision not to cut interest rates. The events leading to this public rebuke of RBI started unfolding in the week before the policy. In the pre-policy meeting with him, I told Chidambaram of my decision to stay pat on the policy rate in view of the inflation situation and the continued concern about the fiscal situation which was undermining the fight against inflation. He was clearly unhappy with my proposed decision, was upfront with it and argued strongly for a rate cut. I did not believe I could yield.

Not one to give up so easily, Chidambaram took the battle forward by unveiling the government's road map for fiscal adjustment in a hurriedly convened media conference just a day before the Reserve Bank policy meeting. The finance minister's prerogative to release the government's fiscal road map any time he chooses is unquestionable, but the timing of this particular unscheduled announcement, just a day before the policy, was clearly an unsubtle message to the Reserve Bank.

While releasing the statement, Chidambaram said: 'Well, I am making the statement so that everybody in India acknowledges the steps we are taking and also acknowledges that the government is determined to bring about fiscal consolidation.' When he was asked if the Reserve Bank would cut rates based on his announcement, he used the opportunity to send a loud message from Delhi to Mumbai via the media: 'I sincerely hope everybody will read the statement and take note of that.'

I have high regard for Chidambaram's competence; if there was one person who could deliver on the demanding fiscal deficit target in an admittedly complex and challenging political scenario, it was he. Even so, I was disinclined to change my decision based on his fiscal road map as it was a mere reaffirmation of the targets with no indication of the steps that would be taken to deliver on those targets.

I was also not prepared to be let down yet again by the government's promise on fiscal targets. Just six months earlier, in April 2012, I cut the policy rate by 0.5 per cent instead of by 0.25 per cent as was widely expected, on the assurance of Pranab Mukherjee that he would aggressively prune subsidies and deliver a fiscal performance better than he had indicated in the budget. If that was the case, why indeed did he not make a tougher commitment in the budget itself, I asked. He could not show such drastic fiscal consolidation in the budget, he told me, because of political compulsions. It so happened that he moved on from the finance ministry to Rashtrapati Bhavan two months later, even as fiscal deterioration continued to put pressure on prices. With that experience still fresh in my mind, I was clearly unwilling to front-load another rate cut by relying entirely on the promise of fiscal rectitude. I consulted my senior colleagues and found that we were all on the same page.

My refusal to fall in line had evidently upset Chidambaram enough to do something very unusual and uncharacteristic—to go public with his strong disapproval of the Reserve Bank's stance. In his 'doorstop' media interaction outside North Block about an hour after the Reserve Bank put out its hawkish policy statement expressing concern on inflation, he said: 'Growth is as much a concern as inflation. If the government has to walk alone to face the challenge of growth, we will walk alone.'

Sure enough, Chidambaram's ire at having been abandoned to 'walk alone' created quite a flutter in the media. I was on notice therefore for the first question put to me in the scheduled post-policy media conference later that afternoon. Clearly reluctant to fan controversy during a difficult economic period, I papered over the differences, saying: 'The government and the Reserve Bank have shared goals. Both of them want high growth and low inflation. Differing perceptions on how to achieve these goals are common across many countries in the world.'

Chidambaram and I were together in Mexico less than a week after that for a G20 meeting. The ambassador of India in Mexico, Sujan R. Chinoy, graciously hosted a dinner for the Indian delegation to provide an opportunity for the finance minister to meet some of the leading public figures and businesspersons of Mexico. When Chidambaram arrived, he greeted everyone, but pointedly ignored me all through the evening, leaving me with an uncomfortable feeling.

Even though this public show of disagreement was a one-off, tension between the government and the Reserve Bank persisted even after that. One particularly contentious disagreement arose in the context of the mid-quarter policy of June 2013 when

Chidambaram was of the view that the Reserve Bank should cut the CRR to stimulate bank lending. This was at a time when the rupee was under intense pressure because of the taper tantrums. Any monetary easing in this situation, no matter how carefully explained, was sure to accentuate the downward pressure on the rupee and undermine the credibility of our exchange rate defence. He called me up and we had our usual disagreement. Showing once again that he wouldn't give up so easily, he fielded his entire team of officers and advisers to canvass the government's case. I stayed with my decision, and as later events would prove, this was well advised as less than three weeks later, we had to actually tighten policy in order to arrest speculation on the rupee.

Why Do Governments and Central Banks Differ?

Maybe, it will be instructive to step back a little and reflect on why indeed governments and central banks have differences. They differ mainly because they see the growth–inflation balance differently, as I said earlier—and this has to do with differing horizons. Governments are typically swayed by short-term compulsions whereas central banks are expected to take a long-term perspective. Central banks can do so only if they are free of political compulsions.

Surely, the autonomy of a central bank on monetary policy cannot be boundless. After all, the source of that autonomy is the mandate granted by politicians. There is wide agreement that it is the government that should set the inflation target, but having set the target, leave it to the central bank to determine the strategy for achieving the target. In other words, a central bank cannot have goal independence; it has to defer to the inflation target set by the government. At the same time, a central bank should have instrument independence; the government should not meddle in how the central bank goes about achieving the inflation target.

It is, in fact, a muted understanding of this principle that was at the heart of a widely reported public spat in early 2013 between the Government of Japan and the Bank of Japan. The Bank of Japan resisted the doubling of the inflation target by the government from 1 to 2 per cent even though the government was well within its right to do so. The Abe government, on its part, was widely seen as having transgressed the principle of separation of powers by not only setting the inflation target, but also prescribing that the Bank of Japan resort to quantitative easing to achieve that target.

The Price to Be Paid for Asserting Autonomy

There is a price to pay, of course, for not falling in line. The government has several ways of showing its displeasure, and the way it chose to do so with me was by going against my recommendations in the reappointment of deputy governors in the Bank.

As the head of the Reserve Bank, enjoined with a public responsibility, the governor should have the privilege of selecting his team just as the prime minister has the prerogative of choosing his Cabinet. There is no question, of course, that under law, it is the government that has the authority to appoint the governor and deputy governors of the Reserve Bank. There are rules about eligibility and tenure, which have to be complied with, and the system of selection has to be fair, transparent and contestable. Within that framework, a healthy convention should be to defer to the governor's recommendation on the appointment of deputy governors. That privilege was denied to me.

Usha Thorat, whose term as deputy governor was expiring in October 2010, was eligible for reappointment for another two years in accordance with the convention followed till then of reappointing deputy governors till they attained the age of sixty-two years. Even as I was planning to formally write to the government recommending and requesting her reappointment, the secretary of the Department of Financial Services, R. Gopalan, called one evening to say that the finance minister had approved the constitution of a committee to select Usha's successor. I was pained that even if the government had decided to deviate from the standard practice of consulting the governor on the reappointment of an incumbent, they had not even told me about it before constituting a selection committee. There was speculation that Pranab Mukherjee was irked by some regulatory decision taken on Usha's watch which, of course, came on top of his general unhappiness with me.

I sought a meeting with Pranab Mukherjee—incidentally one of only two occasions when I met him one-on-one[1]—and requested that Usha be reappointed because of her competence, track record and because she met the eligibility criteria for reappointment. He knew that he could not call into question Usha's competence or track record; it would have been presumptuous on his part to override my judgement on this issue with his own. He pleaded rules instead, but I was prepared for that point. I told him that the government had reappointed Shyamala Gopinath, another deputy governor, an identical case, under the same rule, and added for effect that he was the finance minister who had approved it. He didn't budge and Usha became a part of the price we had to pay for asserting the autonomy of the Reserve Bank.

We had a replay of the same story in the case of reappointment of Subir Gokarn whose three-year tenure as deputy governor was expiring in December 2012. By this time, Chidambaram had returned as finance minister. As early as in August 2012, I requested Chidambaram to reappoint Subir for two more years and told

---

[1] The other one-on-one meeting was in the context of the ordinance on ULIPs which I will come to a little later.

him and that I would send a formal recommendation accordingly. I reiterated the request in October 2012. Chidambaram was clearly disinclined to accede. The reason he gave was that all of us who entered the Reserve Bank laterally had become hostage to the technocrats in the Reserve Bank and the government felt it necessary to bring some fresh thinking into the Reserve Bank. He was firm that we should go through a *de novo* selection process.

I reminded him that according to the rules framed by none other than him, Subir was eligible for reappointment; the question of opening up the position to other candidates would arise only if Subir was not recommended by the governor, which obviously was not the case. Chidambaram did not budge and insisted that we go through a process of selection. He agreed though that Subir could be considered by the selection committee along with other candidates.

The selection committee, under my chairmanship, went through the due process and agreed on a panel of three candidates, with Subir Gokarn at the top of the list. A couple of days later, P. K. Misra, secretary of the Department of Personnel, who was also a member of the selection committee, called me up to say that the minutes had to be redrafted since the rules did not allow for the committee to rank candidates in order of preference. I was surprised because he, as the 'minder of rules', had not said so when we met in the committee. I told him that I could not agree to the redrafting of the minutes through a bilateral, oral arrangement and that we should follow the due process. He should write to me explaining the rule position, then we should reconvene the committee to review the decision, and if agreed, dispense with the ranking. I did not hear from him again on this.

Subir's tenure was coming to an end on 31 December 2012. But even after Christmas, there was no news from the government. I was hoping that since his name was on top of the list, the finance minister would, even if reluctantly, acquiesce. We had a farewell function planned on 31 December to bid farewell to a couple of senior officers who were superannuating that day. My staff asked if we should cover Subir too under this farewell. I said 'no' in the hope that the reappointment would come through literally even at the eleventh hour. In the event, I underestimated Chidambaram's desire to bring 'fresh thinking' into the Reserve Bank. Later that afternoon, we got the news that Subir's appointment was not being renewed.

In an article titled 'Silencing the RBI' in the *Business Standard* of 9 January 2013, Rajeev Malik, a columnist, wrote: 'In some ways, the government's decision not to extend Mr Gokarn's term appears to be a censure of Governor Subbarao. His second term ends in September this year, so he could not be shown the door before without rattling investors. Perhaps it was unfortunate that Mr Gokarn's term ended when it did. It appears to have made him an easy target. After all, the current government has not been shy of messing around with institutions—the RBI is just the latest addition to that list.'

Another mischievous, if also clumsy, attempt by the government to assault the autonomy of the Reserve Bank came by way of appointing the directors on the central board of the Bank. As per law, it is the government's prerogative to appoint the directors but the law also guarantees the directors so appointed a four-year term. In other words, the government cannot recall any director at will during the four-year tenure. Presumably, the intent behind this provision was to ensure that the directors acted independently without any threat of the government 'showing its displeasure' by terminating their appointment.

It has been the standard practice for the government to conform to the wording of the law with regard to the guaranteed four-year term. While appointing a fresh batch of directors in 2011, however, the government changed the wording in the notification to say: 'xxx is appointed as a Director on the Central

Board of the Reserve Bank for a term of four years or *until further orders whichever is earlier* [emphasis mine].'

We were surprised by this change in wording. Maybe a clerical error, I thought. That didn't seem likely though as all they had to do was copy the standard wording of the previous notifications. Having worked in the government, I am aware of the power of precedents; breaking a precedent requires a clear application of mind. Here, someone in the government did apply his mind to incorporate a new provision so as to keep the directors on the board of the Reserve Bank on leash, not realizing that it was against the law. We pointed this out to the government and they issued an amendment to bring the wording back to the standard format. Yes, we held our ground, but it would have been better if the matter hadn't arisen at all.

Global Experience

As I said before, differences between governments and central banks are not unique to India. They are much more common than we think but they play out differently in different countries and different contexts. And they are also managed differently.

The European Central Bank, the monetary authority for the nineteen members of the eurozone, is, in theory at least, supposed to be the most independent central bank in the world if only because it is not answerable to any single government. But even the ECB gets enmeshed in political controversy more often than we think. The irascible German Finance Minister Wolfgang Schäeuble has for long been critical of the ECB's policy cocktail of low interest rates, large bond purchases and generous liquidity for banks. Even as I write this in early 2016, Schäeuble has gone so far as to blame ECB President Draghi for the rise of the Alternative for Germany (AfD), a new anti-immigration, anti-euro party that surged into three regional parliaments with stunning victories.

In his autobiographical book, *The Age of Turbulence*, Alan Greenspan, the former chairman of the Federal Reserve, writes extensively about his strained relationship with President Bush Senior. According to Greenspan, the Bush administration and the Fed differed on managing the economic downturn, and the administration faulted the Fed's tight monetary policy for all its economic troubles. Greenspan writes that President Bush publicly challenged the Fed's hawkish stance by saying: 'I do not want to see us move so strongly against inflation that we impede growth.' Treasury Secretary Nicholas Brady in the Bush administration reportedly resented Greenspan's reluctance to support growth by slashing interest rates, and bluntly complained of lack of forceful leadership at the Fed. Bush himself blamed Greenspan for his loss in his bid for a second term when he told an interviewer, 'I reappointed Greenspan and he disappointed me.'

I was also struck by the fact that the Federal Reserve and its policies get embroiled in sharper political controversies unlike anything we are used to in India. Recall that Rick Perry, who campaigned for the Republican party candidature in the presidential elections of 2012, had attacked the then Fed chairman, Bernanke, charging him of printing money to play politics, which according to him, amounted to 'nothing less than treason'!

Most political systems would deem such a harsh attack as being outrageous, but strangely the US political system took that in its stride and moved on. In India, in particular, it is inconceivable that any politician would attack the Reserve Bank so sharply, which is a tribute not just to the Reserve Bank but also to our political institutions. Recall that during the campaign for the Parliament elections in 2014, even a hint that the highly regarded Governor Raghuram Rajan could be replaced should a Bharatiya Janata Party (BJP) government come into office, was widely criticized for embroiling the office of the governor of the Reserve Bank in electoral politics.

Autonomy Battles Beyond Monetary Policy

The Reserve Bank's battles for autonomy on my watch extended beyond purely monetary policy issues into other domains. By far the most high profile of these, although it was not as dramatic as depicted in the media, came in the context of an ordinance issued by the government setting out a procedure for resolving disputes between financial sector regulators. The trigger for this was a spat between the Securities and Exchange Board of India (SEBI) and the Insurance Regulatory Development Authority (IRDA) in April 2010 on the jurisdiction over regulating ULIPs.

After due deliberation, the government determined that the resolution of the dispute required a statutory change. But instead of just restricting the legal change to this specific dispute, the proposed legislative amendment sought to establish a generalized mechanism of a joint statutory panel under the chairmanship of the finance minister to resolve all future disputes between regulators. I was given to understand that it also became necessary to amend the Reserve Bank Act in the process to make the amendment consistent with all existing laws. As Parliament was in recess, the government issued an ordinance to settle the dispute on hand without delay. The ordinance would, of course, need to be ratified by Parliament at its next session.

At face value, the government's legislative initiative was unexceptionable, in some sense even wise. Instead of addressing just the immediate issue, the government was establishing a generalized mechanism for resolving all regulatory disputes in the future. Ironically, it was this very broad-based action—the statutory sanction to readily convene a committee whenever there was a dispute between regulators—that triggered disquiet among all regulators, including the Reserve Bank, about how it could potentially be abused to compromise the autonomy of regulators.

There were several concerns. First, the bar for invoking the statutory intervention was set very low. All that was required was a complaint by any of the regulators or either of the secretaries, of economic affairs or financial services, in the finance ministry. For a future finance minister intent on misusing the authority of the committee to settle scores with regulators or to trim their wings, this would be an easy enough prerequisite to meet. Second, it would also make it possible for interested parties to pay regulatory arbitrage by deliberately engineering a dispute to invoke the committee's jurisdiction. Finally, whether or not the mechanism was misused, the very possibility of misuse was a concern. The mere existence of an enabling provision of a statutory committee would keep regulators anxious, besides strengthening the perception of potential investors about the fragility of regulatory autonomy in the economy.

I consulted my colleagues and all of us agreed that I should formally take up this issue with the government. The result was a letter that I wrote to the finance minister listing the Reserve Bank's concerns and requesting the government to let the ordinance lapse by not seeking parliamentary approval for it.

The letter received extensive media coverage, with the Reserve Bank getting both approval and reproval. On the positive side, the Reserve Bank was complimented for upholding an issue of larger public interest by trying to prevent politicization of regulatory oversight. As governor, I was praised for the courage I showed in taking a firm and principled position on protecting the autonomy of not just the Reserve Bank but of all financial sector regulators. In an article titled 'Subbarao learns to call a spade a spade', the *Economic Times* of 4 July 2010 wrote: 'Mr. Subbarao's public expression of displeasure has put to rest months of speculation on where his heart lies. The Mint Street clearly trumps North Block.'

On the flip side, some people thought that the Reserve Bank's concerns were unrealistic and that we were seeing a deep conspiracy where none existed. Some had alleged that the Reserve Bank was simply fighting a turf battle under the cover of a grand cause. There were a few comments about how it was governors who were drawn from the IAS that had problems managing differences with the government, whereas the non-IAS governors evidently had no trouble in functioning independently or in establishing a harmonious working relationship with the government. In its editorial titled 'RBI's Consternation', the *Hindu BusinessLine* of 14 July 2010 wrote: 'Nor is it a coincidence that the RBI which is the oldest of the financial sector regulators by far has always exhibited a predilection for greater independence when non-IAS officers have been governors . . . It is the regulatory heads from the IAS who have problems with the notion of standing up to the government which is understandable because it is hard suddenly to jettison your *sanskaras* (training).'

The Reserve Bank's locus standi on this issue was also called into question on the argument that initiating a legislation was the government's prerogative and that the Reserve Bank could not demand to be consulted on every legislation relating to it. This last bit of criticism was clearly misinformed because we were not questioning the government's prerogative to initiate legislation; nor were we demanding that the Reserve Bank be consulted. We were agitating against the content of the proposed legislation as an interested party.

The media saw blood and sensationalized the stand-off between the government and the Reserve Bank. The issue was, of course, serious but the actual 'battle' was much less dramatic. Far from being annoyed or agitated, Pranab Mukherjee was gracious and understanding about the whole matter. He invited me to a meeting in Delhi where we had a very frank and cordial conversation. I made it clear to him that my concerns were as much about the potential misuse of the statutory committee arrangement as about the perception such a statutory provision would convey about regulatory autonomy which, among other things, would erode India's attractiveness as an investment destination. From his side, the finance minister talked about the damage regulatory disputes could do to investor confidence and the need for an established and predictable mechanism to resolve disputes before they blew up into public spats.

Pranab Mukherjee did not concede the main issue but agreed to remove one possible source of misuse—which was that the secretaries in the ministry of finance who were also members of the committee would not be able to register a complaint to invoke the committee's jurisdiction; it could only be invoked by a complaint by one of the regulators. He also tried to assuage me personally by designating the governor of the Reserve Bank as the vice chairman of the statutory committee. This was not something I demanded, nor was it an issue that mattered to me personally.

The autonomy tussle arising from the ULIP ordinance segued into a contention over the establishment of the Financial Stability and Development Council with a remit to deal with issues relating to financial stability, financial sector development and inter-regulatory coordination. The finance minister would be the chairman and all financial regulators would be members of the FSDC.

Some background is necessary to see the FSDC issue in perspective. Financial stability came centre stage in the aftermath of the global financial crisis with the realization that it was the neglect of financial stability by governments and regulators that was the root cause of the crisis. The world view before the crisis was that if governments and regulators took care of price stability and macroeconomic stability, financial stability would obtain as an automatic by-product. The crisis, coming as it did in the midst of an extraordinary period of macroeconomic and price stability, demolished that view. The received post-crisis wisdom is that financial stability has always got to be on the radar of governments and financial sector regulators.

This big lesson of the crisis set a new direction for financial sector regulation, but it also raised new questions. How should financial stability be defined? What are the policies and instruments available to preserve financial stability and when and how should they be deployed? Who should be in charge of what? In other words, in any given jurisdiction, what role should the government play and what should the division of responsibilities be across the several regulators? What should the mechanism be for coordination among them? Should that mechanism be different in normal times and in crisis times?

This is a long list of questions about safeguarding financial stability but as yet there are no definitive answers. What complicates understanding is that the crisis hit virtually every country in the world, showing that there is no clear best practice in regulatory architecture. Even so, several countries, led by advanced economies, instituted changes involving a redesign of the regulatory architecture, redefining responsibilities of various agencies for financial stability and establishing institutions for coordination. India's FSDC initiative was in line with these global developments.

Even as central banks around the world were struggling to adjust to the received wisdom on financial stability, they were also agitated about the possibility of the new arrangements creating a conflict of interest for them and impinging on their autonomy. Abstracting from all the technical details, their concern arose from the understanding that policies for price stability and policies for financial stability are interlinked. What this means is that it might sometimes be necessary to deploy monetary policy to preserve financial stability. Similarly, an action taken by the central bank to preserve financial stability would impact its monetary policy stance. Would that not create a conflict of interest? Besides, there was the possibility that consultation and coordination with the government on policies for financial stability could easily spill over into the government interfering in monetary policy decisions under the cover of preserving financial stability. What would that mean for the central bank's monetary policy autonomy?

These apprehensions at the global level were equally relevant in the Indian context. Having been through the crisis, I was deeply conscious of the critical importance during crisis times of coordination among the regulators, with the government in the driving seat. This was the standard practice in virtually every country during the crisis and India was no exception. But did we need to set up a permanent body like the FSDC? Wouldn't existing mechanisms have been sufficient to take care of financial stability during 'peace' times? Would the proposed FSDC do more harm than good?

I must admit that I had greater reservations about the institutionalization of the coordination mechanism for financial stability under the FSDC umbrella than on the dispute resolution committee envisaged under the ULIP legislation, mainly because it can make the government's transgression into regulatory autonomy appear seamless and even justified. We already had in existence a High Level Coordination Committee on Financial Markets (HLCCFM) under the chairmanship of the governor and comprising all the financial sector regulators and the secretaries of economic affairs and of financial services from the government. The HLCCFM was meeting regularly to coordinate on regulatory issues. The mandate of this committee could easily have been redefined to explicitly include financial stability. The government's concerns on financial stability could be pursued by the two secretaries who were members of the committee. On the other hand, under the proposed FSDC structure, with the finance minister in the chair, there is the risk of financial stability issues transgressing into the domain of monetary and regulatory policies.

On the FSDC issue too, like on the ULIP issue earlier, Pranab Mukherjee was broad-minded and gracious. He invited me for a meeting where we exchanged views and discussed possible safeguards against the FSDC encroaching into regulatory autonomy. He did not concede the main issue but held out several assurances—that there would be a subcommittee of the FSDC under the chairmanship of the governor which would be more active and meet more frequently; the FSDC itself would play an active role during crisis times only. He recalled that during the Parliament discussion on the ULIP ordinance, he held out an assurance that the government would not interfere with the autonomy of the regulators, and added that the same assurance would also hold in respect of the FSDC.

As I look back on the developments of those days, it sometimes occurs to me that I may have possibly overreacted and that my apprehensions were more imagined than real. On the other hand, one cannot rule out the possibility that the sensitivity to regulatory autonomy will erode over time, there could be mission creep and we could end up in a situation where FSDC will routinely discuss monetary policy in the context of discharging its responsibility for financial stability. All this is in the realm of speculation and I do hope that we will build robust and credible institutional protocols to prevent the FSDC from trespassing into the regulatory domain even inadvertently. The FSDC structure will add value only so long as the finance minister and all the members constantly guard against these risks materializing.

The Financial Sector Legislative Reforms Commission, set up as part of a budget decision of 2011, raised the autonomy issue again, although indirectly. Again, let me give a brief background.

Just as the governor informs the finance minister of his monetary policy decision in advance, the finance minister too briefs the governor ahead of the budget on proposals that have relevance for the Reserve Bank. Both Chidambaram and Pranab Mukherjee respected this convention. In such a pre-budget briefing in 2010, Pranab Mukherjee told me about his proposal for the FSLRC. He was preaching to the converted. I had myself strongly canvassed, both in my public speeches as well as internal conversations with the ministry of finance, the need to recast all our financial sector laws—in order to streamline and simplify them. I readily endorsed the finance minister's proposal but cautioned him that the committee should restrict its task to recasting the existing laws but should not, in the process, attempt to change the basic framework of our regulatory architecture.

In fact, I took the opportunity of my inaugural speech at BANCON in December 2010, to indicate my position on the FSLRC. Here's what I said: 'It is important, however, to recognize that bringing about changes in policy or in the regulatory architecture cannot be the remit of a legislative reforms commission. Such changes have to be debated and decided upon as a prelude to the work of the commission so that the commission has a clear mandate on the policy directions. In short, policy directions should drive the work of the legislative reforms commission, not the other way round. That underscores why it is important for all of us—the banks and the banking regulator—to deliberate on the policy directives. I hope this conference will set the ball rolling by discussing the various aspects of legislative changes required in the banking sector.'

Pranab Mukherjee assured me that my concern would be taken care of while drafting the terms of reference of the committee and that he would also brief the committee on this sensitivity before they set out to work.

In the event, the FSLRC interpreted its mandate in a much broader context and went about proposing some fundamental changes to the regulatory architecture. I must say for the record, although it may not matter since I am no longer governor, that I endorse some of the recommendations of the FSLRC, such as its emphasis on consumer protection and the establishment of a Monetary Policy Committee to decide on monetary policy. But I have reservations about some others like the division of responsibilities for capital flows—the government regulating inflows and the Reserve Bank regulating outflows—and entrusting systemic risk management to the FSDC.

Apart from the content of the recommendations, I also have a grievance with the committee over the very minimal opportunity it gave to the financial sector regulators to present their point of view. The committee held just one joint meeting with all the financial sector regulators, maybe of about three hours' duration. There was no prior indication of the specific issues on which the committee wanted to hear the regulators' views; we were simply asked to present our respective briefs in an open-ended manner. The meeting was also one-sided, since they heard us but did not engage us.

I was not too perturbed at that time because I thought this was only a preliminary meeting and that the committee would give each regulator a separate and exclusive opportunity after they had reached some preliminary conclusions. It did not exactly unfold that way. The committee put all these preliminary recommendations straightaway in the public domain, calling for feedback without any further engagement with the regulators.

In the Reserve Bank, we had reservations about several of the recommendations contained in the preliminary FSLRC report and requested a meeting with the committee to represent our point of view. They did not concede our request. All we got was an informal, off-the-record meeting with the chairman and just one other member of the committee where they heard us out without actively engaging us on any of our reservations. For me, the whole experience was very unsatisfactory.

There has been a high-decibel debate on the FSLRC recommendations since I left the Reserve Bank in September 2013. The government is moving forward on implementing some of the committee recommendations. Drawing presumably from the FSLRC report, it has also put out a draft Indian financial code in the public domain, calling for suggestions and feedback. Given all this flux, I am not inclined to use this space to debate the issues on which I disagree with the FSLRC. I do also concede that as an RBI insider, I could be seen as an interested party, with my objectivity open to question.

However, I do have persisting questions about the way the FSLRC interpreted its terms of reference, giving itself scope to alter the fundamental fabric of the financial sector regulatory architecture. It was a Financial Sector *Legislative Reforms* Commission, not a Financial Sector *Reforms* Commission. My understanding was that its job was to recast the financial sector laws to make them simple, streamlined and consistent with a modern financial system. If indeed the committee was right in giving itself such a sweeping mandate, it should have engaged the financial sector stakeholders, particularly the regulators, more actively to debate the pros and cons of their proposals instead of the summary way in which it went about its task.

Payment of Dividend to the Government

The Reserve Bank is not a commercial institution, nor is profit-making one of its objectives. Nevertheless, the Reserve Bank generates a 'surplus profit' which, as per statute, is transferred to the government. This is roughly the pattern across most countries in the world which explains why governments have a stake in how efficiently and profitably central banks manage their finances.

The main source of income to the Reserve Bank is the interest it earns on its holdings of government securities, its overnight lending to commercial banks and the returns on its foreign currency assets. Its main spending commitments are the costs of printing currency, agency commission paid to commercial banks acting on its behalf for government transactions, and employee cost.

The Reserve Bank typically makes a 'profit' from its operations, and from this profit, allocations are made to two reserve funds. The first reserve fund is meant mainly to absorb losses from its operations in money, securities and forex markets, and to absorb shocks arising out of variations in exchange rates and gold prices. The second reserve fund is maintained for meeting internal capital expenditure and making investments in the bank's subsidiaries and associated institutions. The 'surplus profit' after allocation to the reserves is transferred to the government. For a cash-strapped government, the surplus transfer from the Reserve Bank, typically of the order of 0.5 per cent of GDP, is a significant source of revenue in managing its fiscal responsibility mandate. For example, during 2014–15, the Reserve Bank transferred a surplus of ₹660 billion, equivalent to 0.6 per cent of GDP.

In the last few weeks before the budget, it is common practice for the finance ministry to shore up revenues by pressuring public sector enterprises to raise dividend payments. The Reserve Bank too comes under pressure to scale down its allocations to the reserve funds so as to leave a higher 'surplus profit' for transfer to the government. Ironically, I was on both sides of this tug of war. As finance secretary, I pushed the Reserve Bank to raise the payment to the government—much to the consternation of Governor Reddy—and as governor, I resisted similar pressures.

The standard argument of the government is that the Reserve Bank is far too conservative in its estimate of contingent liabilities and is building reserves beyond any reasonable requirement. The Reserve Bank's position has been that the reserves are being built as per a formula recommended by a technical committee which took into consideration, among other things, the point that the Reserve Bank's income can be quite volatile, dependent as it is on both domestic and global macroeconomic developments. No more is being put away, the Reserve Bank maintains, than is required by minimum levels of prudence. These arguments go on every year and a settlement is reached with both sides showing some flexibility. It is notable though that even as this issue is contentious, it has never turned acrimonious.

Central banks are typically apprehensive about threats to their balance sheets for mainly two reasons. Even though they can almost always discharge their financial obligations by creating money if necessary, large exposures and sustained losses can weaken their ability to conduct policy effectively. Second, mounting losses can make it necessary for a central bank to approach its government for capital infusion. This is a contingency that a central bank wants to avoid, as negotiation with the government could erode its independence. This might look like paranoia but some central banks, more so, surprisingly, central banks in mature democracies, take this threat quite seriously.

In India though, even as the autonomy of the Reserve Bank is an issue, the amount of surplus transfer or the capital requirement of the Reserve Bank have never been variables in defining the government–central bank relationship.

Government Intrusion into Bank Regulation

The Reserve Bank is the regulator of banks, while the government owns as much as 70 per cent of the banking system. This has been another area for friction between the government and the Reserve Bank.

The Reserve Bank's regulation is ownership neutral in the sense that the regulatory norms are uniform as between public and private sector banks. Equity holders in banks, as owners, have rights and responsibilities; there are also rules and established conventions about how those rights may be enjoyed and responsibilities may be redeemed. Problems arise if the government believes and acts as if it has 'ownership' privileges extending beyond those of private owners.

The most conspicuous way in which the government had overstepped its ownership privileges was the way in which it regularly 'advised' public sector banks on how to set their interest rates in response to the Reserve Bank's monetary policy stance. It had almost become a standard practice for the finance minister to call a meeting of the public sector bank chiefs following each monetary policy review of the Reserve Bank and advise them not to raise their lending rates even if the Reserve Bank had tightened the policy rate. This overt repression of monetary policy transmission undermined the Reserve Bank's efforts to contain inflation. As the owner of public sector banks, the government's prerogative to influence the way in which a public sector bank responds to the monetary policy signal of the Reserve Bank is unexceptionable. But that prerogative must be exercised through its nominee directors on the boards of these banks, not through a high-profile meeting in the North Block chaired by the finance minister. I must admit that this happened more during my predecessor Reddy's time than mine.

But I had problems of my own. In 2011–12, D.K. Mittal, who was secretary of the Department of Financial Services, started taking a more activist role in managing public sector banks. He started issuing instructions to these banks on a variety of issues, like cautioning them in raising funds through bulk deposits and asking them to be more restrained in loan restructuring. He also forayed into the regulatory domain by asking public sector banks to convert every banking correspondent (BC) outlet into an 'ultra-small' branch.

In sections of the media, Mittal was praised for his zeal to jolt the 'lethargic' public sector banks into action, while he was also criticized for his micromanagement. I also got reports that public sector bank chiefs were unhappy with this meddling, but being 'public servants', refrained from speaking up. Needless to say, in the Reserve Bank, we were clearly unhappy with this activism.

In July 2012, at a public event in NABARD (National Bank for Agriculture and Rural Development) where I had gone to give its silver jubilee lecture, I was asked what I thought about all this micromanagement of public sector banks by the government. I had clearly indicated the Reserve Bank's position. First of all, ownership or no ownership, this government creep into the regulatory domain was wrong. On issues outside the regulatory domain too, the government does not enjoy any privileged ownership position. It should pursue its policies by projecting them in the boards of the banks through its nominee directors. I added that the government should establish best practices for exemplary and responsible corporate behaviour.

Rendering Accountability

Accountability is the flip side of autonomy. An institution like the Reserve Bank that jealously guards its autonomy should also zealously render accountability for results.

Curiously, the Reserve Bank of India Act does not prescribe any formal mechanism for accountability of the central bank. Over the years, however, certain good practices have evolved. The bank explains the rationale of its policies, and where possible, indicates expected outcomes so that the public has a framework for evaluating its performance. The governor holds regular media conference after every quarterly policy review, which is an open house for questions related not just to monetary policy, but the entire domain of activities of the Reserve Bank. The Reserve Bank also services the finance minister in answering Parliament questions relating to its domain. Importantly, the governor appears before the Parliament's standing committee on finance whenever summoned, which happens, on average, three to four times a year.

It has often struck me that for a public policy institution with such a powerful mandate, these sporadic and voluntary mechanisms for accountability are inadequate. Voluntary initiatives for rendering accountability, no matter how effective and earnest, are no substitute for clearly prescribed formal mechanisms.

There have been some positive developments in this regard since I left the Reserve Bank in 2013. Importantly, the Monetary Policy Framework Agreement between the Government and the Reserve Bank, signed in February 2015, prescribes an inflation target, and in the event of failure to deliver on the target, enjoins the governor to send a report to the government explaining the reasons for the failure and the remedial steps being taken to return inflation to the targeted zone. This formal accountability mechanism for delivery on the inflation target is a substantive step forward. But is this enough? It falls short on at least two grounds. First, the accountability is restricted to the Reserve Bank's inflation mandate. What about all the other functions of the Reserve Bank, such as, for example, external sector management, bank regulation, and printing and distribution of currency? Second, a written communication from the governor to the finance minister is a one-way channel, whereas effective accountability should warrant two-way engagement.

I used the opportunity of the Palkhivala Memorial Lecture I delivered in August 2013 to voice my concerns about the absence of a formal accountability mechanism for the Reserve Bank. I argued that in India too, we must institute a practice like in the US where the chairman of the Federal Reserve testifies before a Congressional committee on a regular basis. On those lines, in India, the governor of the Reserve Bank should go before the Parliament's standing committee on finance twice a year to present a comprehensive report on the Bank's policies and their outcomes, and respond to questions by the committee. This can be in addition to the current practice of the standing committee sporadically summoning the governor on specific issues. Besides establishing a formal and comprehensive structure for accountability by the Reserve Bank, a statutorily enshrined procedure like this, I believe, will deliver another significant benefit. By rendering accountability directly to the legislature, the Reserve Bank will be protected from potential assaults on its autonomy by the political executive.

I had, in fact, made this suggestion to the FSLRC, but in the event, they did not accept my advice. I gather informally that some members of the FSLRC thought that such a prescription would not accord with our Constitution!

Instead, what the FSLRC recommended is that the annual report of all financial agencies, including the Reserve Bank's, contain a statement by the chairperson, the governor in this case, on the activities and performance of the institution and that the government lay the annual report on the table of Parliament. This is far short of what I believe is necessary in the case of a public policy institution like the Reserve Bank whose policies have such a wide impact on people's everyday lives.

Walking Alone

All through my occasional skirmishes with the government over the five years I was at the Reserve Bank, I refrained from confronting it on the autonomy issue in the public domain. It was only in the Palkhivala Memorial Lecture I delivered on 29 August 2013, a week before I stepped down, that I rendered an account of my experience of leading the Reserve Bank for five turbulent years, to issue a repartee. This is what I said:

'A final thought on the issue of autonomy and accountability. There has been a lot of media coverage on policy differences between the government and the Reserve Bank. Gerhard Schröeder, the former German chancellor, once said: "I am often frustrated by the Bundesbank. But thank God, it exists." I do hope Finance Minister Chidambaram will one day say: "I am often frustrated by the Reserve Bank, so frustrated that I want to go for a walk, even if I have to walk alone. But thank God, the Reserve Bank exists."'

The standing ovation that I received remains one of the most treasured and enduring memories of my time as governor.

10

Two More Years

Reappointment as Governor in 2011

My first appointment as governor in September 2008 was for a term of three years. When I went to see Finance Minister Chidambaram the morning after the appointment was announced, I had many things on my mind to check with him, almost all of them of immediate concern, such as the logistics of the transition. There were also many issues on which I had to brief him before handing over to my successor as finance secretary. The term of my appointment was nowhere on my agenda. However, he himself kindly volunteered: 'You know, we appointed you only for three years. But don't worry too much about it. You'll surely get an extension.' Worry about it? I had far too many more immediate worries. I forgot about that bit of conversation even before I exited his office.

The inevitable speculation about my extension[1] and the kite-flying on a putative successor started as early as March 2011, a full

---

[1] Grace Koshie, the secretary to the Reserve Bank board, used to reprimand anyone who used the phrase 'extension of the governor's term'. Technically, the governor's term is not extended; she or he is reappointed. I am resorting to the more common phraseology for ease of communication. Grace, since retired like me, will, I hope, pardon the liberty I am taking.

six months before the close of my term. I was not much distracted by this; indeed, I was surprised by my own indifference because it was so unlike me. I wouldn't admit to being a careerist, but all through my career, I had clear aspirations and cared very much about my career progression. So, what explains this uncharacteristic nonchalance? I figured that by way of a career, I got more than my due from the government, and should they decide to replace me, I was prepared to hang up my boots and move on.

But was I prepared to accept an extension if it were offered? Only a few people were close enough to ask me this bluntly, Urmila among them. My answer was a clear yes. I had weathered the global financial crisis and was in the midst of fighting a raging battle against inflation. Going away at this time would have felt like walking away from the battlefield, no matter that it would have been involuntary. Besides, I had started enjoying the job of the governor. When I came into the Reserve Bank three years earlier, I did so—as I wrote earlier—with some trepidation and fear of the unknown. By now, I was in a comfort zone. I had invested in learning and understanding, getting to know the issues and the people, and setting my agenda and priorities. Leaving all this midway would have felt incomplete at a deeply personal level. I had established personal friendships and professional bonds; it felt too soon to tear them asunder. We had, in the previous year, celebrated the Reserve Bank's platinum jubilee which was—I cannot fully capture this in writing—a very fulfilling experience for me. It gave me a keen sense of the history, traditions and ethos of this great institution. Leaving an institution that grew on me so much in the previous year would have left me in an emotional vacuum.

Maybe at some level, I was not completely agnostic about an extension! Because there was a nagging feeling at the back of my mind that not being given an extension would have felt like a seal of disapproval on my performance. That would have been difficult to countenance at any stage of my career, and would have been even more so at the very end. But I had no illusions either. I was by no means irreplaceable. I might miss the Reserve Bank, but the mighty Reserve Bank would move on under a new leadership.

~

Under the Reserve Bank Act, the governor can be appointed 'for a term not exceeding five years' and can be reappointed. Except in the case of Y.V. Reddy, my immediate predecessor, who was given a straight five-year term, the normal practice of the government had been to make the initial appointment for three years and give an extension. This was the case with the two governors before Reddy—Rangarajan and Bimal Jalan; my initial appointment for three years was in accord with this practice.

Note also that contrary to popular perception, the law imposes no term limit; in theory, it is possible therefore for someone to serve as governor for life. There were several governors, especially in the early years after the Reserve Bank was established in 1934, who served longer than five years. James Taylor, the second governor (1937–43), served for nearly six years, and C.D. Deshmukh, the third governor (1943–49) for close to seven years. Benegal Rama Rau (1949–57), who succeeded Deshmukh, had the longest tenure—nearly eight years.

Most governors served out their terms of appointment although there were a few exceptions. L.K. Jha (1967–70) resigned when he was appointed India's ambassador to the United States. K.R. Puri (1975–77) relinquished office midway through his term when the Janata government came into office post-emergency. Manmohan Singh (1982–85) resigned when he was appointed by Rajiv Gandhi as deputy chairman of the now-defunct Planning Commission, while Bimal Jalan (1997–2003) resigned a few months before the expiry of his term when he was nominated to the Rajya Sabha.

Two governors resigned in protest and therein lie two interesting tales.

Sir Osborne Smith, the first governor of the Reserve Bank (1935–37), was an Australian national and remains the only professional banker to date to have been appointed to this high office. His tenure came at an interesting political-economy juncture in our history when the colonial administration seemed open to yielding to greater self-rule. Top officials in the British Indian bureaucracy, already irked by this impending power shift, were upset by the Reserve Bank of India Act which, far from making the governor play 'second fiddle' to the government, had in fact, made him all too powerful.

Percy Grigg, the then finance member in the government, was particularly upset with Governor Smith's working style and had serious differences with him on monetary policy issues, especially on lowering the bank rate. Their relationship deteriorated so much that while Smith, then only an year into his office, said he was 'sick to death' by the government's desperation to dominate the Reserve Bank, Grigg started suggesting that the governor was acting in unison with 'devaluationists and currency speculators'. The already antagonistic relationship took an ugly turn when there were allegations that the government was tapping the governor's telephone and mail. And when no evidence came out of these 'interventions', Grigg forced the issue by asking the government to choose between him and Smith, and decide who stayed on and who moved out. The government sided with Grigg, forcing Smith to resign, which he did on 1 November 1936. After proceeding on eight months' leave, he laid down office on 30 June 1937.

Sir Benegal Rama Rau, the fourth and also the longest-serving governor to date, served as India's ambassador to Japan and the United States before being appointed to the Reserve Bank. His relationship with Finance Minister T.T. Krishnamachari, popularly known as TTK, was frosty right from the time he succeeded C.D. Deshmukh in July 1956.

The first serious tussle between the two erupted when TTK introduced a supplementary taxation proposal for hiking the stamp duty rate on bills, a 'fiscal measure with monetary intent', as TTK himself described it, but which ran counter to the Reserve Bank's Bill Market Scheme. Taking umbrage at this encroachment into monetary turf, Rama Rau took the issue to the board of the bank which passed a resolution of protest. When requested by Rama Rau to rethink his stance on the proposal, TTK responded with 'professional discourtesy'. As B.K. Nehru recollects in his autobiography, *Nice Guys Finish Second*, the finance minister 'let fly in no uncertain terms and in the loudest of voices' at Rama Rau.

Matters escalated further when Rama Rau's memorandum expressing deep concerns about the independence of the central bank and RBI's ability to exercise statutory responsibility for 'monetary policies and other matters' made its way to Prime Minister Nehru. Nehru reportedly took serious exception to this 'improper and agitational' memorandum, which he saw as 'practically an indictment of Government's policy'.[2] Rama Rau stood his ground, and deeming it not possible to continue under the circumstances, resigned on 14 January 1957.

The tussle between the government and the Reserve Bank has long historical traditions, after all!

~

A few of the possible contenders, including some who did not figure in the media's speculation, came to see me to probe. My answers were straightforward. No, the finance minister had not spoken to me about it. No, I had not raised the issue with the

---

[2] *History of the Reserve Bank of India*, vol. 2 (Mumbai: RBI, 1998).

finance minister. No, I did not intend to go and request the prime minister. Yes, I would accept an extension were it to be offered. To remove any awkwardness from the conversation, I also told them forthrightly that should they be interested in the job, they should go and request the prime minister or the finance minister, and I would not misunderstand.

It was more important for me to address the awkwardness and discomfort of my staff with regard to this situation. I kept scheduling appointments, meetings and travel, and accepting external speaking commitments as if I would continue beyond the three-year term. This set the staff speculating on whether I might have got an inside tip on an extension. I decided to lay my cards on the table and levelled with the senior staff at one Top Management Group (TMG) meeting in early July 2011. I told them the same thing that I had told the possible contenders. I added that no inferences should be drawn from my accepting commitments beyond my term; I was doing that only for maintaining continuity. Should I be replaced, my successor could always rework the schedule. Managing abrupt transitions has traditionally been one of the strengths of the Indian bureaucracy, and this would be no exception.

~

The media did a comprehensive job of analysing why I might or might not get an extension, which, of course, ran along predictable lines. Pro-extension arguments were that I had steered the Reserve Bank through some very challenging times, that my experience would be handy in managing the continuing global uncertainty, and that a change in leadership would be unwarranted at a time of persistent high inflation and stalling growth.

The case against my extension was stronger and centred around my record of aggressively asserting the Reserve Bank's autonomy, contrary to the expectation when I was appointed that I would act as per the government's bidding. I botched up my chances, it was said, by differing with the government on the criteria and timing for issue of new bank licences, openly questioning the government's attempts to encroach on the autonomy of the regulators—for example, during the ULIP controversy, an issue I wrote about in an earlier chapter—and by my strident criticism of the government's fiscal laxity on the ground that it was exacerbating inflation pressures, as well as my open opposition to the establishment of FSDC. Most importantly, why would the government reward me with an extension when I kept interest rates high, completely unmindful of their pleas for a softer interest-rate regime?

An intelligent person would have surmised from the media reports that my extension was certainly not assured, but neither did it seem impossible.

There was an interesting side story running alongside around the time my extension came up for a decision, and that had to do with the unfolding 2G Scam which embroiled the UPA government in charges of mammoth corruption. The scam erupted when the CAG (comptroller and auditor general) pointed out in his audit report of 2010, huge undercharging, massive irregularities and grave procedural manipulation by the Department of Telecommunication in giving licences to telecom companies for 2G spectrum.

At the time the licences were given away in 2007–08, I was finance secretary in the Central government and was an important player in the decision process. I had written to the Department of Telecommunication in November 2007, questioning their proposal to give away 2G spectrum licences in 2007–08 at a price fixed in 2001 without any fresh effort to rediscover the price. I suggested that the pricing issue, instead of being decided unilaterally by the Department of Telecommunication, be brought before the

Group of Ministers. This letter received quite a lot of play in the media, with the suggestion that the UPA leadership's inaction in preventing the issue of licences at questionably low prices despite its own finance secretary questioning the pricing formula, was evidence of its complicity in this alleged wrongdoing.

It was not as if I was a completely unblemished hero in the 2G drama. Both the PAC (Public Accounts Committee) and the JPC (Joint Parliamentary Committee), while acknowledging my diligence in raising the pricing formula, pulled me up for not sufficiently following up on my letter. But all that is a different story and a deviation from my main narrative here. In the context of the main story—my extension—the speculation was that the government would not give me one because it was cut up with me for the embarrassment my letter had caused to the UPA leadership.

~

I went to meet the prime minister at his official residence at 7 Race Course Road on 21 July 2011 as part of my regular pre-policy briefing ahead of the quarterly policy review scheduled for 26 July. This was roughly seven weeks before my three-year term was to expire. After we finished the substantive business of the meeting, he asked me if I had met the finance minister and briefed him on the policy. I told him I had. He paused for a while and I remained quiet, as gaps of silence were quite common in one-on-one conversations with Dr Manmohan Singh. 'Has the finance minister spoken to you about your extension?' he then asked me, and I said no. 'You are doing well at RBI and there is no reason why you should not serve a full five-year term like others.' This was more of self-musing rather than a question. After another awkward pause, I stood up to take leave, and then he said, 'Let me know as soon as the finance minister speaks to you.'

I returned to Mumbai and got caught up in the hurly-burly of the policy review and follow-up tasks. It was not as if the uncertainty of an extension was burdening my mind. There was still more than a month to go, and given the government's standard practice of eleventh-hour appointments, I knew it was too early to feel at a loose end.

T.K.A. Nair, principal secretary to the prime minister, called me on 28 July to check if the finance minister had spoken to me about my extension, and I told him no. The prime minister wanted to know, he said, adding, 'Let me know as soon as the finance minister speaks to you.' I knew Nair quite well as I used to deal with him on a regular basis both when I was in the prime minister's Economic Advisory Council and later as finance secretary. He was a warm, friendly and affable person, and I knew he regarded me highly and was my well-wisher. He called me again, I think on 4 August, with the same inquiry. He sounded a bit puzzled at what he thought was an impasse. The only signal I got from these phone calls was that the government was actively engaged in a decision on my extension or in identifying a successor. That was comforting, as the last thing I wanted was for the issue to go to the wire.

On the morning of 9 August, at about eleven, I was in my office working on a speech that I was scheduled to deliver in Kathmandu later that week at a conference organized by the Nepal Rastra Bank, when Susobhan Sinha, my executive assistant, walked in to tell me that he had just seen a scroll on the TV, saying: 'Subbarao gets two-year extension'. We switched on the TV in my office and saw it too. I dismissed that as a continuation of the ongoing media speculation. My logic was that the finance minister, or at any rate, someone high up in the government would call and give me the news before putting it out in the public domain. Within fifteen minutes, Nair called to give me the news and congratulated me on behalf of the prime minister and on his own behalf.

I tried to call the finance minister, Pranab Mukherjee, to thank him for the reappointment, but managed to connect with him only late in the evening, at about ten. I thanked him for the confidence reposed in me and he said something to the effect of: 'Oh, that was just a formality. You've earned the extension by your performance. There was never any question of replacing you at this stage. All the best.'

One issue in this whole process of reappointment that provided grist for the media mill was the way in which the announcement came from the prime minister's office, on its website, rather than from the ministry of finance. Did this indicate a tussle between the prime minister and the finance minister? Did this suggest that the prime minister uncharacteristically pushed for my extension overruling the finance minister's reservations? If indeed Pranab Mukherjee was against an extension for me, wouldn't that impair the already fraught relationship between the two of us?

I am no wiser than anyone else on the first question of whether the prime minister prevailed over the finance minister's opposition, but if it were true, it would have marked another turnaround. Recall that I wrote earlier about how Chidambaram may not have been inclined to take me in as finance secretary in 2007 but the prime minister had nudged him; and later in 2008, it was Chidambaram who reportedly backed my candidature for the governor's job even as the prime minister was not too sure. And now it was a case of the prime minister backing me against Pranab Mukherjee's wishes. But all this is surely in the realm of speculation.

On the second question, I must say that my relationship with Pranab Mukherjee remained exactly as before. He continued to be friendly and gracious, just as before, and he continued to be upset with my interest-rate policies just as before.

The media and the financial sector endorsed the decision. The *Economic Times* wrote that a fresh two-year term for Subbarao was a 'reflection of the confidence in the way he has handled the monetary policy and also signalling continuity at a time of turmoil in global markets'. In an editorial titled, 'Mr. Crisis', the *Financial Express*, while endorsing the extension, said that 'few RBI chiefs have handled two crises like Subbarao'. The *Mint* hailed the government's decision and complimented me for coming into my own as a central banker. 'The July policy,' it wrote, 'demonstrated that Subbarao had graduated from being a Finance Secretary sent to the RBI to take up the Government's job, to being a central banker.'

Those endorsements came with plenty of advice too. Analysts, asked for their opinion by the media, said that I must move away from my 'baby-step' rate action to a more aggressive interest rate-setting policy, that I must improve my communication 'to convince households and markets that my commitment to inflation control stood above all else'. In its editorial, 'Central Bank Rerun', the *Indian Express*, dated 10 August 2011, wrote: 'In the next two years, apart from negotiating through the expected global uncertainty, Subbarao's biggest challenge will be to reorient the multi-instrument, multi-objective, non-accountable, non-transparent, RBI into a central bank that promises and delivers price stability. He has now been given another chance to change the RBI and help it fit the needs of a rapidly growing India.'

At the dinner table that evening, Urmila said to me, 'Now that you've got an extension, I suppose you can be more independent.' I was surprised by this statement-cum-question. I believed and continued to believe that standing by your conviction and doing what you think is right is more a matter of personality than opportunistic behaviour. I would be no less or no more independent, I told Urmila, than I had been in the first three years of my term.

~

When I next ran into the media at some event, a reporter asked me: 'Are you reconciled to living in Mumbai for two more years?' Both the question and the way he phrased it surprised me. It struck me that the question was not the expected one about my challenges and goals for the next two years; nor was it about life in Mumbai. It was about being '*reconciled* to living in Mumbai'.

I figured out where he was coming from. In the early days of my shift from Delhi to Mumbai, I had felt distinctly uncomfortable. That had nothing to do with Mumbai, but with the sanitized life that the governor is expected to lead. I had lived and worked in Delhi for several years. I had gone around by bus, by auto and by car; I had walked the streets of Delhi. I was familiar with the city and felt comfortable in it. Although I had visited Mumbai dozens of times in the past, I had never lived there. Indeed, I couldn't recall staying in Mumbai more than three consecutive nights.

Early in my term, on my way back from office one evening, I asked the driver to stop in Colaba, got off the car and walked around for about half an hour just to get a feel of the place. The next morning, the protocol and security officer attached to the governor's office told me: 'Sir, next time you want to go anywhere on your way back home, let me know. I'll come along with you.' Evidently, the driver was under instruction to keep the security officer informed in real time about my movements, and he himself was uncomfortable with my gallivanting on my own.

In conversations with colleagues and acquaintances, whenever the topic came up, I would express my frustration at not being able to explore Mumbai on my own. But somehow, that reaction took on life as 'the governor doesn't like Mumbai'. Perhaps this is where 'being reconciled to living in Mumbai' came from.

This is hardly the place to go into the usual Delhi–Mumbai squabble. There are differences between the two, both subtle and striking, that I got to notice as I spent time in Mumbai. Delhi is the nation's capital and you can't miss the very essential political undertone in your everyday work life there. Its history and grandeur—especially the Raisina complex where my office was—are overpowering; its art and culture scene is lively. But Delhi is also guilty of an exaggerated air of self-importance and an all-pervading sense of self-righteousness.

Mumbai is different. The leafy streets and colonial buildings of South Mumbai add to its charm. The city oozes energy and vitality from every nook and corner. Mumbai is a city of stark contrasts—providing opportunities to millionaires to pursue their riches and millions of poor to pursue a livelihood. For many, Mumbai is a city where their dream begins; for many others, it marks the end of a dream.

Contrary to the perception conveyed by the reporter's question, I actually came to like Mumbai—the allure of the city grew on me. There are many things I recall with fondness and nostalgia—the Mumbai rains, walking along the Worli Seaface, eating in the hole-in-the-wall vegetarian Maharashtrian eateries in Tardeo, strolling in High Street Phoenix Mall, and watching plays in Prithvi Theatre.

One of my most enduring memories of Mumbai is of the Walking Tour of South Mumbai that Urmila and I took along with a few Reserve Bank colleagues on a pleasant Sunday morning. The young, knowledgeable and enthusiastic guide walked us along some of the historic precincts of Mumbai, telling us enchanting stories about those magnificent buildings and the rich and sometimes hidden tapestry of their cultural heritage. It was a wonderful lesson in history and a crash course on the evolution of architectural styles—neoclassical, neo-Gothic, Indo-Saracenic, and of course, art deco—which you can't miss along Mumbai's iconic Marine Drive.

And since this is also a 'tell all' book of sorts, I might as well add that on a few occasions, although not too often, Urmila and I would tell the staff that we were going for a walk, take a taxi from down the street and wander off to explore the colours and sounds, and experience the hustle and bustle of Mumbai, taking cover under the volume and crowds of this megapolis.

~

All directors on the board of the Reserve Bank, including the governor, sign an official declaration of fidelity and secrecy as laid out in the Bank's general regulations. Earlier on, the declaration used to be taken in a register, but in time, an elegant tradition has evolved—of signing on a scroll. The governor and deputy governors sign when they assume office, while the part-time directors sign before their first board meeting.

This reappointment meant that I was going to sign the scroll for a third time. I signed it the first time when I was appointed to the Reserve Bank board in my capacity as finance secretary, and the second time at the beginning of my first term. Grace Koshie, the meticulous and diligent secretary to the board, took great pride in maintaining and honouring the traditions of the Reserve Bank. She suggested a small ceremony around my signing the scroll after the reappointment, but she acceded to my request to keep it low key and I signed it in the quiet of my office.

As I mentally prepared for two more years, I was hoping that the global uncertainty would wind down, inflation would trend down and growth would trend up, freeing me to focus on the longer-term agenda of the Reserve Bank. But that was not to be. My interesting times continued, justifying the moniker of 'Mr. Crisis' that the *Financial Express*'s editorial had given me.

11

What Does Your Promise Mean, Governor?

Reflections on Currency Management

Most people associate the Reserve Bank with the printing of currency. When I travelled around the country, especially on outreach visits, I used to be fond of visiting primary schools. It was easy to make a connection with the children as they recognized the visiting VIP as the one who signs on the currency notes. Soon enough, the conversation with the children turned to currency matters. Little children would ask if the reason we don't have enough money is because the governor is not able to sign fast enough! Slightly older children would give these little ones a reproving look of 'how can you be so dumb?' and come up with their own question: 'Why doesn't the Reserve Bank just print more money so that everyone in the country can have more of it and India can become a rich country?' Explaining to the children that it does not work that way, what really matters is not how much money we print but the value of goods and services we produce in the country, and that if we just printed more money without increasing production, all we would get is higher prices, is a pedagogical challenge I have never successfully mastered.

The Governor's Promise

Our currency notes[1] carry a promise by the governor. For example, a ₹10 note has a promise on it, saying: 'I promise to pay the bearer a sum of ten rupees.' A woman actually having a ten-rupee note in her hand can be quite perplexed by this promise. What does it mean for the governor of the Reserve Bank to promise to pay you ten rupees when you actually have ten rupees in your hand? Tautological as it might seem, it is simply an old-fashioned way of saying that the currency note is legal tender and will be accepted as a medium of exchange on the trust of the Reserve Bank.

The critical word here is 'trust', which is the core of any system of money. Paper money originated on the basis of trust, trust that the holder of a note could go to a bank and exchange the note for an equivalent value of gold or silver. If that trust—that the bank would redeem its pledge without fail—held, the note would circulate as a medium of exchange without anyone ever going to the bank to exchange the note for precious metal.

Sure, that explanation of the evolution of money based on trust is persuasive enough. But, is there a deeper meaning to the trust underlying the governor's promise on the currency note beyond the assurance that the note is legal tender? Shouldn't trust also extend to an assurance that the Reserve Bank will maintain the purchasing power of the currency by keeping inflation under check? Isn't price stability, in fact, the reason why almost everywhere in the world, the power to print currency is entrusted with unelected

---

[1] The technical phrase for currency issued by central banks is 'bank notes'. I am using the phrase 'currency notes' since it is more easily understood.

technocrats in a central bank rather than with elected politicians in the government? Wouldn't central banks forfeit the trust of their people if they failed to maintain the purchasing power of their currency?

These questions surrounding this broader interpretation of trust become all the more meaningful if we note that the issuance of currency by central banks is no longer governed by the theology of the gold standard—the belief that a central bank must issue currency equivalent only to the value of the precious metal in its vaults. The gold standard was abandoned during the Great Depression of the 1930s and what central banks issue today is fiat currency—that is, currency which derives its value not from any gold or precious metal held by the central bank but from a government decree.

The Reserve Bank too has been part of this global shift from the gold standard to fiat currency. In fact, the original Reserve Bank Act which, coincidentally dates back to 1934, the Great Depression era, prescribed a proportional reserve system whereby, of the total value of notes issued by the Reserve Bank, at least 40 per cent was to be backed by gold bullion and sterling reserves. Subsequent amendments to the Reserve Bank Act have relaxed that provision, and today gold provides only a very small part of the asset-backing for the currency issued by the Reserve Bank; the rest of the cover comes from the domestic and foreign securities held by it.

This breaking of the historical link between the issue of currency by a central bank and its gold holding redefines the basis of public trust in a central bank. The restraint on a central bank to issue currency without bounds is no longer its gold holding but the obligation to preserve the value of the currency by keeping inflation in check. All through my Reserve Bank tenure, I firmly believed that it is this broader interpretation of trust that underlies the governor's promise to pay the bearer 'the sum of ten rupees'.

Security Features of Our Currency

By far the most important facet of currency management is building in security features to prevent counterfeiting.

There are several considerations that go into the design of a currency note, such as reflection of the culture, history and ethos of the nation, a pleasing and appealing look and feel, sensitivity to the needs of differently abled people, particularly those with vision deficiencies, and amenability to mechanized processing. An overriding consideration, of course, is to make counterfeiting difficult and expensive. Keeping ahead of counterfeiters by constantly enhancing the security features is the only way by which central banks can confront this constant occupational hazard.

The most effective deterrent to counterfeiting is wide public awareness of the security features so that people are able to tell a counterfeit note from a genuine one. This is the motivation for the extensive awareness campaign that the Reserve Bank runs in the media to educate people on the security features of the currency. That shopkeepers routinely hold up high denomination notes to the light with the confidence of people who know how to tell the true from the false is everyday proof of the success of this scheme.

In managing this awareness campaign, the Reserve Bank faces two dilemmas. The more straightforward dilemma is that the campaign has to educate people without unduly alarming them, which is the reason why the Reserve Bank has opted for a soft campaign rather than a hard-hitting one. We knew it would take longer to create the necessary impact but it would be more lasting.

The second dilemma, and a more complex one, is that the awareness campaign aimed at educating the public also provides handy information to the counterfeiters. The Reserve Bank manages this tension by making the replication of security features technically complex and prohibitively expensive, and also by incorporating some additional security features that can be detected only by sophisticated equipment.

On an issue like counterfeit currency, there can be nothing short of a zero-tolerance policy but there is a gap, as always, between the policy and the reality. The incidence of counterfeit notes has, of course, come down because of greater awareness and improved systems for detection, but the problem is far from totally eliminated. It shouldn't be surprising also that the problem of counterfeit notes is more acute in our states which have international borders.

Counterfeit currency is primarily a law-and-order and enforcement issue with the responsibility for detection and prosecution lying with the police and security forces. The Reserve Bank has the responsibility to ensure that counterfeit currency does not circulate in the banking system; it does so by detecting and eliminating it at the entry level itself. Importantly, the Reserve Bank has invoked its regulatory power to instruct banks that all currency notes of ₹100 and higher denomination should be checked for genuineness and fitness before they are reissued into circulation. The Reserve Bank regularly trains commercial bank staff and police personnel in detecting counterfeit notes.

The legal provisions governing prosecution for counterfeit currency are quite comprehensive, but the underlying prescription regarding the procedure to be followed distorts the incentives for enforcement. In particular, if a currency note that a customer brings to a bank counter is suspected to be counterfeit, the bank is mandated to file a First Information Report (FIR) with the police. This drags both the customer and the bank into extensive paperwork, and in the case of the customer, confirming that she was unaware of the counterfeit nature of the note in her possession forms the first layer of investigation. This prima facie suspicion and the associated paperwork deter reporting of counterfeit currency.

We tried our best to rectify this perverse incentive structure but met with only limited success. Simplifying the process required amendments to the criminal procedure code (CrPC). We proposed to the home ministry amendments to the CrPC that will absolve the customer of prima facie responsibility, as that will remove the fear and apprehension underlying the current provisions of the law. The ministry, however, was unwilling to relax the process for fear that it would compromise internal security. We did win some concessions though in the matter of rationalizing the procedure for reporting of counterfeit currency. First, in every district of the country, one police station was to be designated as a nodal station for counterfeit currency cases so that the training and specialization could be focused; second, the immediate filing of an FIR was required only if the number of counterfeit notes detected in a single transaction exceeded four, or else, banks could pool cases and file a combined FIR once in a month. This rationalization has improved reporting and provided some relief to common people who unknowingly come into possession of counterfeit notes.

Clean Note Policy

The Reserve Bank is committed to a 'clean note' policy. It exchanges soiled and mutilated notes for clean ones. In pursuit of our clean note policy and also to check counterfeiting, in 2011, we prescribed that all bank branches with cash receipts of over ₹5 million per day be equipped with a note-sorting machine so that every high-denomination currency note is checked for fitness and genuineness before it is put back in circulation. Subsequently, the requirement of machine-processing of cash has been extended to all bank branches, irrespective of the value of receipts.

I noticed early on that there was an urban bias in the implementation of the clean note policy. Urban areas get relatively clean notes and all the soiled notes end up in the villages. The common complaint when I visited villages, more than the absence of banking facilities, was about how they always got only soiled notes. We tried to redress this grievance, at least partly, by including the distribution of notes and coins in the scope of the activities of a banking correspondent in addition to her regular tasks of cash remittances and withdrawals, although I am not sure to what extent this initiative could mitigate the problem. I must also admit that I did not pay as much attention to this issue as I should have, but do hope that the Reserve Bank takes more active interest in correcting the urban bias in its clean note policy.

Plastic Currency

Cost and longevity are important considerations in currency management. We are a large cash economy; in fact, India is the second-largest producer and consumer of currency in the world, next only to China. Producing such a large amount of currency is expensive. One option for economizing is replacing paper currency with plastic currency as some countries, such as Australia and Singapore, have done. For some years, the Reserve Bank has been planning on introducing plastic currency in India, starting with the ten-rupee note on a pilot basis.

Plastic currency offers several advantages. It makes counterfeiting more difficult, the notes stay clean and last longer, therefore entailing lower costs by way of handling and replacement. As against these advantages, we had to test the durability of plastic currency in India's harsh and heterogeneous climatic conditions. Whether they would get 'cultural acceptance' was also a question mark.

I spoke about the Reserve Bank's plans to introduce plastic currency in one of my public speeches which was widely reported in the media. Within ten days after that, I got a letter from an eighth-class girl from a remote village in Jharkhand, asking me whether plastic currency was environmentally positive. I was both touched and impressed. The Reserve Bank, of course, had already taken care of that by commissioning a study by TERI (The Energy and Resources Institute) on the carbon footprint of plastic currency. The TERI report found that plastic currency would be about five times more environment friendly than cotton fibre-based currency mainly because of the longevity of the notes and low-resource consumption. During my term, we initiated a bid process for outsourcing the production of plastic currency of ₹10 denomination. The understanding was that if the pilot process succeeded, the initiative would be mainstreamed.

India towards a Cashless Society?

India, as I have said earlier, is a large cash economy, which is to say that a preponderant proportion of all financial transactions are conducted in cash as opposed to electronic payments. Both the government and the Reserve Bank are keen on moving India towards a less cash economy by encouraging people to shift from cash to electronic payments for all transactions. This will not only reduce the cost of printing and handling cash but also make transactions faster and safer. Electronic payment systems also enable an audit trail of money, which would help in the detection of money laundering and terrorist funding.

This shift from cash to electronic payments is a continuous process and is happening all the time, but its scaling up will depend on some important factors. The first is public acceptance, which is, in part, a question of removing the fear of the unknown, and also a question of making it convenient for people to use electronic payment systems. The second is a significant expansion of the payment infrastructure, and in the nature of supply creating its own demand, this expansion of the infrastructure may itself encourage more people to shift from cash to electronic payments.

In the ultimate analysis though, facilitating the shift to a less cash economy is a question of meaningful financial inclusion.

There has been much talk recently in some rich countries of scrapping cash altogether so that they can become 'cashless societies'. In this futuristic world, all payments will be made by contactless cards, mobile phone apps and other electronic means, while notes and coins will stand abolished. Denmark is reportedly in the forefront in this regard where, under a new proposal, paper money transactions will be disallowed, except, for now, in places like hospitals. The Danish central bank will stop printing currency, and banks will stop carrying cash. In Sweden, it is common practice already for parents to pay pocket money to their children electronically.

There are three main motivations behind this aspiration to a cashless society. The first is the straightforward incentive of avoiding the cost of printing money in the expectation that people will embrace electronic payments once they discover how easy, convenient and efficient they are. Second, forcing people into electronic payments will enable an audit trail of all financial transactions and minimize tax evasion. Third, increasingly, an important motivation for scrapping cash is to choke drug dealers and terrorist organizations who typically use high-denomination notes for their financing.

The case for doing away with cash has gained currency in recent months in the context of some advanced economy central banks, with the ECB and central banks of Japan, Sweden and Switzerland embarking on negative interest rates. In the midst of a contentious debate on the merits and demerits of negative interest rates, an argument has been made that the way to make negative interest rates effective is to ban cash altogether. The objective of negative interest rate is to make people spend rather than save. But, as long as there is cash, people can thwart negative interest rates by hoarding their savings in a safe or under the proverbial mattress. In the absence of cash, on the other hand, people will be encouraged to spend, as the alternative is to lose value by saving in a bank.

Some people have even argued that abolishing cash will give traction to monetary policy even in the normal world of positive interest rates. Since all savings will be in the banking system, it is argued, central banks can manage the business cycle more efficiently as its interest-rate calibration will have a bigger impact. When the economy is slowing, it will cut interest rates to encourage people to spend more; conversely, when the economy is overheating, it will raise interest rates to discourage spending.

There is, of course, opposition to abolishing cash altogether and going completely online. People apprehend invasion of privacy. The very audit trail that allows the checking of illegal activities can turn into an Orwellian nightmare where citizens' every step is recorded in a Big Brother database for tax, financial and monetary purposes. Worse still, should some hackers tap into the information base, the consequences can be disruptive. People argue that the anonymity of cash keeps them free from government snooping and that some criminality is a price worth paying for this liberty.

The economic case for a cashless economy on the argument that it enables the central bank to run a countercyclical policy more efficiently is also contested by some experts who argue that it will deliver results no better than the conventional monetary policy, and may in fact, do worse.

A debate such as this is far too premature for India. We are hardly ready to contemplate the elimination of cash. Our objective is more limited—to shift from a cash-intensive economy to a less cash-intensive economy since the benefits of this shift, at our stage of development, unarguably, outweigh the costs.

Meanwhile, physical currency with the governor's promise will continue to be around, reminding the governor of his dharma.

12

Goldfinger Governor

Foreign Exchange Reserve Management

I authorized the Reserve Bank's purchase of 200 tonnes of gold from the IMF in November 2009. There was deep irony in this for two reasons.

The Purchase of Gold from the IMF

First, back during the 1991 balance of payments crisis, it fell to my lot as a joint secretary in the finance ministry to sign the agreement on behalf of the government, authorizing the Reserve Bank to pledge our gold reserves to secure foreign exchange for our rapidly depleting coffers. By sheer accident, this purchase of gold in 2009 from the IMF to buffer our foreign exchange reserves happened to take place on my watch as governor. The second irony surrounding this transaction was that even as the Reserve Bank eagerly bought gold in 2009, in the later years of my governorship, we were not only preaching to the public to desist from buying gold, but had actually instituted regulations to discourage the practice.

Well, the irony, if any, was superficial, and to understand why, I must tell the full story. The Reserve Bank's foreign exchange reserves comprise foreign currency assets, gold and SDRs (Special Drawing Rights) issued by the IMF.[1] When I took office as governor in September 2008, I inherited 357.7 tonnes of gold, which was about 3.5 per cent of our total forex reserves of that time. There was a view within the Reserve Bank that we must raise the proportion of gold in the reserves as a risk-diversification measure since gold and dollar values move in opposite directions in global markets. The counterargument was that gold, in contrast to foreign currency holdings, is a non-income-generating asset and it will be difficult to justify spending foreign currency to buy gold. Buttressing this argument was the fact that during the global boom of 2002–06, the appeal of gold as an asset had diminished even further.

Besides financial prudence, there were also logistic issues that inhibited the purchase of gold. The problem of putting through a transaction in a transparent manner is always a challenge. Not just the price of purchase, but the counterparty risk involved, the quantity of gold that can be bought without adversely tipping the price, due diligence, including the time gap between paying for and receiving gold, could all be potentially controversial.

Both the economics and logistics changed in 2009, presenting us a 'golden' opportunity to bolster our gold reserves. Importantly, the global financial crisis called into question the long-term health of the dollar as a stable asset, reinforcing the argument for diversification away from the dollar. More crucially, in September 2009, the IMF announced that it would be selling 403.3 tonnes of gold from its holdings to finance its lending to low-income countries and partly also to defray its own operating expenses.

---

[1] Included in the SDRs is also the Reserve Tranche position of India with the IMF.

The IMF also indicated that before going for open market sales, it would make a preferential offer to official reserve holders, including central banks, to buy the gold at the going market price. The offer was on a first-come, first-served basis within a three-month window.

Given the size of the transaction, we confronted the classic Hamletian dilemma: 'to buy or not to buy' the gold on offer from the IMF. What made the decision even more difficult was that all of this had to be done in great secrecy since any leak would have moved the global price of gold, thereby exposing the Reserve Bank to heavy pecuniary and reputation risk. This ruled out the possibility of consulting any external expert. In fact, the initial discussion involved just three of us—Deputy Governor Shyamala Gopinath, an epitome of quiet competence and sturdy confidence, and Executive Director Harun Khan of unquestionable integrity and discretion. The other deputy governors were brought into the loop only after the three of us reached an 'in principle' view.

On the positive side was the rare opportunity to buy a significant quantity of gold from an official international institution, a consideration that had to be balanced against the potential censure we would attract should the price of gold fall steeply in the future. Time was of the essence too since there could be competition from other central banks. And how much should we buy? All 400 MT on offer? Or should we bid only for a part of it? It appeared from the reaction when the news hit the market that I'd have pulled off a coup of sorts if we had bid for the total quantity. But by then, over one year into my tenure as governor, I had become enough of a central banker to take a conservative approach. Considering all the pros and cons, I told Shyamala to go ahead and place a bid for 200 tonnes of gold. In the next few days, I informed only the prime minister and the finance minister, that too in person, when I happened to meet them in some other context.

A small team in the Reserve Bank, led by the affable and intelligent Chief General Manager Meena Hemachandra, worked on the logistics with the IMF. The arrangement was that we would pay the IMF the average price in the London bullion market over the following fifteen working days. Since secrecy was critical, the whole operation had to be conducted on an entirely 'need-to-know' basis. In fact, beyond me and the deputy governors, no more than half a dozen Reserve Bank staff were involved in the transaction. The IMF too instituted a similar code of diligence and secrecy on its side.

The transaction was completed on 3 November 2009, with 2 November being the last of the fifteen working days. As per the agreement, we paid the IMF through the US Federal Reserve by wire transfer at 6 p.m. IST that day, while the Bank of England, the custodian of IMF holdings, transferred the gold to our account by 9 p.m. the same day.

The contract with the IMF also included an agreement that both sides would issue simultaneous press releases on completion of the deal, which meant that the Reserve Bank release would be on 4 November. However, late evening on 2 November, our media spokesperson got a call from a press reporter saying that he was releasing a story the next day, 3 November, on the Reserve Bank's purchase of gold unless we denied it. This report would not have had any impact on the purchase price since the fifteen-day period was over. However, we needed to ensure not only that the public heard it first from the Reserve Bank, but also that they got accurate information, which made it imperative to advance the press releases. Our staff coordinated overnight with the IMF and we issued press releases simultaneously, in the early morning of 3 November in Mumbai, and late evening 2 November in Washington.

This purchase of 200 tonnes of gold raised our gold holdings from 4.1 per cent of our forex reserves on 30 October 2009 to 6.7 per cent on 6 November 2009.

The manner in which the entire transaction was conducted in extreme secrecy and with utmost diligence, taking care at every step of the way to contractually protect India's interests, is a tribute to the competence, professionalism and integrity of the Reserve Bank staff under the overall guidance of Shyamala Gopinath. The *Financial Times* commended the Reserve Bank for putting through the deal 'like a hedge fund manager, leaving many countries red faced'. For me personally, it felt good to have pulled off such a complicated piece of theatre to conclude what some market experts labelled as the largest official deal in history.

The commentariat welcomed the gold transaction with enthusiasm and saw it as the Reserve Bank 'redeeming the honour' of the country nearly two decades after we were pushed into the ignominy of pledging gold to raise money to pay our foreign creditors. The *Guardian* of 4 November 2009 wrote: 'The deal underlines how India's economy has been transformed since 1991 when a financial crisis forced the country to take a loan from the IMF and ship its gold reserves to London as security.' And in an article titled 'India flexes its foreign reserve muscles', the *Financial Times* of 3 November 2009 reported Finance Minister Mukherjee describing the gold stock build-up as soothing the outrage that Indians had felt when 'we had to pledge gold to the Bank of England just for borrowing to support our imports'.

I was pleased with all the praise for the Reserve Bank's acumen but I was discomfited by compliments for me at a personal level, tempting though it was to believe that having signed away the pledge of gold back in 1991, I was now having the opportunity of redeeming the honour of the country as the governor of the Reserve Bank. But redeeming the honour of the country, an unquestionably laudable objective, was not a consideration in the decision. The only consideration that informed my decision was financial prudence. This was exactly what I told the prime minister when, with glowing eyes, he complimented me generously after the deal went public.

Reserve managers invest in gold for the long term. Even so, I am only too conscious that should the price of gold drop significantly in the future from the purchase price of $1041.80 per troy ounce, the very same people who praised me would pan me. It is fortuitous that the price of gold has held so far!

What about the other irony that even as the Reserve Bank itself invested in gold, we preached to the public not to invest in it? Some context is necessary to appreciate this apparent contradiction.

As I wrote earlier, the allure of gold for Indians is legendary. We absorbed nearly a quarter of worldwide gold supplies in 2012. Changes in Indian demand, therefore, have a significant impact on the world price of gold. During 2011–13, our gold imports had increased abnormally, pushing the current account deficit beyond the sustainable limit. The Reserve Bank investigations revealed that the domestic demand for gold had gone up in part because people were investing in gold as a hedge against inflation, and in part because the secular increase in the world price of gold was encouraging speculators to invest in gold. It was inevitable that we had to restrain the import of gold as part of our overall strategy to manage the exchange rate during the taper tantrums in 2013, a topic I wrote about earlier. Yes, it was ironic that I bought gold myself but stopped others from doing so, but it was part of the dharma of the governor's job.

Foreign Exchange Reserve Management

Although I have so far written only about gold, it is important to note that gold is only a small proportion of our foreign exchange reserves. The bulk of the reserves is foreign currency which the Reserve Bank invests as deposits with other central banks, official international institutions and overseas branches of commercial banks, driven by objectives of safety, liquidity and returns, in that order. The broad strategy for investment is decided by a high-level committee chaired by the governor and comprising the relevant deputy governor, the secretary of economic affairs and the chief economic adviser from the finance ministry. Within the broad strategy, the operational details are left to the staff of the Reserve Bank.

A frequent question any governor confronts is whether our forex reserves are sufficient. It's also a tricky question because no matter how the governor replies, it is bound to be overinterpreted to draw inferences on the rupee movement, thereby fuelling speculation. If, for example, the governor answers that the reserves are sufficient, the market would infer that the Reserve Bank would not intervene in the forex market for the purpose of buffering the reserves. That would bring the rupee under appreciation pressure. If, on the other hand, the governor says that the reserves are not sufficient, there would be speculation about the ability of the Reserve Bank to defend the exchange rate should it become volatile, thereby pushing the exchange rate down.

Back in the 1980s, the yardstick, in part enshrined by the IMF, used to be that a country should have reserves sufficient to provide at least three months of import cover. But that was when trade flows dominated the balance of payments and determined the exchange rates. Today, global capital flows are several multiples of trade flows, and floating exchange rates are more a function of the capital account in the balance of payments rather than the current account. Any measure of reserve adequacy in today's world has to factor in not only the current account balance, but also, at the minimum, debt with a residual maturity of less than one year.

The economics literature has several models and formulae for estimating reserve sufficiency. The time-tested truth on reserves, though, is that in good times, no amount of reserves is too much, and in bad times, any amount of reserves is too little.

Another FAQ that a governor faces is about why the Reserve Bank is not fully transparent about its reserve holdings. In particular, why doesn't the Reserve Bank put out its reserve position in real time and why doesn't it give out the currency composition of its reserves?

Actually, the Reserve Bank puts out the data on foreign exchange reserves every week with a lag of one week. It also publishes a half-yearly report on the management of foreign exchange reserves indicating several details, including the objectives of the reserve management strategy, and the adequacy of the reserves as measured by several metrics, risk management practices and the like. However, it does not disclose the currency composition of the reserves because, as the forex reserves manager, the Reserve Bank is like any other commercial entity in the market. The information is market sensitive and disclosure could potentially impact our commercial interests adversely. Disclosure also has wider implications for our international relations. Furthermore, market efficiency is in no way affected by this non-disclosure. Indeed, non-disclosure is the norm around the world; a majority of countries, particularly the large reserve holders, do not disclose the composition of their foreign exchange reserves.

The Reserve Bank has, however, progressively moved towards a greater degree of disclosure in line with international best practices. It is among sixty-eight central banks from around the world to have adopted the Special Data Dissemination Standards (SDDS) template for publication of detailed data on foreign exchange reserves, including some information on currency composition, investment pattern and forward positions. These data are released on a monthly basis on the Reserve Bank's website. The Reserve Bank is also one of the very few central banks which publish their market intervention numbers; it does so in its monthly bulletin with a lag of two months.

Use of Reserves for Domestic Capital Expenditure

For a cash-strapped government like ours with huge and compelling expenditure needs, there is a big temptation to dip into the foreign exchange reserves in the custody of the Reserve Bank to finance capital expenditure. The idea was most actively canvassed by Montek Singh Ahluwalia, deputy chairman of the Planning Commission during 2004–14, who argued that we should design a scheme for lending our forex reserves to public and private enterprises engaged in infrastructure projects, as it was irrational for Indian entities to be borrowing abroad at high cost while the Reserve Bank was earning such low returns on its reserves. And if the Reserve Bank allowed its reserves to be put to use like this for domestic capital expenditure, it would earn more by way of return, and the borrowing entities would pay less by way of interest and we would have a win-win situation.

The Reserve Bank did not see the cost-benefit calculus that way, and rightly so, for several reasons. The most important concern was that India is a current-account-deficit economy and our reserves, accumulated mainly through capital flows, are actually in the nature of borrowing. This is in sharp contrast to China, for example, whose reserves, earned through current account surpluses, are unencumbered. Moreover, frittering away reserves like this would compromise the Reserve Bank's ability to defend the exchange rate in times of volatility and also erode its external credit rating. There were also concerns that any relaxation like this would, in fact, be the thin end of the wedge. Once the Reserve Bank lets go of caution, there would be no end to similar proposals for spending away the reserves, which could severely hurt our external sector viability.

Paying Iran for Oil Imports during the Sanctions

In the area of foreign exchange management, a sensitive task I had to handle as governor related to payments to Iran for the oil we imported from it while remaining in compliance with the sanctions the country had come under. The point to note is that the UN sanctions did not prohibit buying oil from Iran, but payment for the imports became increasingly difficult as first the US, and later Europe, tightened the use of their currencies for settling these transactions. Here is how the situation developed.

Since India and Iran are both members of the Asian Clearing Union (ACU), net trade settlements were generally routed through the ACU mechanism. The ACU comprises nine countries—Bangladesh, Bhutan, India, Iran, Maldives, Myanmar, Nepal, Pakistan and Sri Lanka—which have mutually agreed that trade payments among them will be settled on a multilateral netting basis which would help economize the use of foreign exchange reserves and transfer costs, as also promote trade among the member countries. Import and export of oil was brought under the ACU umbrella in 1985. The currency used for net settlement under the ACU mechanism was originally only the US dollar, but the euro was added as a settlement currency in January 2010.

Amidst misinformed and speculative news reports in America that the ACU mechanism was being used as a conduit for payments on behalf of Iranian companies that were blacklisted by the US for supporting nuclear proliferation activities, starting 2008, the US authorities heightened their scrutiny of payments under the ACU mechanism, gradually making it difficult and eventually impossible to use the dollar as a settlement currency for Iranian transactions.

To get around this, the ACU shifted to using the euro to settle payments to Iran. However, that channel too got choked in the wake of EU regulations issued in 2010 that any bank in the euro area effecting a transfer to Iran on behalf of the ACU had to obtain prior authorization from the euro area authorities by showing that the proposed transfer would not contribute to Iran's nuclear proliferation or other sensitive and prohibited activities. With the dollar out of the ACU since 2008 and euro following suit in 2010, Iran's continuation under the ACU arrangement became virtually impossible. The inevitable consequence of taking payments to Iran out of the ACU mechanism followed in December 2010.

Given India's significant reliance on Iranian oil, the lack of a payment channel landed us in a near-crisis situation. The challenge for us—the government and the Reserve Bank—was to identify a payment mechanism that was in compliance with the Iranian sanctions, but did not involve any American or European bank. The Iranian authorities who were in constant touch with us suggested several alternatives, but none of them materialized, as the parties involved were wary of the consequences of getting hit themselves by sanctions.

Eventually, as a result of the joint efforts of the government and the Reserve Bank, we zeroed in on two payment mechanisms. The first was to pay a part, albeit a small part, in euros through a Turkish bank which came forward; and the second was to pay the remaining amount owed to Iran in rupees. But where would Iran keep the rupees and what will it do with them?

The straightforward option would have been for Iran to open an account with one of our banks into which the rupee payments could be made, but that wasn't as simple as it seemed. Most of our banks were reluctant to accept this business, not being sure of the impact of US sanctions on their overseas business, particularly given the dominance of the dollar for trade settlements. After much effort, we were able to persuade one of our public sector banks with minimal overseas presence to take on this task.

But what was Iran to do with the rupees in its Indian account? It was agreed that they would buy goods from India and use the rupees to pay for them; and the balance, if any, would be remitted to them in hard currency once the sanctions were lifted. Subsequent to the activation of the Rupee Payment Mechanism by the Reserve Bank, India's exports to Iran had increased from $2.4 billion in 2011/12 to $5.0 billion during 2013/14.

The resolution of the Iran oil payment impasse was a testimonial to the strong friendship between our two countries as well to as the ingenuity of senior officials of both the government and the Reserve Bank to find a solution to what seemed like an impossible cul-de-sac situation.

13

'Keep Your Ear Close to the Ground'

The Reserve Bank's Outreach

When I went to call on Prime Minister Manmohan Singh in his South Block office before assuming office as governor in September 2008, the meeting lasted just about fifteen minutes. As I stood up to leave, he graciously walked me to the door, and literally at the doorstop, gave his bit of advice: 'Subbarao, you are moving from long experience in the IAS to the Reserve Bank. That's a big change. Unlike in the civil service, in the Reserve Bank you risk losing touch with reality. Your mind will be so full of numbers like inflation, interest rate and credit growth that you will tend to forget how all this matters to people and their livelihoods. Remember to keep your ear close to the ground.'

Tribal Indebtedness

I could relate very much to that advice. Let me give just one example to explain why.

I have already written about how tribal welfare dominated my job chart in my first posting as subcollector of Parvathipuram division in north coastal Andhra Pradesh in the mid-1970s. The tribal people there suffered from a chronic curse of indebtedness. It was far from uncommon for them to lose what little assets they had to moneylenders and then end up as bonded labour.

How households living at a subsistence level end up in a debt trap is easy enough to understand at a conceptual level. But why tribal people should suffer this misery was initially a mystery to me. The reason is that since colonial times, tribal people have been protected by a debt relief regulation. The regulation, applicable to what were popularly called 'agency areas' in the erstwhile Madras Presidency—hill tracts inhabited by tribal households and designated as scheduled areas—was, by far, one of the most sympathetic laws that I had come across. It provided that any and all debt owed by a tribal to a non-tribal stood completely annulled. It was summary justice at its simplest. All it required for an indebted tribal person to free himself of debt was to come forward and report that he owed a non-tribal a certain amount of money, and I, as the subcollector, could then issue an order that all that debt was cancelled. What was more, if the non-tribal still pressed for repayment, he could be jailed. By way of affirmative action, the debt relief regulation was remarkable for its extraordinary clarity of purpose and simplicity of process.

The regulation was also most ineffective. My first instinct was to believe that all tribal debt would have been written off since the regulation had been in force since colonial times. But during my visits to villages, I realized that nothing had changed. The moneylenders were still there, tribal households were still borrowing from them, and generations of them were still going into bondage. I thought maybe my predecessors didn't pay attention to this task, and I would make amends for past negligence.

In all my youthful enthusiasm, I went around tribal hamlets and encouraged tribal households to report their debt so that I could then write it off and free them from debt and bondage. I simply didn't make a dent. Not one would come forward. It took me several months to understand why. Their total silence had to do with the dependence of the tribals on the non-tribals. Imagine a tribal actually coming forward and getting his debt written off by the subcollector. From that very moment, not only he, but his entire village, would be ostracized by the moneylender community. The net result of my misguided heroism would have been to cut off tribal households from their only source of loans.

Consider these scenarios. Where would the tribals go for an emergency loan if they had a sick child who had to be taken to a doctor in the nearest town in the middle of the night? Where would they go if their animals died in a drought or their crop got washed away by floods? Where would they go for a loan to meet lumpy expenditure on weddings and festivals? The moneylender, never mind his usurious interest rate, was the tribal community's safety net. It was vacuous on the part of the government to believe that it could free the tribal people from the clutches of the moneylenders without first instituting an alternative.

The Reserve Bank's Outreach

This early experience with tribal indebtedness taught me an important lesson in managing public policy. Competence and commitment are necessary to successfully execute development policies and programmes, but not sufficient. Those working at the field level, in particular, need to have a keen understanding of the psychology of poverty and the sociology of village life.

The prime minister's advice to keep my ear close to the ground, when juxtaposed with my civil service experience, struck a deep chord in me. I made a conscious effort to keep this in mind all through my tenure in the Reserve Bank. I am by no means suggesting that the Reserve Bank is cut off from the real world of everyday people. Far from it. Many, if not most, of the

Reserve Bank staff come, like me, from modest backgrounds and have grown up with middle-class anxieties and aspirations. They are also intelligent enough to understand that they must think through all the consequences of their actions, especially keeping in view the levels of poverty and illiteracy in our country.

At the same time, there was also much truth to what the prime minister had told me. The Reserve Bank is an insular institution with not much public interface. In the normal course of their work, the staff do not have occasion to travel into the hinterland of the country. Data and numbers on the economic and financial sector are so much a part of everyday work that real-world perspectives risk being pushed into the background.

It became quite clear to me, early in my term, that deepening the real-world exposure of the Reserve Bank—the outreach—had to be one of my priorities. The platinum jubilee celebrations of the Reserve Bank during 2009–10 provided an opportunity to get started on this. At a meeting with the top management of the bank where we were discussing the layout of the events and programme for the whole year, we agreed that we should embark on something that would have an enduring value extending beyond the platinum jubilee year. The outreach programme emerged out of this brainstorming. The idea was that all of us in the top management of the Reserve Bank would visit at least two villages each during the year, spending a good part of the day there, connecting with ordinary people and understanding their concerns, their problems and their way of life.

It was not as if we meticulously choreographed the outreach programme in all its detail before rolling it out. On the contrary, the programme got off the block with only a hazy structure and evolved over time, based on early experiences. The twin objectives of the programme too crystallized more clearly only down the line—first, to demystify the Reserve Bank which is to tell people what we do and how it makes a difference to their lives in a language and idiom that they can relate to; and second, to listen to them and understand their concerns so that decision-making in the Reserve Bank gets to acquire a human face.

A picture, they say, is worth a thousand words. Similarly, visiting a village, even if for half a day, and even if not seeing it in its everyday unrehearsed setting, is more valuable than studying dozens of books and reports on village life. It gives a perspective, a sense of reality, if also greater meaning to what the Reserve Bank does. Imagine, for example, that the issue before a deputy governor of the Reserve Bank is whether the area of operation of a banking correspondent should be increased from a radius of ten kilometres around the core village to fifteen kilometres. In the normal course, this issue would be decided by studying an analysis on paper of the pros and cons of doing so. Now imagine that the deputy governor actually sees a BC operate in a village and has an understanding of how a transaction is carried out on a handheld machine, the time it takes for each transaction, the volume and flow of work for the BC through a workday and the logistics involved in moving from one village to another. She would then have a much better sense of what it means to extend the radius of operation of a BC. And if the deputy governor also visits villages in the North-east, she will be able to appreciate why the area of operation there should be different from that in the rest of the country.

Whenever I went to see the prime minister, I would often tell him about the various initiatives of the Reserve Bank towards financial inclusion and how the technology of a handheld machine was proving to be a game changer in barefoot banking. I also used to urge him, during his travels across the country, to just side step into a village, any village, to see a BC in operation. He and I, both knew that this was not a practical idea. The prime minister's travels are so well choreographed and the security so intense that it is virtually impossible for him to make an impromptu visit to a village. In the event, we settled for the second-best alternative. I offered to bring a BC to his office and demonstrate the operation to him.

Anyone who has seen a BC operating a handheld machine, which is just like a credit card reader, would have noticed that the technology is far from robust. Because the palms of villagers are typically soiled, it takes several attempts to get the machine to respond to their fingerprints. In the manner of learning by doing, BCs acquire rich experience in making these stubborn machines work. Given this situation, it would have been best for us to choose a couple of BCs from the vast hinterland of the country for the demonstration before the prime minister. But that wasn't to be. Demonstrating barefoot banking before the prime minister was such a rare and prized opportunity that the chairmen of public sector banks offered their own services.

So it transpired that one afternoon in September 2010, deputy governors Usha Thorat and K.C. Chakrabarty, O.P. Bhat, chairman of State Bank of India, and K.R. Kamath, chairman of Punjab National Bank, and I, along with three villagers, appeared at the 7 Race Course Road residence of the prime minister to give him a demonstration of the handheld mission. Imagine the situation. None among the five of us had any prior experience of touching a handheld machine, let alone operating it. I am sure both Bhat and Kamath were intensely tutored by their staff and had practised on the machines for days on end for this impending test before the prime minister.

But, of course, Murphy's Law[1] came into full play. The machines refused to respond notwithstanding the villagers' hands having being sanitized clean before this demonstration. As his face and hands started sweating, Bhat even blurted out light-heartedly that performing before the prime minister was making him

---

[1] Murphy's Law: If anything can go wrong, it will.

nervous. Only after much huffing and puffing did the machines oblige and save our collective reputation. The prime minister, of course, was very pleased and asked some very searching questions about financial inclusion before we all trooped out triumphantly.

The Value of Getting Your Hands Dirty

Consider the following sample of questions. Can a bank branch operate out of a village panchayat office? How popular or useful is the kisan credit card? How do poor people with irregular incomes and lumpy expenditures manage their finances? Is the interest rate charged by microfinance institutions usurious? If yes, why are people still borrowing from them? If we make borrowing against the pledge of gold more difficult, who gains and who loses? What do schoolchildren learn about finance? Is that learning effective? Is it the case that villages end up with only soiled currency? How big a grievance is that? Why and how are poor people lured by Ponzi schemes?

These are just a sample of hundreds of questions over which the Reserve Bank could take a more informed view by looking at things from the trenches, as it were. Simply put, the outreach gave a real-life context and a human face to Reserve Bank decision-making.

Personally, I had a lot of fun going on outreach visits to villages. I was always touched by the warmth and affection of the villagers. In Lalpur Karauta village of Uttar Pradesh, I went into a house with a newly built toilet and asked the woman of the house how she felt. *'Meri izzat vaapas aa gayi'*—'I have regained my honour'—was what she told me. I visited the primary school in Jalanga, a village near Bhadrak in Odisha, and chatted with the girls in the school. I was impressed by how their aspirations had grown. One girl told me she wanted to be an astronaut like Kalpana Chawla, another said she wanted to be like me—become the governor of the Reserve Bank. I do hope that in not too distant a future, the Reserve Bank will be headed by a female governor with a rural background.

While the outreach programme was widely commended, there were a few critics who said that an initiative like this was out of character for a central bank which should remain in the background, and see and learn quietly. There was criticism also that there was too much of show and festivity and that it was just a vacuous attempt by the Reserve Bank to play to the gallery, and had little learning value. I remained sensitive to this criticism and was concerned that the outreach programme should not degenerate into an empty pageant; that it should retain its freshness and spontaneity, and continue to enrich the Reserve Bank's collective understanding of the sociological context of our policies. Just to make sure that we remained on track, I frequently did a reality check with the senior management, both in formal meetings as well as informal conversations.

Town Hall Meetings

Although I have gone on at length on the outreach programme, this was only one of the several initiatives that we launched during my tenure at the Reserve Bank in order to keep our ears close to the ground.

The town hall meetings I wrote about earlier were a particularly rich hunting ground for insights and understanding. I recall vividly the very first town hall meeting we held in Chennai, on the steps of the museum in Egmore, one pleasant January evening, as part of the Reserve Bank's platinum jubilee celebration. This was shortly before Pongal in 2010, and Chennai was in a festive mood, matching with the celebratory mood of the Reserve Bank's platinum jubilee. Vikram Chandra of NDTV was the moderator, and seated on the dais along with me were the four deputy governors—Shyamala Gopinath, Usha Thorat, K.C. Chakrabarty and Subir Gokarn. The audience for the show, which was telecast live nationally, was entirely middle class comprising both the young and the middle-aged.

As a warm-up for the questions from the audience, Vikram set the conversation rolling by asking me to explain the basic functions of the Reserve Bank, why we were in Chennai and why indeed were we doing a town hall meeting on live TV. Thereafter, we fielded a variety of questions from the audience centred expectedly on soaring prices, low interest rate on savings accounts and fixed deposits, the myriad problems in getting loans from banks, poor customer service, and vexatious KYC (know your customer) requirements. Obviously, we tried our best to respond to all these questions in as simple and direct a language as we could muster.

Midway through the show, I asked for an audience poll on how many thought that the Reserve Bank should be supporting growth even if it risked higher inflation as against those who thought that the Reserve Bank should firmly keep prices under check even if that meant some sacrifice in growth in the short-term. I was aware I was oversimplifying a complex dilemma but I wanted to get the pulse of the public. The votes by show of hands were roughly even for either option. But it struck me immediately, even through only a rough, visible check, that the youngsters in the audience predominantly voted for growth—reflecting, I thought, their concerns for job prospects and career opportunities—while the middle-aged voted for the Reserve Bank giving priority to controlling inflation over all else.

The town hall meetings were a rewarding learning opportunity; they were also big mood elevators. Encouraged by our happy experience with the initial town hall meetings, I started urging senior staff, both in our central office in Mumbai as well as our regional offices spread across the country, to hold focus group meetings in tier-2 cities and district towns with various categories of stakeholders—pensioners, bank depositor associations, microfinance institutions, banking correspondents and small and medium industries. I soon realized that I didn't need to coax the staff any more; they seemed to have embraced the idea with energy and enthusiasm.

Financial Inclusion

We would often discuss the issue of financial inclusion with chairmen and CEOs of commercial banks. These meetings were useful for understanding the major challenges in deepening financial inclusion and for reaching a shared understanding on the broad strategy forward. But these meetings lacked depth because all of us operating at the top management of our institutions did not have a full grasp of the problems at the front end. To fill this knowledge gap, we embarked on what came to be called a 'front-line bank managers conference'.

The format was to get together about fifty people—a dozen front-line bank managers from branches in small towns and villages, banking correspondents, MFIs (microfinance institutions), NGOs and some low-income households—in an informal setting for a whole day to talk about financial inclusion. These meetings were an eye-opener on the many gaps between policy and its implementation at the field level: How long and how many visits does it take for a low-income household to get a bank loan? How difficult is it for them to meet all the documentation requirements for a loan? How much do they have to spend out of pocket to secure a loan? Are the poor treated courteously and kindly in the bank? These and other similar questions that came up in the front-line managers' conference were pointers to what we from the Reserve Bank should be doing to take banking services to the poor.

One of the things that used to impress me, both during outreach visits and front-line managers' meetings, was how confidently rural women would speak up, not at all overawed by the occasion or the unfamiliar setting. At an outreach visit to Chapro, a village in Himachal Pradesh, I recall one woman taking the mike in front of maybe 2000 people to tell me that her local bank had introduced a monthly recurring deposit scheme that would yield a lump sum at the end of the year. She said she was attracted by the scheme as the lump sum return on maturity would come in handy to pay the school fees of her children in June–July. But the problem was that the bank had a rigid calendar for the recurring deposit—it started in January and matured in December, whereas what she wanted to do was to start in June so that the lump sum would be available the following year in time for school reopening. All that was needed was a simple fix that would have made a big difference to her and to the bank. But the bank did not oblige her!

When in Ernakulam in November 2012 for a conference, I went for a morning walk. I noticed that hundreds of labourers were gathered at the main street corner. Just from their appearance, it was clear that they were not locals. On inquiry, I found that they had come from the North-east for manual labour in Kerala. I struck up a conversation with them and learnt about the work they do, how much they earned, where they ate and lived in Ernakulam, and why indeed they had travelled 3000 kilometres across the country for eking out a livelihood.

I was particularly curious to know how they were sending money back home to their families. I gathered that out of hundreds of them, only a dozen or so could meet the KYC requirement to open a bank account in Ernakulam, but they got around that with some resourcefulness. Each of the dozen or so account holders would service dozens of others, who did not have bank accounts. Each of them would deposit the amount he wanted to send to his family back home into a designated bank account, and the account holder would text his wife about the respective shares. At the North-east end, his wife would withdraw the money with her ATM card and disburse amounts to each family in accordance with the remittances made in Kerala.

I was impressed by their enterprise. I was also embarrassed by my ignorance. Here was big phenomenon—massive migration of labour across a 3000-kilometre diagonal of the country—and I, as the governor of the Reserve Bank, was not even aware of it.

I happened to go back to Ernakulam after stepping down from the Reserve Bank. The regional director of the Reserve Bank there told me that they have since started disseminating material on financial literacy in Bengali and Assamese and that it would soon extend to other languages.

Portfolios of the Poor

By way of keeping my ear close to the ground, one book that impressed me was *Portfolios of the Poor*[2] where the authors tracked 100 poor rural households each (living below the World Bank poverty norm of less than $2 a day) in three countries— Bangladesh, India and South Africa—for one full year and maintained a financial diary of each household's daily income and expenditure.

The findings in the book are revealing and touching. One of the least understood problems of poverty is that the poor have not only low incomes but their income streams are irregular and unpredictable. Living on less than $2 per day does not mean that you earn $2 every day. That is the average over time. At the same time, the poor have to cope with loss of employment, illness and

[2] Darryl Collins, Jonathan Morduch, Stuart Rutherford and Orianda Ruthven, *Portfolios of the Poor: How the World's Poor Live on $2 a Day* (New Jersey: Princeton University Press, 2010).

death in the family and lumpy expenditure needs. One of the stereotypes about poverty is that 'the poor don't save because they have no money to save'. That is a false stereotype. The poor need to save precisely because, like the rest of us with a present and a future, they too have to put aside a part of what they have today, little as it might be, to provide for tomorrow. The sophisticated financial planning that the poor adopt to smooth their incomes constitutes the fascinating story of portfolios of the poor.

The reason I am referring to 'portfolios of the poor' is because of the powerful way in which the book reinforces the importance of keeping one's ear close to the ground. Let me elaborate.

All through my tenure in the Reserve Bank, we would occasionally get reports from banks as well as state governments that some districts have achieved 100 per cent financial inclusion. These claims would not, of course, stand scrutiny. When you actually check, you would find that thousands of households had not been covered. And even where they have a bank account, the accounts would not be actively used. In other words, our financial inclusion programme was going the way of all other target-driven programmes—compliance in letter but not in spirit.

While visiting Vengoor village near Ernakulam, on an outreach trip in March 2011, I had thrown a challenge to Union Bank of India (UBI), the lead bank of Ernakulam district, that they should make it the first district in the country to achieve 100 per cent 'meaningful' financial inclusion—i.e. not only should every household have a bank account, they should also be using the account actively and regularly.

The choice of Ernakulam was significant. Ernakulam was the first district in the country to have achieved 100 per cent family planning, in the 1970s; it was the first district in the country to have achieved 100 per cent literacy, in the 1980s; achieving 100 per cent financial inclusion would therefore be a logical sequel. UBI set about the task with impressive diligence, and working along with the state government and the Unique Identification Authority of India (UIADI), reported by mid-2012 that they had achieved 100 per cent 'meaningful financial inclusion' in Ernakulam. We planned a big celebration, together with the state government and UBI, to mark this achievement, in part to showcase Ernakulam as an example for other districts in Kerala and indeed in the country. Chief Minister Oomen Chandy, Nandan Nilekani of UIADI, Debabrata Sarkar, chief of UBI, and I attended the celebration in November 2012.

Even as we were planning the celebration in Ernakulam, I had my own doubts about the claim of 100 per cent 'meaningful' financial inclusion. So, three months ahead of the launch, I asked our staff to commission a study in Ernakulam district on the lines of 'portfolios of the poor'.

We found that financial inclusion in Ernakulam was more meaningful than elsewhere in the country, and since the launch of the drive, the banking habit had certainly increased. Even so, there was a significant segment of households still operating in the informal markets. They were still saving through chit funds, and borrowing from moneylenders.

I realized that we were quite some way away from 100 per cent meaningful financial inclusion. All that we need to do to achieve cent percent 'meaningful' financial inclusion remains an open question. Keeping our ear close to the ground will take us closer to an answer.

14

Sleeping at the Wheel?

Regulation of Non-Banking Financial Companies

Since I left the Reserve Bank over two years ago, several people, especially from the financial sectors of Hong Kong, London and Singapore, have asked me why the Reserve Bank is institutionally biased against the non-banking financial sector. This question has always surprised me, not only because there is no such bias but, on the contrary, the Reserve Bank believes that non-banking financial companies add to the financial intermediation function by reaching out to borrower segments left out by banks. As governor, I myself have publicly acknowledged several times that NBFCs perform a valuable function in the financial space.

So, why the misperception? I can only conjecture that it probably arises from the Reserve Bank gradually tightening the regulation of NBFCs over the years for reasons of financial stability and consumer protection, which regulated entities may have perceived as a systemic bias. It is important to understand the context in which the Reserve Bank has moved in the direction of tighter regulation of NBFCs.

Evolution of Regulation of NBFCs

NBFCs differ from banks in a number of important ways. Banks have access to the Reserve Bank's repo window for overnight liquidity management, whereas NBFCs have to depend entirely on the regular financial markets and therefore suffer higher cost of funding. NBFCs are not also entitled to access the 'lender of last resort' facility of the Reserve Bank, and are therefore less able to protect themselves against liquidity crunches in an emergency situation. NBFCs are not part of the payment and settlement system, and cannot issue cheques drawn on themselves. Unlike banks for whom retail deposits are the mainstay, NBFCs typically depend on borrowing wholesale from banks as also the money and bond markets. Only a relatively small number of NBFCs are allowed to mobilize deposits, and to the extent they do, those deposits are not covered by deposit insurance unlike retail deposits with commercial banks.

The business models of NBFCs have evolved reflecting these constraints. As their source of funding is narrower and costlier, NBFCs finance niche segments where they have a comparative advantage in contrast to banks which maintain a diversified portfolio of loans and investments. Because they pose less of a systemic risk compared to banks, NBFCs have historically faced lighter regulation than banks. That perspective has, however, changed over time because of developments in the financial sector having implications for financial stability and consumer protection, resulting in tighter regulation of NBFCs in some respects.

Take financial stability first. We know from the experience of the crisis that the interconnections in the financial system are by far the biggest threat to financial stability. As NBFCs grew in number and size, their interconnection with the rest of the financial sector, and with banks in particular, had not only increased but had also become more complex. Being under lighter regulation, NBFCs were becoming conduits for routing bank finance into risky activities where the banks themselves were restrained from lending, such as real estate development and stock market investment. The Harshad Mehta and Ketan Parekh scams where bank finance had allegedly found its way into stock market speculation are high-profile examples of this regulatory arbitrage. To prevent this leakage of bank money into risky activities via NBFCs, the Reserve Bank had tightened the leverage and reporting requirements for those NBFCs that largely depend on bank financing for their business.

The second reason behind the gradual tightening of NBFC regulation was a growing concern for consumer protection. Because they do not suffer bank-like regulation, NBFCs are able to offer a higher interest rate on the deposits they mobilize, thereby providing a saving option for people willing to accept higher risk for higher reward.[1] While the existence of such a saving avenue to cater to higher-risk segments may be appropriate, it does pose problems in a country like India with widespread poverty and low awareness levels. There have been several cases where low-income households have been lured by the high returns offered by NBFC deposits only to have lost all their money as the NBFC defaulted on paying interest or even returning the principal. Besides, in the absence of sufficient vigil, a number of 'fly by night' operators, masquerading as NBFCs, have mobilized money from gullible people and run away with it.

As a measure of consumer protection therefore, the Reserve Bank has decided that deposit mobilization by NBFCs should be gradually minimized and eventually eliminated so that deposit-taking remains restricted to banks which are more tightly

---

[1] The Reserve Bank imposes a ceiling on the interest rate that NBFCs can offer on the deposits they mobilize, but this ceiling is typically higher than the maximum interest that banks offer.

regulated. The Reserve Bank has, in fact, not accorded registration to any new NBFC for deposit mobilization since 1997, and has even asked already licensed NBFCs to scale down deposit mobilization. To get a perspective on the share of NBFCs in the retail deposit space, note that of over 12,000 NBFCs registered with the Reserve Bank as of May 2015, only about 220 were authorized to collect deposits. These deposit-taking NBFCs are also subject to more stringent Reserve Bank regulation than their non-deposit-taking counterparts.

The perception about the Reserve Bank's alleged bias against NBFCs may also have been shaped in part by the general antipathy at the global level towards shadow banks in the aftermath of the global financial crisis. Shadow banks had a sizeable role to play in abetting, if not actually causing, the crisis as banks transferred their risky assets to these shadow banks, thereby freeing up space for themselves for further lending which led to an unsustainable debt build-up and the near-total implosion of the global financial system. Unsurprisingly, one of the big post-crisis reform initiatives is to plug this loophole by bringing shadow banks too under the regulatory purview, and thereby minimizing the chances of contagion from shadow banks to regular banks.

Are NBFCs in India shadow banks? They are shadow banks in the sense that they perform bank-like intermediation; but they are also not shadow banks because, unlike shadow banks elsewhere which emerged and flourished beyond regulatory oversight, India's NBFC sector has always been regulated, although less tightly than the banking sector.

Even though our NBFCs are not shadow banks, reflecting the global unease about financial sector entities outside of the banking system, we too felt that there was a need to review our regulatory approach to the NBFC sector in the context of the shrinking difference between banks and non-banks, and their increased interconnection. This was the motivation for my

decision to appoint a working group under the chairmanship
of retired Deputy Governor Usha Thorat in November 2010 to
advise on the broad principles that must underpin the Reserve
Bank's regulatory approach to the NBFCs keeping in view the
economic role performed by them, their heterogeneity as well as
recent international experience.

The thrust of the Usha Thorat Working Group (UTWG)
recommendations was that the Reserve Bank must use its
regulatory and supervisory resources more efficiently by relaxing
the regulation on smaller NBFCs and focusing more on larger,
systemically important NBFCs.

The UTWG recommendations were eminently rational and
the Reserve Bank subsequently accepted and implemented most
of them. But one recommendation that remains in abeyance has
been the one regarding exempting smaller NBFCs—those with
asset sizes of less than ₹500 million—from the requirement of
registration with the Reserve Bank. Just to get a perspective on
this, note that of the 12,000 NBFCs registered with and regulated
by the Reserve Bank, over 11,000 fall into this category of asset
size below ₹500 million.

I would have thought that any relaxation like this which
sought to exempt over 90 per cent of the NBFCs from the
requirement of registration would be welcomed by the sector.
On the contrary, they were quite agitated as they were afraid of
foregoing the credibility and reputation that came with registering
with the Reserve Bank. In any case, the public outcry following
the Saradha scam also turned opinion strongly in favour of more
regulation rather than less regulation of NBFCs.

The Jolt of the Saradha Scam

I was deeply distressed by the Saradha scam that erupted in
West Bengal in April 2013 in which hundreds of thousands of

low-income households who had invested their entire life savings in the Saradha Group of companies lost all of that money when the operations of the companies collapsed.

Although the details of the various schemes run by the Saradha Group with the money mobilized from the public and their legality are the subject matter of criminal prosecution currently under way, media reports indicate that the group collected around ₹200–300 billion from over 1.7 million depositors on the promise of investing the pooled funds in collective investment schemes, popularly but incorrectly called 'chit funds' in eastern India.[2] The group companies pooled the money they mobilized and invested it in a range of enterprises—tourism packages, forward travel and time share credit transfer, real estate, infrastructure finance and even motorcycle manufacturing. Reportedly, investors were not properly informed about what use their money was being put to, but were repeatedly assured that they would get handsome returns after a fixed period.

Here is a report titled 'Sen's "bluff", in a nutshell' that appeared in the *Telegraph* of Kolkata on 9 May 2013: "'Soon after the acquisition, Sen held an agents' meeting at the Science City auditorium to inform everyone how his group was investing in the agro industry and hence, there should be no cause for concern about the future of the investments," said a senior officer of the

---

[2] According to the definition given by Chit Funds Act 1982, 'chit' means a transaction whether called 'chit', 'chit fund', 'chitty', 'kuri' or by any other name by or under which a person enters into an agreement with a specified number of persons that every one of them shall subscribe a certain sum of money (or a certain quantity of grain instead) by way of periodical instalments over a definite period and that each such subscriber shall, in his turn, as determined by lot or by auction or by tender or in such other manner as may be specified in the chit agreement, be entitled to the prize amount. (See more at: http://business.mapsofindia.com/investment-industry/chit-funds. html#sthash.ONkcMyph.dpuf.)

investigation team. "As with his other investments in industry, he knew from the beginning that there would be no production from the company. The move was aimed at encouraging his agents to bring in more funds. He would often tell the agents that Saradha's assets were ten times that of its liabilities," the officer said.'

The first signs of the impending collapse appeared in January 2013 when the group's cash flow was, for the first time, less than its cash payout, an inevitable outcome in a Ponzi scheme that runs its full course. Sudipto Sen, the chairman of the group, tried to raise additional funds but failed. In the face of the rapidly intensifying investor agitation, he wrote an eighteen-page confessional letter to the CBI admitting that he had paid large sums of money to several politicians and was blackmailed into investing money mobilized from the public in dubious and loss-making investments. Sen fled on 10 April after posting his confessional letter, and in his absence, the Ponzi scheme unravelled. Despondency quickly spread across Bengal, leading to massive street rallies and angry protests targeting both the state government and Saradha agents. In a story titled 'Banking on Lies', the *Business Standard* of 26 April 2013 said: 'While Sen is in prison, it is left for his agents to face the ire of the depositors. Kalipada Naskar, 60, looks disturbed as he stands facing Saradha's registered office in Salt Lake's Sector V. He became a Saradha agent a year ago after he was told that he could earn up to ₹15,000 a month in commissions and also get retirement benefits. Ever since Sen's business went belly up, depositors have hounded Naskar and 3,00,000 other Saradha agents. Some call him names, others threaten him with dire consequences. "I am helpless, I am sick," says Naskar. A few blocks away, about fifteen people have assembled outside another office of Saradha. These are the depositors who have come to inquire about the fate of their investments. The crowd includes old and young people, mostly poor. It's a heart-wrenching scene.'

An arrest warrant for Sudipto Sen was issued the next day. By 20 April, the news of potentially the largest Ponzi scheme in India became front-page news nationally. After evading the authorities for a week, Sudipto Sen and two of his associated were arrested in Kashmir on 23 April 2013. On the same day, SEBI announced that both chain marketing and forward contracts were forms of collective investment schemes and officially asked the Saradha Group to immediately stop raising any further capital and return all deposits within three months.

Although Saradha was a high-profile implosion, it was by no means a stand-alone episode. For many years, eastern India, particularly West Bengal, had been a fertile ground for firms and outfits of questionable credentials luring unsuspecting low-income households to part with their hard-earned savings by promising enticing returns. No matter what the advertised business model, all these were, at their core, pyramid schemes programmed to implode sooner rather than later. 'Why eastern India' was an issue we used to discuss internally in the Reserve Bank although a clear answer eluded us. Was it that there was traditionally a culture of saving in eastern India among low-income households, thus providing an opportunity for exploitation by clever operators? Did such operators enjoy more political patronage than elsewhere? Was the lack of access to the formal financial sector more egregious than elsewhere? Was it the relative weakness of the cooperative structure?

As its name indicates, a pyramid scheme is structured like a pyramid. A straightforward version typically starts with one person—the initial recruiter—who is on top at the apex of the pyramid. This person then recruits a second who is required to 'invest' a certain amount that is paid off to the initial recruiter. In order to get his money back, this second recruit must now recruit two more people; from the 'investment' made by these latest recruits, he pays himself off first and the balance goes into a pot.

The pyramid keeps building up, with money brought in by fresh recruits used to pay off the recruiters above them such that the entire stake, at any point of time, is borne by the bottom-most layer of the pyramid.

The problem is that it is impossible to sustain this cycle. These operations seldom involve any production of goods and services; no wealth is created and no revenue is generated. Very soon, the only way a pyramid can survive is by recruiting additional members. But that possibility hits a limit very soon—remember the power of compounding—when people at the bottom of the pyramid find themselves unable to recruit the next layer of investors to pay themselves off, and the scheme closes in on itself. This kind of chain, pyramid or Ponzi schemes, whatever name they are called by, are illegal in most countries of the world. But fraudsters manage to get away by creating an illusionary legality.

When the Saradha scam exploded spectacularly and made front-page news in national newspapers, the Reserve Bank was on the block to explain how such dubious schemes were allowed to not just operate, but even flourish, on its regulatory watch. I was not surprised by being put in the dock as the Reserve Bank is quite used to being the default defendant for any irregularity or malpractice in the financial sector, no matter where the lapse lay and who was responsible. We did a quick check and found that none of the companies of the Saradha Group were registered with the Reserve Bank, nor indeed did the advertised activities of these companies require them to register with the Reserve Bank.

It would, of course, have been callous on the part of the Reserve Bank to wash its hands off with the argument that the activities of the Saradha Group fell outside its regulatory ambit when tens of thousands of poor households had lost their financial lifeline. I was very sensitive to the fact that as a public policy institution, the Reserve Bank has a larger responsibility, extending beyond the letter of its regulatory remit, of protecting the public from dubious and fraudulent schemes by spreading investor awareness and by working with other regulators and state governments to tighten the policing of illegal activities.

I do not want to give the impression that the Reserve Bank woke up only after the Saradha group imploded. For years, indeed even before I came in as the governor, the Reserve Bank has been urging state governments to tighten laws to protect depositors, enhance policing of fraudulent schemes, prosecute some of the fraudsters and get stiff punishments for them so as to deter the mushrooming of such schemes. In fact, this would be a standard item on my checklist whenever I met the chief minister of a state.

When we were in Kolkata for the Reserve Bank's board meeting in December 2012, in the media interaction that followed, I was asked about the alarming increase in the incidence of pyramid schemes in West Bengal and what the Reserve Bank was doing about it. Incidentally, this was just a few months before Saradha exploded. I explained how such schemes operate below the regulatory radar, and took the opportunity to urge the state government to increase its vigil and take suo moto action against companies indulging in fraud and financial malpractices.

The standing committee on finance of the Parliament had an exclusive meeting on the Saradha case to understand what caused the collapse of the group and what steps governments, both at the Centre and in the states, and financial sector regulators must take to prevent a recurrence. They summoned officials from several ministries of the government and all financial sector regulators, including myself.

As I was preparing for my deposition before the standing committee, with help from my staff, I noticed for the first time what an appallingly complex and confusing regulatory web we had created in the non-banking financial sector. There are several regulators operating in this sector—the Reserve Bank, SEBI, IRDA, the National Housing Bank, the ministry of corporate affairs of Government of India and state governments, each with compartmentalized responsibility, each with its own set of complex rules and regulations, with no one having a full picture, and with a whole lot of regulatory overlaps and gaps, thereby providing a fertile ground for illegal and fraudulent schemes to flourish. If I found it so difficult to comprehend the big picture and the small print, even with my expert staff tutoring me, how could we expect non specialists, let alone rural, semi-literate households, to understand what was legal and what was illegal, what was safe and unsafe, and what to trust and what not to trust? Whom could they turn to for advice? Whom could they turn to if they found themselves defrauded?

I had faced the parliamentary standing committees in the past as finance secretary, and several times as governor too, and in the process, developed enormous respect for the knowledge, understanding and grass-root wisdom that members of Parliament bring to bear on public policy issues through the committee process. No matter how much I prepared, I always went into these meetings with a great deal of trepidation. The meetings are invariably adversarial; the members grill you to the point of exhaustion for lapse of responsibility and dereliction of duty. To be sure, there was never anything personal in this. Typically, when the meeting breaks up and the chairman of the committee invites you to have tea with the members, the hostility just witnessed in the formal meeting instantly melts away. There were several occasions when individual members of Parliament even came and apologized to me for being so harsh in the just concluded meeting and requesting me not to misconstrue their questions and comments. I never failed to be amused by the members' apparently high regard for me at an individual level and their eagerness to criticize the Reserve Bank as an institution as if I had nothing to do with the Reserve Bank's decisions and actions.

When it came to the standing committee meeting on Saradha, I was, as always, impressed by the concern shown by the members. I was even more impressed by how they zeroed in on the root of the problem by juxtaposing the regulatory gaps and confusion with the ignorance and poverty in Indian villages. My session with the committee spanned a wide range of issues, but at its core, the parliamentarians' question to me was: 'Why was the Reserve Bank sleeping at the wheel and allowing such frauds to go unchecked?'

I admitted to the committee that our balkanized regulatory structure in the non-bank financial space, straddling so many different regulators and regulations, was bewilderingly complex and confusing with regulatory overlaps and cracks. All of us regulators have a basic responsibility to protect the larger public from malpractices and frauds. At the same time, I emphasized to the committee that cases like Saradha were not so much the result of a regulatory lapse but of a policing lapse. Ponzi and pyramid schemes, no matter how they are camouflaged and marketed, are illegal. They operate below the regulatory radar, in part by taking advantage of our complex regulatory maze. We can comprehensively deter such frauds only by more stringent policing and prosecution. National-level regulators like the Reserve Bank and SEBI do not have the reach, penetration or the comparative advantage to effectively police such activities in the financial space across the vast hinterland of the country. It is state governments, with their local presence and vast police force, that have to be the bulwark of surveillance and deterrence. Regulators such as the Reserve Bank have a responsibility, of course, to work alongside state governments to disseminate financial awareness and to train their police and other vigilance personnel in detection and prosecution of financial frauds. As happens in such meetings, we went back and forth several times, and even after nearly five hours, I was not certain I had convincingly made my points to the committee.

As the meeting was closing, I told the committee that the ultimate defence against malpractices and fraud was greater public awareness. I told them that I would review the Reserve Bank's approach to financial literacy and see how it could be expanded and improved. I also told them that we would streamline our training of grass-root police and bank personnel about frauds and malpractices. Finally, I offered that the Reserve Bank would take the initiative to come out with a comprehensive list of FAQs and put it up on our website. Some members thought this response was too non-specific and inadequate compared to the severity of the problem. One member even ridiculed my suggestion of FAQs by asking whether it was realistic to expect semi-literate villagers to go to the Reserve Bank's website to understand the NBFC sector. I could relate to that criticism. I assured the committee that we would translate all the material into vernacular languages and work with state governments to disseminate that knowledge widely and deeply.

The result of this assurance was a comprehensive and exhaustive list of FAQs on the NBFC sector, the first of its kind for any sector or activity within the Reserve Bank's mandate. As per my assurance to the standing committee, we also translated the material into local languages for dissemination across the country. I must admit though that as all these developments took place in the closing months of my tenure, I did not have the time or the mind space, given my almost total preoccupation with rupee tantrums, to follow them through. But I am happy to note that the Reserve Bank has carried the action plan forward in all its dimensions.

In line with the 'every cloud has a silver lining' viewpoint, a positive outcome of the Saradha scam has been the tightening of the vigil at the field level on fraudulent schemes, fly-by-night operators and unauthorized deposit mobilization. In fact, as far back as in 1999, the Reserve Bank enjoined state governments to constitute state-level coordination committees (SLCCs) comprising relevant government officials, police and regulators for regulatory oversight. However, the SLCC meetings were irregular, and even when they did meet, ineffective. The Saradha scam shook the authorities out of complacency. As I write this more than two years after leaving the Reserve Bank, I checked with my former colleagues, and they told me that SLCCs across most parts of the country have been energized and are proactive in sharing economic intelligence and expanding financial literacy and awareness.

Although the business model of Saradha was predominantly that of a collective investment scheme, the scam nevertheless highlighted the issue of regulatory oversight of chit funds. The basic point to note is that chit funds are not illegal. However, and in some way adding to the confusion, even when chit fund firms are incorporated as companies and are therefore NBFCs by definition, they are not regulated by the Reserve Bank. As per a Central law, the power to regulate the chit funds has been vested in the state governments. I can say from my own experience as finance secretary in the Government of Andhra Pradesh and also as governor of the Reserve Bank, that regulating chit funds is nowhere near a priority for state governments. This neglect typically encourages fraudulent and dubious schemes to project themselves as chit funds so as to escape scrutiny. Indeed, a big lesson from the Saradha case for state governments is not only to regulate chit funds more actively, but also to monitor activities in the chit fund space closely to curb illegal activities masquerading as chit funds.

The Blow Up in the Microfinance Sector

The blow up in the microfinance sector in Andhra Pradesh in 2010 was the other major episode in the non-bank sector during my tenure that has had significant regulatory implications.

In some ways, the growth of the microfinance sector in India has been a remarkable success story of recent years; in some other ways, that very rapid growth had raised concerns about the quality of income-generation support that microfinance institutions were offering. Although the microfinance sector had presence across the country, it was particularly prominent in the southern states, with the erstwhile combined state of Andhra Pradesh itself accounting for as much as 40 per cent of the country's microfinance activity.

In late 2010, Andhra Pradesh became the scene of a severe backlash against the microfinance sector, with a flood of allegations about the usurious interest rates charged by the MFIs, their coercive recovery practices and their unscrupulous business practice of luring borrowers with multiple loans, in the process pushing low-income households into the deep end of indebtedness. There were reports too of some microfinance borrowers having committed suicide to escape the debt trap. At around the same time, there were also exposés of the grotesquely huge profits of some of the larger MFIs which was seen, unsurprisingly, as exploitation of the poor.

The growing anger at the harassment by MFIs and resentment at their fat profits at the expense of the poor, galvanized into a widespread public agitation across Andhra Pradesh, prompting the state government to promulgate an ordinance in October 2010,[3] imposing stringent restraints on both the business models and the business practices of MFIs operating in the state. All MFIs were required to register with the state government on an annual basis. They were barred from visiting the houses of borrowers; instead, they were required to conduct their borrower meetings only in public places like the village panchayat office or the village

---

[3] Converted into law with the approval of the state legislature in December 2010.

school. The recovery cycle was lengthened from one week to one month. In an attempt to prevent household indebtedness, the law stipulated that the total interest on a microfinance loan could not exceed the principal. To restrain aggressive lending, MFIs were proscribed from lending to self-help groups (SHGs) that were already covered by the formal banking system, without the prior approval of the bank.

As a result of this clampdown, the microfinance activity in Andhra Pradesh came to a grinding halt. Not only was there no fresh lending, but even recovery of existing loans plummeted as word spread across villages that microfinance loans need not be repaid. Both MFIs and the banks that loaned funds to MFIs were agitated about this deepening default. And in the Reserve Bank, we were getting inside track reports that several other states too were considering following the Andhra Pradesh example to restrain microfinance activity, thereby putting a big question mark on the future of the ₹250-billion ($5-billion) microfinance industry across the country.

Once again, the Reserve Bank was in the dock for having acquiesced in these excesses by MFIs. To be sure, what happened was a matter of deep concern and consternation for all of us in the Reserve Bank. At the same time, we were also worried about how the backlash might impact the future of the microfinance industry. There were, of course, excesses and malpractices but we could not risk throwing away the baby with the bath water. How we could get rid of the bad and keep the good was the big challenge.

The Andhra Pradesh law also posed a legal dilemma for us. Under the Reserve Bank Act, MFIs, incorporated as companies, were NBFCs falling within the regulatory ambit of the Reserve Bank. By seeking to regulate MFIs, the Andhra Pradesh law was encroaching into the Reserve Bank's jurisdiction.

The prime minister called me to inquire about the imbroglio in the microfinance sector. He, like me, believed that while we should come down heavily on malpractices, we should not overreact by killing a sector which has provided livelihood support to millions of households across the country. I also explained to the prime minister the legal issue of the overlapping regulation brought on by the Andhra Pradesh law and the possibility of this snowballing across other states. The prime minister suggested that I speak to the chief minister of Andhra Pradesh and resolve the legal complication.

Belonging to the Andhra Pradesh cadre of the IAS as I do, I had known chief minister Konijeti Rosaiah for several years, in fact right from the time of my early career in the late '70s and early '80s when I was holding field jobs in the Government of Andhra Pradesh. He was already a senior politician by then. More importantly, when I was posted as finance secretary to the Government of Andhra Pradesh in September 1993, he was the finance minister in the then Congress government. But that relationship lasted just about ten months, as NTR won the subsequent election in mid-1994 and Rosaiah metamorphosed into a feisty opposition leader.

Rosaiah is a seasoned politician; he is a warm and friendly person too. He is also one of the most effective legislators that I had come across in my career. There were several occasions during that ten-month period when we would be in a meeting with him in his office in the assembly building when the legislative assembly was in session. Even as he would be listening to us, he would have one eye on the CCTV in his office, watching what was going on in the House. Once in a while, he would abruptly get up, excuse himself, walk into the House, reprimand the Opposition in chaste, firm Telugu with humorous overtones, and tiptoe back to his office, all in a matter of minutes, to resume where we had left off.

I spoke to Rosaiah and requested him to withdraw the microfinance ordinance because of the several practical complications it would create. I levelled with him on my apprehensions about how the Andhra Pradesh initiative might snowball across the country and jeopardize the future of the entire microfinance industry. I assured him that I would take action to comprehensively review the situation in the microfinance sector and take appropriate remedial action that would protect the borrowers, typically women who pursue an income-generating activity, without killing the microfinance industry altogether. Rosaiah did not budge though. I could understand his predicament. There was such deep rancour against the microfinance sector that it wouldn't have been possible for any political leader, much less the chief minister of a state in a vigorous democracy like ours, to backtrack on his action in such an emotionally charged atmosphere.

I took the microfinance issue to the Reserve Bank board at its meeting in Kolkata in December 2010 where we decided to constitute a subcommittee under the chairmanship of Y.H. Malegam, one of the board's venerable members, to study the issues in the microfinance sector, and recommend reforms in order to prevent excesses and malpractices. The Malegam Committee did a commendably thorough, competent and quick job and submitted its report in just a little over a month with a comprehensive set of recommendations to bring some discipline into the microfinance sector, covering both prudential and regulatory dimensions.

The most important recommendation of the Malegam Committee was to cap the interest rate that MFIs could charge their borrowers and also to limit the margin (mark-up) they could have over their own cost of funds. Accepting this recommendation posed a dilemma for the Reserve Bank, so once again it was up to me to make a difficult judgement call.

Here was the issue. Before the 1991 reforms, odd as it might seem to the 'children of reforms', the Reserve Bank had in place an extensive regulatory prescription on what interest rates could be charged on what type of loans and what interest rate could be offered on what type of deposits. As part of the reform process, the Reserve Bank had gradually dismantled this micromanagement in the belief that the competitive impulses so generated would enhance overall efficiency in the financial sector, and benefit both borrowers and savers. The dismantling started with the deregulation of interest rates on the lending side and then moved to deregulation on the deposit side.

I have already written about my decision in October 2010 to free up the interest rate that banks could offer on savings deposits and how that decision brought this huge task of interest rate deregulation, which had been in progress for nearly twenty years, to a logical closure. But here I was, with the Malegam Committee recommendation, being called upon to reverse what was considered a significant, if also a long-drawn-out reform, and that too, just within months after I brought the curtain down on it. It wasn't an ideological issue. My concern was whether this reopening of the regulation of interest rates, no matter how compelling, would turn out to be the thin end of a wedge and reopen the interest-rate structure in the economy for regulatory tinkering.

I was also weighed down by another important dilemma. The charge against MFIs was that they were charging usurious rates of interest. Is it possible for anyone, including the Reserve Bank, to make an objective assessment of what is usurious and what is not? Consider, just for illustration, a pushcart fruit vendor who might borrow ₹10,000 in the morning, accepting to repay ₹10,200 at the end of the day. That would be 2 per cent interest per day, or between 750–1000 per cent interest per year, depending on how you compound it. That sort of interest rate certainly looks ultra-usurious, and also grotesquely iniquitous, especially when you compare that with the interest rates rich corporates pay on the loans they take from commercial banks. But that pushcart vendor, no matter where in the country, hardly has a chance of getting a loan from a commercial bank. He would only be too happy to pay that 'usurious' interest because access to the loan, never mind the 1000 per cent interest rate, means livelihood to him. By regulating the interest rate that the MFIs can charge, might we be driving them out of business and running the risk of pushing impoverished households once again into the laps of even more usurious moneylenders? That was my concern.

Quite obviously, the internal discussion on the issue within the Reserve Bank was quite intense and impassioned, with the dividing line between objectivity and emotion often blurring. All through this process, I was holding no brief for the MFIs, and there was enough reason to believe from the Malegam Committee report that MFIs, especially the large and established ones, were enjoying scandalously fat margins. I asked my staff to review the cost details in the committee report once again, and after convincing myself that the risk of the entire microfinance industry winding down as a result of any interest-rate regulation was small, I decided to bite the bullet and clamped down on the maximum interest rate that MFIs could charge their borrowers.

Meanwhile, the Andhra Pradesh law on microfinance was challenged in the high court by some MFIs in which the Reserve Bank too was impleaded as a party. By the time the case came up for arguments in 2012, we had already implemented the Malegam Committee recommendation. In our submission to the high court, we took a purely pragmatic position and pleaded that the state law was in conflict with the Reserve Bank's regulatory jurisdiction and would cause a lot of confusion and disruption, eventually hurting larger public interest. We also argued that by carving out MFIs into a separate category of NBFCs (NBFC-MFI) for the purpose of regulation, we had removed the ambiguity, if any, on the exclusive regulations applicable to the MFI sector. In the end, the high court upheld the constitutional validity of the Andhra Pradesh law, but asked the state government to review its statute in light of the comprehensive national-level bill for the regulation of the microfinance sector which was then under the consideration of Parliament.

Ironically, the standing committee of Parliament rejected the comprehensive national-level microfinance bill in its report dated February 2014. It is not clear if the Modi government wants to review the situation and introduce its own version of a bill for a common national-level law to regulate the microfinance sector.[4]

As I look back on the microfinance imbroglio from this distance of time, the question of whether I did the right thing by capping the interest rate does occasionally cross my mind. In the event, I believe that the Malegam Committee recommendation was wise and mature. The microfinance industry did not die—unlike what the opponents of the interest rate cap had argued. On the other hand, the industry is back on track and is growing at a healthy clip. I hope, and I believe too, that someday soon enough there will be sufficient competition in the microfinance sector which itself will act as a check on the interest that MFIs are able to charge so that the Reserve Bank can withdraw its regulation on the interest rate.

Curbing the Excesses of Gold Loan Companies

The last topic I want to write about in regard to matters in the non-bank financial sector is on the tightening of regulation on gold loan companies on my watch. I've already written about the huge demand for gold in India not only because it is an attractive saving option for households, but also because of its liquidity and the ease of using gold as a collateral for borrowing. Companies that lend against the pledge of gold are commonplace across the country although they are more visible in some parts than others. In 2011 going into 2012, we found that the gold loan business

---

[4] The Modi government has since established MUDRA (Micro Units Development and Reform Agency) as an agency to refinance and supervise microfinance operations.

was expanding at an unusually rapid pace. The reason for this was that for a few years before that, the price of gold was increasing steeply and secularly which encouraged the all-too-familiar herd behaviour. Households increased their purchase of gold and were raising loans against that gold to meet their expenditure needs. This growing trend raised concerns for us in the Reserve Bank from both financial-stability and consumer-protection dimensions.

If the price of gold was to correct sharply downwards, the gold collateral available with the loan company would not be sufficient security for the amount of loan. If indeed that happened, borrowers would be tempted to default on the loan and the resulting loss to the gold loan company could potentially cascade across the financial system, threatening financial stability. To safeguard against this downside risk, we reduced the loan to value ratio (LTV) from 75 per cent to 60 per cent. What this meant was that a loan against gold could not exceed 60 per cent of the value of the gold pledged as collateral. We also reset the capital requirements for loan companies primarily engaged in lending against the collateral of gold jewellery so as to prevent contagion from them to the rest of the financial system. As a measure of consumer protection, we imposed regulations on where and how gold loan companies should store the gold pledged with them, their obligation to make the gold available for inspection by the borrowers and the procedure that the loan companies should follow for selling the pledged gold in case of default by the borrower.

Financial Literacy—the Most Robust Defence

I started this story of mine on regulating the non-banking financial sector with the question of whether the Reserve Bank has an institutional bias against the sector and then meandered into talking about Ponzi schemes, MFIs and gold loan companies. The common thread running through all this is my belief, as indeed it is of the Reserve Bank too, that the non-bank financial sector plays a vital role in financial intermediation by channelling money from savers to borrowers, thereby contributing to growth, efficiency and equity in the economy. To those who doubt the Reserve Bank's commitment to the NBFC sector, here is what the RBI says on its website regarding its role in non-banking regulation: 'This role is, perhaps the most unheralded aspect of our activities, yet it remains among the most critical. This includes ensuring credit availability to the productive sectors of the economy, establishing institutions designed to build the country's financial infrastructure, expanding access to affordable financial services and promoting financial education and literacy.'

That said, we certainly need to simplify the regulatory structure; but even more importantly, we need to increase vigil against excesses, malpractices and frauds. The ultimate, and certainly the most robust, defence against excesses, malpractices and fraud is widespread financial literacy.

As of now, financial literacy remains a scarce commodity, even among people who are supposed to be disseminators of financial literacy. Let me illustrate. The legendary Ela Bhatt, founder of the Self Employed Women's Association (SEWA) and pioneering social activist, was on the board of the Reserve Bank during my tenure and brought a tremendous amount of grass-root sensitivity to bear on the Reserve Bank's policies. She presented me a copy of her book, *We Are Poor but So Many: The Story of Self-Employed Women in India*, which I read avidly. One incident that Ela related in her book remains etched in my memory. She took a vegetable vendor to a bank for a loan. The bank manager quizzed both Ela and the applicant in several sessions over several days, but was unable to make up his mind. Ela says that after all that vacuous and vexatious interrogation, she realized that 'financial literacy was on the other side of the table'!

15

Footloose in the World of Central Banking

International Meetings and Global Policy Issues

The governor's annual calendar contains a host of international commitments round the year, much more than I had thought and much more than is possible to cope with. Missed connections, security checks, jet lag, sleep disorder, frequent flyer miles and airport lounge food, are all a part of the job content.

The regular meetings on the governor's annual calendar include the meetings of the IMFC (the International Monetary and Financial Committee of the IMF), the G20 meetings of finance ministers and central bank governors, the bimonthly BIS meetings of central bank governors in Basel and at least one meeting each year of the Asian Consultative Committee, the Asian Currency Union and SAARC governors. There are also regular meetings of finance ministers and central bank governors of BRICS (Brazil, Russia, India, China and South Africa) that are typically held on the sidelines of the G20 or the IMFC meetings. An incidental by-product of the crisis has been an increase in the number and frequency of these meetings with the result that deciding which meetings to attend and which ones to skip becomes a complex scheduling challenge.

Fund–Bank Meetings

The meetings of the World Bank and the IMF, Fund–Bank meetings, as they are popularly called, are, as I mentioned at the beginning of this book, held twice a year—the spring meetings in April and the annual meetings in October. The meetings are held in Washington, the headquarters of these two Bretton Woods institutions, except every third year when the annual meetings are held in another country capital which is determined on the basis of some geographical balancing formula. The finance minister is India's nominee on the board of governors of both the IMF and the World Bank; the governor of the Reserve Bank is the alternative governor on the IMF board while the finance secretary is the alternative governor on the World Bank board.

Over the years, the Fund–Bank meetings have evolved into a nucleus for a host of other multilateral and bilateral meetings, regional briefings, conferences and seminars, some organized by the IMF and the World Bank, either jointly or separately, and some organized by think tanks and global financial institutions focused on the global economy, international development and world financial markets. This ever-expanding activity brings to Washington during the meetings week about 15,000 participants comprising finance ministers and central bank governors, and their staffers, chief executives of banks and financial institutions, investors and investment advisers, economists, corporates and consultants, and many well-known and also not-so-well-known experts, all milling around the Fund–Bank complex of office blocks and the numerous cafeterias around in the Foggy Bottom area of downtown Washington DC, just a couple of blocks from the White House. And, of course, the media from all around the world is present in full force—with their mikes, cameras and lights—beaming images, filing stories and reports, and eagerly chasing any minister or senior official in sight for a sound bite.

The IMF has a membership of 188 countries, organized into twenty-four constituencies, with each constituency represented by an executive director. Just as owners of a company hold shares in it, countries hold 'quotas' in the IMF, with each country's quota based largely on its relative position in the global economy. Quota subscriptions are a central part of the IMF's financial resources. A member country's quota determines its maximum financial contribution to the IMF, its voting power and its access to IMF financing. The five largest quota holders—the US, Japan, Germany, the UK and France—as also China and Russia are single-member constituencies with an exclusive executive director, while the majority of the countries are grouped into multi-country constituencies. India, for example, is the lead country in a constituency that also includes Bangladesh, Bhutan and Sri Lanka.

The main official event for the congregated finance ministers and central bank governors is the meeting of the IMFC which deliberates on the principal policy issues facing the IMF, held over half a day in a large, harshly lit conference hall in the IMF headquarters. Each executive director constituency is allowed a delegation of ten people at the meeting. While the delegation leaders occupy the front-row sofa seats, the rest of the delegation is seated in the rows behind. Together with the IMF staff, there are typically around 350 people in the meeting hall.

The IMFC is chaired by the finance minister or the central bank governor from one of the member countries, elected typically for a three-year term. During my tenure as governor, Youssef Boutros Ghali, the finance minister of Egypt, was the chairman till he resigned in 2011 following the defeat of his party in the elections in Egypt. He was succeeded by Tharman Shanmugaratnam, the finance minister of Singapore. Tharman, who has since been elevated as the deputy prime minister of Singapore, is intelligent, suave and articulate. I was always impressed by the way he steered the discussions, and especially for the special effort he made to bring emerging-market perspectives on to the issues, and for the maturity and skill he showed in coalescing a consensus on what were very divisive issues.

The format of the IMFC meeting has changed over time. Earlier, the meetings used to be quite staid, with the leader of each delegation reading out a prepared statement, with not much discussion or engagement with one another. That format has since yielded to a new pattern. The statements are now taken as read and are recorded. Under the new format, the meeting starts with a presentation by the chief economist of the IMF on the global economic outlook and by its financial counsellor on the global financial conditions. This is followed by a briefing by the IMF's managing director on policy issues that need to be addressed by the IMF, such as global growth prospects, exchange rate movements and financial conditions. Thereafter, there is a general discussion on three or four topics identified in advance. Even as this format allows for a more structured discussion, the sheer size of the meeting makes it unwieldy for active engagement on any specific issue. Also, since the meeting proceedings are recorded and its minutes are kept, it remains formal and somewhat choreographed.

Partly to compensate for this, the IMF has introduced a new event on the regular schedule—a breakfast meeting—bringing together finance ministers and central bank governors from systemically important countries and large economies, about thirty to thirty-five in all, along with the managing director of the IMF, the president of the World Bank and their senior deputies, for a freewheeling discussion on the global economic and financial situation. This meeting is informal, more participative and engaging, and decidedly more interesting than the formal IMFC meeting that follows this breakfast meeting. While Chidambaram attended these meetings, Pranab Mukherjee usually chose to skip them, and I often found myself to be the sole representative of India. I profited from these breakfast meetings, both for the insights into global policy issues and the opportunity to present emerging-market perspectives.

Neither the formal IMFC meeting nor the informal breakfast meeting was ever acrimonious, but one could easily sense undercurrents of strain on certain issues. In terms of these undercurrents, there was a clear distinction between the earlier period (2008–10) when the global financial crisis dominated the agenda and the later period (2011–12) when the eurozone sovereign debt crisis was the focus of these meetings. In the earlier period, America was at the receiving end of the blame for the economic and financial turmoil it foisted on the world because of its poor policies and loose regulation. Except on QE, a topic to which I will return later, on most other issues, the American tendency was generally not to contest the blame. It was instead more pragmatic: 'OK, let's put that behind us and see how we should move on.' The Europeans, in contrast, were given to vehemently pushing back on any suggestion of blame for the spillover impact of their sovereign debt crisis or of their ineptitude in managing it. Nor did they tolerate any advice on how they could improve their policy response to mitigate the costs to them and to the rest of the world.

Governance Reforms at the IMF

Governance reforms at the IMF came to be a standard item on the agenda of virtually every IMFC meeting in the post-crisis period. Emerging markets and developing countries (EMDCs) have long nursed a grievance that the Bretton Woods twins—the IMF and the World Bank—are controlled and managed by advanced economies to serve their own economic and political interests, consistently denying EMDCs voice and representation commensurate with their growing role in the global economy. The harsh, and often counterproductive, conditions imposed by the IMF and the World Bank when extending aid to EMDCs, it was believed, was a reflection of this asymmetric relationship. That grievance went largely unheeded.

Until the crisis changed the dynamics of international economic power play. The stereotypical view before the crisis was that EMDCs repeatedly brought on financial crises on themselves because of their poor economic management and venal governance. The crisis destroyed that stereotype. Here was America, the largest and most advanced economy in the world, which was the epicentre of this crisis, the deepest since the Great Depression. The causes of this America-centred crisis were the same as those for which the EMDCs have historically been reprimanded—inept economic management and poor governance. Post-crisis, advanced economies found themselves in an unfamiliar and vulnerable spot, of receiving a scolding rather than giving it, and depending on the EMDCs, particularly China, for leading the world out of a potentially deep recession.

The changed dynamics presented an opportunity to the EMDCs to press for a redressal of their grievances—for a bigger say in the running of the Bretton Woods institutions. After protracted negotiations, extensive backroom diplomacy and several iterations, the EMDCs extracted two concessions. First, it was agreed that the historical monopoly of the US on the position of the president of the World Bank and of Europe on the position of the managing director of the IMF would be ended; instead of the traditional process so obscure that it made a papal election process seem transparent by comparison, these two pivotal positions would, in future, be filled through a merit-based international selection process. The second concession, enshrined as the '2010 quota and governance reform', was that the quotas in the IMF would be adjusted to shift the voting power in favour of dynamic EMDCs. In particular, the new formula would push the BRIC countries to be among the top ten IMF shareholders, while at the same time protecting the voting shares of the poorest 110 member countries.

The first reform of opening up the selection of the chief executives of the two institutions to global competition is yet to be tested. The second, the 2010 quota and governance reform, was held up for over five years almost entirely because the US Congress took that long to approve it. The problem was that as per the IMF regulations, quota reforms require an 85 per cent majority of the total voting strength. Even though most countries had approved the reform, that was not sufficient for passing it, as the US had a voting share of 16 per cent and therefore a virtual veto. The issue of US approval for the quota reform came up unfailingly at every IMFC meeting. And all that US treasury secretary would offer each and every time was that it was yet to be approved by the Congress. Evidently, an issue that was a clear priority for EMDCs remained low priority for the US Congress for over five years. It was only in December 2015, as I write this, that the US Congress is reported to have at last approved the IMF quota reform.

~

As I wrote earlier, one big criticism of policymakers post-crisis was that they remained indifferent to the incipient signals of financial instability in the markets in the lead-up to the Lehman collapse. To remedy this, the IMF introduced another regular meeting into the Fund–Bank meeting schedule—'the early warning exercise'—which is a briefing to select finance ministers and central bank governors by the IMF and the BIS on potential threats to economic and financial stability. The discussion in this 'early warning exercise' meeting remains confidential and no record is maintained on the premise that disclosure of what global policymakers think of as potential threats might actually trigger those threats into materializing!

The Fund–Bank meetings provide a convenient venue for a variety of bilateral meetings. Several people—from global financial institutions, especially large investment banks, think tanks, the academia and the media—seek to meet the Indian authorities. The finance minister and the governor meet them either together or separately depending on the issue and their respective schedules. Running in parallel with the formal meetings is a beehive of intellectual activity—conferences, seminars and panel discussions. The finance minister and the governor of the Reserve Bank are typically featured speakers at some of these events.

BIS Bimonthly Meetings of Governors

The bimonthly meetings of central bank governors convened by the BIS in Basel were among the most productive and interesting that I attended as governor. Set up in 1930, originally to facilitate German World War I reparations, the BIS has had a chequered history, and it has today transformed into a premier organization to serve central banks in their pursuit of monetary and financial stability, to foster international cooperation in those areas and to act as a bank for central banks.

In all the uncertainty surrounding the governor's work and travel schedule, the BIS calendar of meetings was a rare item of certainty. The dates for the six bimonthly meetings every year are determined a year in advance and are not shuffled around. The two-day meetings are typically scheduled on Sunday and Monday with the result that even for those of us who had to take a transcontinental flight, the trip could be managed with an absence from the office of just one workday.

The flagship event in the two-day choc-a-bloc schedule of BIS meetings is the Global Economy Meeting (GEM) convened on Monday mornings, which brings together about thirty governors from advanced and large emerging-market economies to gather around a big circular table—indeed the biggest circular table I have seen—discussing the global economic situation and exchanging their own country perspectives.

The code of conduct governing the BIS meetings is that what is discussed within the room stays within the room. No record or minutes are kept and no attribution is to be made to anyone in any discussion beyond the meeting room. This format allows for a frank expression of country situations and policy dilemmas, and a freewheeling exchange of perspectives and ideas. The GEM was an excellent forum to get a clear and candid briefing on the developments in the advanced economies from their respective governors. This heads-up was particularly useful during the global financial crisis as it helped those of us from emerging markets to be better prepared to respond to those developments.

I feel quite nostalgic about this bimonthly trip to Basel on many counts; they were also memorable for the efficiency with which the BIS ran the logistics of the meeting—right from the time of receiving each governor at the airport on arrival to dropping us back there at the end of the meetings, they demonstrated the best practice for understated deference and unfailing courtesy.

G20 Meetings

Let me now turn to the G20 meetings of finance ministers and central bank governors which I found useful but also taxing.

The G20 is an informal club with nineteen member countries and the European Union that together represent 90 per cent of global GDP, 80 per cent of global trade and two-thirds of the global population. Contrary to popular perception, the G20 is not a new international grouping triggered by the global financial crisis. It was, in fact, triggered by an earlier crisis, the Asian crisis of 1997.

The G20 has been meeting regularly since 1997, twice a year, at the level of finance ministers and central bank governors. One important change brought on by the crisis was to elevate the level of the meeting with the introduction of an annual meeting of leaders—the Leaders' Forum—which India's prime minister attends. The frequency of finance ministers and governors meetings went up to four per year during the peak of the crisis in 2009 and 2010, but has since reverted to the standard pattern of two meetings every year.

The chair of the G20 rotates every year from one member country to another. All the G20 meetings are typically held in, and hosted by, the chair country. The chair country takes the lead in formulating and driving the agenda and providing logistic and secretarial support. The president of the World Bank and the managing director of the IMF also attend the G20 meetings, thereby ensuring that the activities of the G20 are integrated into the agenda of the Bretton Woods institutions where necessary. There are also other invitees such as the OECD, UNDP and the regional development banks like the Asian Development Bank.

The G20 was in the forefront of battling the global financial crisis of 2008–09. Indeed, when the history of this crisis is written, the London G20 Summit in April 2009 will be acknowledged as the clear turning point when world leaders showed extraordinary determination and unity in addressing the biggest economic and financial crisis of our time. There were differences, of course, but they were debated and discussed, and compromises were made in order to attain the shared goal of restoring market confidence. In fact, the entire range of crisis-response measures—accommodative monetary stance, fiscal stimulus, debt and deposit guarantees, capital injection, asset purchases, currency swaps—all derived in varying degrees from G20 decisions.

The sense of purpose and vaunted unity that the G20 had shown in managing the crisis all through 2009 and 2010 started dissipating in 2011 as the agenda shifted from crisis response to agreeing on post-crisis reforms. The fault lines ran along several dimensions: between advanced and emerging economies over the responsibility of the former for the spillover impact of their policies that were adversely impacting the emerging markets; between America and Europe on the management of the eurozone sovereign debt crisis; and largely between America and the rest of the world on banking regulation reforms that eventually led to the Basel III standards.

Managing these fault lines raised a contentious issue within the G20 about how transparent it should be about these differences. A large majority of the G20 members felt that these differences, if exposed, would be exaggerated in the global media which would dent the credibility of the G20, spook the markets and undermine the as-yet fragile recovery from the crisis. They would contend that these differences should remain within the conference room and we should all present a picture of unity to the outside world, much like the code of conduct of collective Cabinet responsibility in a parliamentary system. Ranged against this was a minority view that any such cover-up attempt would be pretentious. Differences, they argued, are inevitable in a world divided by nation states with no natural constituency for the global economy. There was no need, therefore, to be secretive about them. Besides, being upfront about differences of views would help the G20 get larger public inputs into global policy issues and give us a more informed basis for decision-making.

~

The G20 meetings typically started with an extended working dinner hosted by the chair country which provided an informal, freewheeling discussion on the global economy. That would be followed by the formal full-day meeting the following day.

The last item on the agenda would be approving the communiqué of the meeting. The communiqué process itself was quite interesting. It was not that someone sitting in the meeting drafts the communiqué on the basis of the discussion there. In fact, a draft communiqué, based on the agenda, is circulated to the members in advance of the meeting. Even as the G20 meeting is in progress, the deputies of the G20 delegations convene in a parallel session negotiating the draft communiqué regularly, but informally, checking with their respective principals on the content as well as the nuancing and messaging. This process ensured that a pre-final draft of the communiqué was available to the G20 delegates as soon as they completed the agenda of the meeting.

Sometimes, the communiqué approval used to go through quickly and easily. But there were several occasions where it took much longer, often extending beyond an hour, in order to arrive at the language and nuance that all members felt comfortable with. It then became as much a test of English as of economic diplomacy.

I often wondered if the G20 meeting was degenerating into a communiqué-driven process with members focused more on messaging through the communiqué rather than on discussing and resolving the underlying issues. But I was in a minority. A majority seemed to feel that the prioritization was right: that putting effort into the communiqué was a productive use of G20 time given how crucial the communiqué was to shaping global sentiment.

Currency Wars

Two issues that regularly figured on the G20 agenda, either directly or indirectly, were currency wars and the dollar as the global reserve currency.

Although 'currency wars', as a phrase, is of relatively recent origin, and largely attributed to Guido Mantega, the former finance minister of Brazil, as a phenomenon, they have been part of international trade and finance ever since the 1980s when Japan had several run-ins with the US on the exchange rate of the yen against the dollar. Currency wars represent a situation when countries competitively depreciate their currencies against those of their trading partners so as to boost their exports and restrain imports, in a classic beggar-thy-neighbour attitude. Currency wars are ultimately self-defeating as they depress trade and raise the costs for all trading partners involved.

The origin of the latest round of currency wars lay in the ultra-easy monetary policies of advanced economies—zero-interest rates topped up by quantitative easing—aimed at reducing interest rates, stimulating domestic demand and helping economic recovery. In the event, this huge liquidity unleashed by QE found its way into emerging markets in search of quick returns. But emerging markets too did not have the capacity to absorb these large and volatile capital inflows, with the result that their exchange rates appreciated out of line with their economic fundamentals, eroding their export competitiveness and threatening their financial stability.

The consistent refrain of emerging markets at the G20 meetings used to be that the unconventional monetary policies of advanced economies were taking a heavy toll on their economies and that advanced economies must factor in this spillover impact in formulating their domestic policies. They argued that these cross-border capital flows were a consequence of globalization—maintaining open borders for trade and finance. Both sides, advanced and emerging economies, benefit from globalization and so both sides also must share the costs of globalization; it is unfair to leave the entire burden of adjustment to emerging markets. Although they did not bluntly make the allegation, emerging markets would strongly suggest that the intent behind QE was for advanced economies to debase their currencies for unfair trade advantage. Otherwise, why would they persist with QE even after it became evident that it failed to deliver the intended results?

Advanced economies, led by the United States, were largely dismissive of these grievances. Their main response used to be that QE was driven entirely by the need to stimulate their domestic economies, and the argument that it was a cover for deliberately debasing their currencies for export advantage was vacuous. They did not deny the existence of the spillover impact but would argue that such spillover was an inevitable by-product of their policy effort to revive their domestic economies. Moreover, the argument went, revival of advanced economies is in international public good inasmuch as emerging markets too benefit from that revival through increased demand for their exports. They would add for good measure that emerging markets should set their own houses in order to cope with the forces of globalization rather than find a scapegoat in the domestic policies of advanced economies.

In the context of this debate, here is what Bernanke writes in his book *The Courage to Act* on what he said at the G20 meeting in South Korea in October 2010: 'I argued that because we are an important trading partner for many countries, the rest of the world would benefit from a stronger US recovery. I said that countries with sound monetary, budget and trade policies could better withstand any short term disruptions from our easing.'

The asymmetry in this dialogue was best captured by the following poser from an emerging-economy central bank governor to Bernanke in one of the G20 meetings. 'You know, Ben, when we formulate our monetary policy, we review not just our domestic macroeconomic situation, but also the global situation. In our policy documents, there is a section on the global economy, and in particular, on the outlook for advanced economies. Do you, when you make monetary policy for the US, similarly review the economic situation in the emerging world?' The answer was a sheepish silence.

Currency wars is an issue where consensus remains elusive.

Dollar as the World's Sole Reserve Currency

The second, almost regular, item on the G20 agenda was the position of the US dollar as the world's sole reserve currency. The risk to global financial stability because of the world depending on a single reserve currency became starkly evident during the global financial crisis.

As far as currency markets go, the aftermath of the crisis actually presented a bizarre situation. The United States was the epicentre of this huge crisis; its financial markets had seized up with deep anxiety and panic; several of its big-name financial institutions were on the brink of collapse and the US economy was headed into a deep recession. That should have sapped confidence in the dollar and the dollar should have plunged in value vis-à-vis other currencies as a consequence. Yet, exactly the opposite happened—the dollar actually appreciated.

The reason for this counter-intuitive surge in the dollar was not far to seek. As a result of the extreme uncertainty in financial markets following the Lehman collapse in September 2008, dollar investors around the world began withdrawing their investments to return to the safe haven of the US, in the process pushing up the dollar exchange rate. The flip side of this capital exodus was a severe dollar shortage everywhere outside the US which threatened the smooth functioning of global payment systems, and exacerbated financial vulnerability. The point is that every country in the world needs dollar reserves just because the dollar is the underlying currency for a preponderant portion of global trade and finance. The turmoil in the currency markets was a result of this total dependence on the dollar as the world's sole reserve currency.

To mitigate the risk of overseas dollar liquidity crunch, the US Federal Reserve provided bilateral swap arrangements for some countries. The aim was to improve liquidity conditions in the US as well as in foreign financial markets by providing foreign central banks with the capacity to deliver US dollar funding to institutions in their respective jurisdictions in times of stress. But such an accommodation was restricted to hard currencies, and largely to OECD countries. We requested a similar rupee–dollar swap arrangement, but the Federal Reserve did not respond positively. Although they never said it in so many words, I believe their reluctance was either because the rupee is not a freely convertible currency or because our financial markets were not important from the US perspective.

Given the turmoil caused by this dependence on the dollar, it was not surprising that when, in early 2009, Governor Zhou Xiaochuan of the People's Bank of China floated the idea that the SDR issued by the IMF could be an alternative to the dollar, it created ripples in global policy circles and financial markets.

The agitation about this excessive dependence on the dollar was not confined to emerging markets. In fact, in 2011, when France was the chair of the G20, President Nicolas Sarkozy had even appointed a task force with a mandate of finding a solution to the sole reserve currency issue, with a not-too-unsubtle message that the task force should explore ways in which the euro could become an alternative reserve currency. As it happened, that task force lost its momentum, as the eurozone sovereign debt crisis erupted in 2011 and continued to convulse the global economy in the following years.

Can the yuan challenge the primacy of the greenback in the global system? After listening to the Chinese authorities in the G20, IMFC, BRICS meetings and indeed at several other international policy forums and conferences, I am not certain if even the Chinese authorities are clear about whether they want to position the yuan as an alternative global reserve currency. This is not to say anything about their active efforts over the last several years to internationalize the yuan, which the Chinese saw as a project quite distinct from positioning it as a reserve currency.

The results of this internationalization effort are clearly evident. The yuan is today second only to the dollar in its use in international trade and finance. Yuan deposits outside China have multiplied more than tenfold in the last five years. Every year, there are dozens of issuances of dim-sum—yuan-denominated—bonds outside China.

What is also clear is that China has set a lot in store by way of the IMF, including the yuan in the SDR basket, along with the dollar, euro, sterling and yen. In November 2015, it achieved that aspiration when the IMF determined that the yuan met its qualifying criterion of being 'widely used and freely usable', and made it part of the SDR basket.

Opinion is divided on the significance of this imprimatur of respectability for the yuan from the IMF, an institution with which China has often had a testy relationship. One view is that this is only of symbolic value as the SDR is no more than an accounting device; it is neither a true currency nor a claim even on the IMF. True, central banks do hold SDRs, but they still have to convert them back into the constituent currencies if they want to use them for intervention purposes. Moreover, being in the SDR basket is neither a necessary nor a sufficient condition for a currency to be widely held in official reserves.

Ranged against this is the view that being part of the SDR basket may make central banks around the world more open to add yuan to their coffers. This could be significant. Excluding China's own pile, global foreign exchange reserves are about $7.8 trillion. Shifting, say, even 10 per cent of this into yuan over the next five years would require central banks to spend about $150 billion a year on bonds and other assets denominated in the yuan. That could mean a significant expansion of the internationalization of the yuan.

Even if this more positive perception about the future of the yuan bears out, it might still be far from being accepted as a global reserve currency at par with the dollar. For that to happen, China will have to meet some demanding preconditions. In particular, the world must become confident that the Chinese authorities will allow the yuan exchange rate to be freely market determined. It will take at least a few years for the Chinese to establish credibility in this regard. Further, the yuan should become fully convertible on the capital account and it is still a far way from that. Also, the financial markets of China should inspire the confidence of global investors about being open, deep, liquid, and credibly and predictably regulated. This too will take time.

Beyond the above preconditions, there is another requirement too. For any currency to be a global reserve, there should be ample amounts of it floating around in global financial markets. The dollar meets this requirement, as the Americans facilitate this by running a consistent trade deficit—a phenomenon that textbook economics call 'the Triffin Paradox'. This is the logic behind the American claim that the dollar being the global reserve currency is not an 'exorbitant privilege', as it is made out to be but, in fact, an exorbitant obligation on them. It is not clear that the Chinese are willing to take on a similar obligation.

Money, as we know, has three functions: it is a unit of account; a medium of exchange; and a store of wealth. A global reserve currency should meet these three criteria at the international level. The yuan is surely a unit of account and a medium of exchange, but far way yet from being a store of wealth.

My own view, from what I gathered from hearing the Chinese authorities both in formal meetings and informal conversations, is that they will promote the use of the yuan in international trade and finance, but are quite agnostic about whether it will actually become a reserve currency.

Basel III Framework for Bank Regulation

Apart from currency wars and the reserve currency issues, the other contentious issue in the post-reform period was banking regulation reform that eventually took shape as the Basel III framework.

Although banking regulation is a domestic issue and every country can, in theory, regulate its banks any way it wants, in practice, the flexibility is much limited as countries perforce find that they have to conform to international standards. Why so? Because in an era of globalization where trillions of dollars cross international borders every day, it is just not possible for any country to remain an outlier in terms of regulatory standards. Markets shun economies which do not meet global standards. The choice in this regard is particularly stark for emerging economies which are dependent on foreign capital for investment.

The international standards for banking regulation are set by the Basel Committee for Banking Standards, BCBS or Basel Committee for short, and for non-banks by the Financial Stability Board (FSB).[1] Before the crisis, both the BCBS and the FSB comprised only advanced economies. In other words, these exclusive clubs of advanced economies set the standards for bank and non-bank regulation, and the rest of the world had to adhere to them. After the crisis, emerging markets protested against being relegated to being hapless bystanders, especially as it was the lax regulation by the advanced economies that was one of the root causes of the crisis. The result was that the membership of these

---

[1] Before the crisis, the Financial Stability Board was known as the Financial Stability Forum.

forums was expanded to admit a few large emerging markets, including India.

As it turned out, this was not as substantive a victory as it looks. In some sense, the advanced economies continue to run the show. Although emerging markets were given a seat at the table, there was no real inclusion. Typically, the advanced economies would stitch up a deal at a conclave ahead of the meeting, and present that at the formal meeting for approval, almost as a fait accompli. In other words, emerging markets had a vote, but not a voice.

The Basel III banking regulation standards emerged out of this 'inclusive' process. Shorn of a myriad of detail, at its heart, Basel III is a requirement for banks to raise the quantum and quality of their capital so that they are better prepared to withstand shocks, thereby bolstering both domestic and global financial stability.

At a theoretical level, the requirement of higher capital standards on banks is unexceptionable; the more fortified an institution, the better it is able to withstand shocks. But bringing in additional capital entails costs, and these additional costs will translate into higher interest rates on bank lending. In short, the question is, how much are we willing to spend to buy insurance against a shock to our banking system?

The cost-benefit calculus is different for advanced economies and for emerging markets. Emerging markets, led by India, argued at the BCBS meetings that the costs of additional capital to be raised by banks would hurt their growth prospects, especially at a time when their growth prospects depended more than before on the availability and cost of bank credit. However, we failed to influence the final Basel III decision in any significant way.

For sure, the Basel III framework includes a 'comply or explain' provision, meaning that if a country is unable to comply with the standards, it can choose to deviate and then explain why it had to deviate. In practical terms though, this choice is a no choice. In the ruthless world of globalization, deviating from global standards, no matter how convincing the explanation, is not an option open to emerging markets.

Going forward, I believe it is important for global-level reforms to factor in emerging-market viewpoints. Emerging markets are undergoing significant transformation, including in their banking and non-banking sectors, technology-led financial inclusion and product development. These developments challenge old banking models, present promising opportunities and pose new risks for financial institutions and financial markets. Ignoring these EM perspectives in global-level financial sector reforms will be collectively suboptimal for the whole world.

Foreign Banks

Way back in 1972, when I qualified for the civil service, I had an option to join the foreign service, but I decided to choose the IAS for a number of reasons, one of which was that I didn't think I had the personality or skills to be a successful diplomat. My self-assessment has not changed in the several decades since. But I could not avoid diplomacy altogether; I was involved in economic diplomacy at several points even in my IAS career, while dealing with multilateral institutions like the IMF and the World Bank, and bilateral donors like Japan.

A successful diplomat, they say, is one who puts the interests of his country above all else, consistency be damned. The truth behind this wisdom came forcefully to me via a big policy issue pertaining to foreign banks that I had to address as governor.

During the global financial crisis, emerging markets found that foreign banks were largely fair-weather friends. A priority for emerging markets during the crisis was to keep bank credit flowing for productive purposes. To persuade banks to keep pumping credit was no easy task when they were seized with such unprecedented fear and uncertainty. In general, emerging markets found that their domestic banks heeded the call but foreign banks remained reticent, almost all of them, in fact, retrenching credit.

The received wisdom among emerging markets in the post-crisis period was that the best way to mitigate the risk of such self-centred behaviour by foreign banks was to require all foreign banks to incorporate in the host country as a subsidiary.

Just by way of explanation, commercial banks typically operate in a foreign country either as a subsidiary or as a branch, and what form they choose depends both on their business model as well as the regulations of the host country. In India, the Reserve Bank allows both models of operation, leaving the choice of a branch or a subsidiary mode to the foreign bank. Curiously, all foreign banks that have come into India have chosen to operate as branches.

We deliberated on the issue of whether the Reserve Bank too should mandate all foreign banks to compulsorily operate only as subsidiaries. For sure, the issue was not black and white, there were pros and cons on either side. To get a broader opinion on the issue, we issued a discussion paper, listing the merits and demerits of both models and calling for feedback. Foreign banks from almost everywhere in the world endorsed the subsidiarization model and indicated their readiness to incorporate in India should the Reserve Bank so regulate. The only country that had a serious objection to this was the US, mainly on the ground that mandatory subsidiarization of foreign banks would erode the efficiency of capital use and therefore raise the costs of banking. International banks, they contended, should be able to freely move capital from one country to another swiftly, depending on the need. This, according to them, was good not only for the bank but for the global financial system as a whole.

We raised the issue of mandatory subsidiarization of foreign banks with the US authorities several times, including in the Indo-US economic dialogue in Delhi in October 2012, when both Treasury Secretary Geithner and Federal Reserve Chairman Bernanke were present. They reiterated their standard position. We argued that they should not be judging the issue from the narrow perspective of their self-interest but also factor in the risks and rewards of emerging markets in determining the cost-benefit calculus. The impasse persisted.

But the US opposition to our proposal for mandatory subsidiarization was not a binding constraint. Considering all the pros and cons, including the fact of broad endorsement from the foreign banking community, the Reserve Bank has since issued fresh regulations on the subsidiarization of foreign banks operating in India.

But that is not my main story. My main story is that the same US authorities who argued against our proposal for mandatory subsidiarization of foreign banks on grounds of efficient use of capital had jettisoned that principle while applying Dodd Frank regulations to foreign banks operating in the US. In particular, the Dodd Frank Act requires foreign bank subsidiaries in the US to hold higher levels of capital at par with domestic US banks. This angered foreign banks and their regulators for the same efficiency reason that the US argued with us—that it amounts to ring-fencing capital and depriving them of the flexibility to move it around as per need. The US authorities did not budge, evidently putting self-interest ahead of all else, inconsistency be damned.

A lesson in diplomacy for me at the end of my career!

16

Moving On

Stepping Down from the Office of Governor

In February 2012, I gave an interview to the online edition of the *Wall Street Journal*. After covering a vast ground on the global and Indian economic outlook, the last question Alex Fangos of the *WSJ* asked me was: 'You were recently reappointed to another two-year term, running out in September 2013. Would you like to serve another term?' My answer was a curt and crisp 'no'.

I was very clear in my mind that not only did I not want to serve as governor beyond the extended term of September 2013, in the very unlikely event of it being offered, but also that I needed to move on from government service into private life. I joined the IAS barely two months after finishing college and it has been the government all the way since. It is where I learnt, matured and was amply rewarded. After over forty years, I now wanted to live without the crutches of the government.

The Succession Story

I first met Raghuram Rajan when I was finance secretary in the government and he was leading a committee on financial sector reforms appointed by the Planning Commission. We had lunch in my office, of idli and dosa, which my staff had ordered from Saravana Bhavan. We also talked a little bit about financial sector reforms.

The Rajan Committee submitted its report to the government in September 2008, shortly after I moved from North Block to Mint Street. I have already written in an earlier chapter about that meeting with the prime minister where the committee presented its report and the inconclusive discussion we had on inflation targeting. Raghu and I kept in touch after that. We met in meetings and conferences, and exchanged emails. As honorary adviser to the prime minister, he used to send occasional notes to the prime minister on economic issues and was always kind enough to share them with me. I also invited him to give a talk in the Reserve Bank on his much-acclaimed book, *Fault Lines*, in May 2010.

In April 2012, Raghu, who was still in his academic job in Chicago, came to see me in my office in Mumbai and asked about my plans, in particular, if I was going to seek another extension of my term. Incidentally, he had been on the probable list of candidates to succeed me in September 2011 if I was not given an extension of two more years. Since that was behind us by the time of this meeting, there was now occasional speculation that he would succeed me when my extended term finished in September 2013. In response to his query, I told him in no uncertain terms that I would not seek an extension, nor would I accept one were it to be offered. I encouraged him to make his plans on that basis.

We met again three days later in Delhi where both of us were featured speakers at a Festschrift for Dr Manmohan Singh, organized by Isher Judge Ahluwalia, chairperson of the Indian Council for Research on International Economic Relations (ICRIER) board, to celebrate twenty years of economic reforms. I had a feeling, and I must emphasize this was just my gut feeling, that Raghu was still doubtful about what I told him in Mumbai regarding my plans. To put those doubts, if any, to rest, I told him in a quiet moment, when there were just the two of us, that I didn't intend to continue as governor beyond my term.

In August 2012, Rajan was appointed as the chief economic adviser (CEA) to the government. The speculation was that this was just a parking slot until he moved to the Reserve Bank a year later, and that this experience as CEA would give him the much-needed exposure to the functioning of the government from within. That sounded very plausible but I am not sure if the government gave him any assurance on the governor's job, nor indeed if Raghu asked for one.

I don't think either the prime minister or the finance minister had even contemplated another extension for me. To make matters absolutely clear though, I told Chidambaram as early as in January 2013 that he should begin thinking about my successor. He passed it over saying it was more than six months away. I reminded him again in March 2013, and also told him that the government should announce my successor three months before the close of my tenure so that the incumbent could understudy during that period. I had in mind my own experience of the abrupt shift I had to make from Delhi to Mumbai and how disruptive such unprepared transitions can be for both the institution and the individual. On the other hand, understudying for the new position can add enormous value to the change of guard.

I knew from working with Chidambaram that he was not only a reformer but also a modernizer. I thought he would readily accept my suggestion, which should mark a welcome departure from the standard, but antiquated, practice in the government of making decisions on high-level appointments at the eleventh hour. But he looked askance at me, surprised, I thought, at my readiness to become a 'lame-duck' governor for a full three months. My own experience in the civil service, however, gave me no reason to believe in the 'lame-duck' theory; in the Indian system, the incumbent prevails till he or she actually signs off.

My term was finishing on 4 September 4 2013, but there was no decision from the government even as we entered July. There was mounting speculation about who my successor might be. Although Rajan was the overriding favourite, there were other names being speculated about as well—Saumitra Choudhury, member of the Planning Commission, and Arvind Mayaram, finance secretary, among them.

The government announced Rajan's appointment as the twenty-third governor of the Reserve Bank on the afternoon of 6 August. Chidambaram, courteous and correct as always, called me earlier that morning to inform me in advance not only about the appointment but also about Rajan being an understudy for one month. I thought he sounded a bit apologetic about the understudy bit even as it was I who had encouraged him on such an arrangement.

The Governor's Office

The governor's office on the eighteenth floor of the Reserve Bank's central office in the Fort area of Mumbai is spacious and comfortable, elegant but not luxurious. There was an ambitious greening project undertaken for the entire tower structure of the

central office in 2009–10 which doubled as an opportunity to
redesign the layout of the executive office floors of the building.
The old small, steel-frame windows were replaced by floor-to-
lintel-level chrome and glass windows which let in a lot of light
but kept the heat out. You look out the window and you could see
the Government Mint, the colonial era customs house and the
ships docked in the Bombay port. I used to joke with my staff
that the Reserve Bank must allow me the use of the governor's
office for at least three months after I stepped down so that I
could enjoy the comfort and elegance of the beautiful office
without the burdens of the job.

The eighteenth floor houses the governor and his front office;
there is also a large, handsomely appointed conference room,
modernized as part of the greening project. Across the aisle from
the governor's office is a private lounge for meeting visitors, with a
separate dining space should the governor be hosting a small meal
for friends or guests. On the wall adjacent to the dining table is
the governor's gallery, portraits of all the past governors, seemingly
keeping an eye on the current incumbent who will, in course of time,
join their club. You look out the window on the lounge side and you
can see several behemoths of the Indian financial sector—SBI, UBI,
BSE (Bombay Stock Exchange)—as well as the high court, the naval
base and the Mazagon Docks. From the air-conditioned comfort and
calm of the eighteenth floor, the hustle and bustle and the chaos and
confusion of Mumbai's financial district looks orderly and organized!

There is an additional small office room on the eighteenth floor,
behind the governor's office, which is allotted to visiting dignitaries.
The Reserve Bank's housekeeping department arranged for this
office to be used by Rajan during the understudy period. He shuttled
between Delhi and Mumbai during the month, but I took care to
keep him in the loop on all important developments, including
managing the exchange rate which dominated my agenda during
that period.

What Would You Have Done Differently?

'What would you have done differently?' is a question that has crossed my mind several times since stepping down. This is also one of the pointed questions that Mythili Bhusnurmath of ETV hurled at me in the only formal, exclusive TV interview that I had done since leaving the Reserve Bank. At one level, this is an incomplete question. The full question, in my view, should be: 'What would you have done differently if you knew what you now know?' With the benefit of hindsight, one may, in fact, do many things differently. On the other hand, if the question were 'What would you have done differently if you were operating within the universe of knowledge available at that time?', the answer may be, 'Not very much.'

The writing of this book involved a lot of introspection into my time at the Reserve Bank to identify in particular what I got right and what I didn't get right. Without getting into the logical fallacy outlined above, I tried to indicate, wherever the context demanded, what I could have done better even with the knowledge available in real time and what I would have done differently with the benefit of hindsight. In one sentence, if indeed I had a second chance, I would pay much greater attention to communicating more effectively.

I still have a fairly vivid recall of one of the topics that came up for discussion when I appeared before the civil services interview board way back in 1972. I wrote in my application that I was on the IIT debating team. 'What was the latest topic you debated on?' a member asked me. That happened to be: 'Man is condemned to be free', a statement from the existentialist philosophy of Jean Paul Sartre. The interview board members pushed me into interpreting that statement. Here is a precis of what I told them.

At the heart of the existentialist philosophy is the premise that all existence is absurd. Life has no meaning and death is the ultimate absurdity. But in the course of this absurd existence, man is forced to make choices, even if those choices may be about absurd issues. But man abhors this freedom of choice, a condition called 'existential angst'. Until we reach a time when most of our life lies behind us, we second-guess ourselves interminably. 'What if I had done this?' 'What if I had done that?' 'Could I have learnt from what others before me have done?' But that is a futile endeavour. It is just not possible to pass on the burden of decision-making to someone else, nor is it possible to learn from other's experiences. Every man has to make choices by falling back on his own experience. In short, man is condemned to be free.

I must admit it didn't exactly go as fluently as that, and to this day I wonder if the wise men (yes, all men, no woman!) on the board were impressed or put off by a cocky twenty-two-year-old pontificating on what is arguably one of the most abstract concepts in the history of ideas.

But why did this memory from over forty years ago come to me when I am thinking about what I would have done differently as governor of the Reserve Bank? Perhaps to remind me that every governor is a creature of the circumstances in which he is called upon to perform. He has to make choices and decisions based on his own learning and experiences. The governor is condemned to be free!

If there was another chance, I could fall back on this experience to do things differently. But then there are no second chances in life.

Looking Ahead

Another omnibus question that I have been asked both while on the job as governor, and after I stepped down, is about the challenges for the Reserve Bank on the way forward. I will highlight, but only briefly, four challenges that the Reserve Bank will need to address in order to remain a premier policy institution.

The first challenge on my list is for the Reserve Bank to learn to manage both economic and regulatory policies in a globalizing world. The global financial crisis, the eurozone sovereign debt crisis as well as the currency market volatility during my tenure, have emphatically demonstrated how external developments influence our domestic macroeconomic situation in complex, uncertain and often capricious ways. In making policies, the Reserve Bank has to factor in external developments, particularly the spillover impact of the policies of advanced economies on our macroeconomy. This will become even more important as India's integration with the global economy deepens.

Even at the risk of sounding clichéd, let me say that the Reserve Bank needs to 'think global and act local'. The idea is not to fight globalization but to manage it to the country's best advantage. Mahatma Gandhi said: 'I do not want my house to be walled in on all sides, and my windows to be stuffed. I want the cultures of all the lands to be blown about my house as freely as possible. But I refuse to be blown off my feet by any.' The Mahatma's exhortation is even truer today than when he said it.

Over the years, the Reserve Bank, as an institution, has learnt quite a lot about managing policy in a globalizing world. Yet the learning curve ahead is steep. My wish is that the Reserve Bank should take the lead in setting standards for how an emerging-market central bank manages its policies in a globalizing world. The Reserve Bank should become the best practice that other central banks emulate.

The second on my list of challenges is that the Reserve Bank must position itself as a knowledge institution. The crisis has shown that knowledge matters. Those central banks which are at the frontiers of domain knowledge and are pushing the envelope in terms of policies and actions will be better equipped to deal with the complexities of macroeconomic management in an increasingly dynamic and interconnected world.

There is obviously no template or manual for becoming a knowledge institution, nor is there a comprehensive list of attributes. Becoming a knowledge institution is a continuous process of learning from the best practices in the world, oftentimes reinventing them to suit our home context, pushing the envelope, asking questions, being open-minded, acting with professionalism and integrity, and encouraging an institutional culture that cuts through hierarchies.

That takes me to the third big challenge for the Reserve Bank—to widen and deepen financial inclusion. We all know from personal experience that economic opportunity is strongly intertwined with financial access. Such access is especially powerful for the poor as it provides them opportunities to build savings, make investments, avail credit, and above all, insure themselves against income shocks. At the aggregate level, financial inclusion provides an avenue for bringing the huge savings of the poor into the formal financial intermediation system, and for channelling them into much-needed investment. One of the big takeaways from the outreach programme initiated on my watch has been that financial inclusion is not just a public good; it is also a merit good. It empowers poor people in diverse ways. If there is to be 'inclusive growth', financial inclusion is the next big idea, as it will at once promote both growth and equity.

The final challenge for the Reserve Bank is to become a more transparent and sensitive institution. As a public institution, it has an obligation to deliver quality service at the cutting-edge level. The bank needs to listen to the people, be sensitive to their concerns and responsive to their needs.

Release of RBI History Volume

The Reserve Bank initiated a project for recording its institutional history from the time of its establishment in 1935, based on archives and oral interviews of key players. The first three volumes covered the period up to 1981, and were released before I became governor. The fourth volume, covering the period 1982–97, was ready for release by early 2013.

All of us in the Reserve Bank were very keen that Prime Minister Manmohan Singh release this volume because it would mark a very unique event. This volume of history covers the period when Dr Manmohan Singh was governor of the Reserve Bank and subsequently, the finance minister, and would be released by him as the prime minister. I requested the prime minister several times but he remained reticent. When I met him before the July 2013 policy review, I reiterated my request, and to my surprise, he agreed, but on the condition that the event should be low key and be held in his official residence at 7 Race Course Road in Delhi. I got a feeling that he agreed just to oblige me since I would be stepping down shortly, and I was grateful to him for that.

The event was finally scheduled for the morning of 17 August. I got a call that morning from his office, saying that the prime minister wanted to see me fifteen minutes ahead of the function. I wondered why, and got a bit anxious. We had already sent the briefing material to his office earlier. Was he annoyed about some misrepresentation of his period of history? Did he just want a personal briefing? Was he upset that the function was not as low key as he had asked it to be? I went to see him with much trepidation because I had not read the full volume myself. I had neither the time nor the mind space in the midst of managing the rupee tantrums. I depended on the same briefing material that we sent him.

The meeting turned out to be for a completely different reason. He said he just wanted to compliment me for the way I led the Reserve Bank during a period of enormous economic and political challenges. Once again, I was touched by his graciousness. He inquired about my future plans. I told him I would be relocating to Hyderabad and that I wanted to take about six months off to decide what I would do next. 'Do let me know if you want anything in the government. I will be happy to consider that,' he added kindly. Thinking that it would be discourteous to tell him that I had decided to keep away from the government and live completely as a private citizen, I thanked and took leave of him.

Subbarao's Mixed Record

Quite expectedly, there was extensive media evaluation of my five years at the Reserve Bank. The general verdict was that my record was a mixed one. Here are some excerpts:

'Had Subbarao stepped down in May [2013], his legacy would have been different. In September 2008, when he took up the assignment, India was one of the many countries hit by the global credit crunch. But the currency crisis is mostly India specific and tackling it has been Subbarao's biggest challenge in his entire career. He hasn't met the challenge with aplomb. Does that mean his has been the worst tenure at RBI? As they say, a governor should be judged over a cycle and not when he leaves.' ('D. Subbarao: The government insider who turned rebel' by Tamal Bandyopadhyay, *Mint*, 3 September 2013)

'The true legacy of Dr Subbarao will be realized . . . down the line. But this much needs to be said: over the years the grand old lady of Mint Street has been wooed by several powerful suitors from Delhi. And she turned them all down. Dr Subbarao sustained that legacy even if at times it required him to tell some of those suitors to take a walk, all alone. That shall remain his biggest accomplishment.' ('Not his master's voice', *The Hindu*, 4 September 2013)

'Fiscal dominance means that fiscal policy dominates monetary policy in terms of its impact. Monetary policy actions lose traction and effectiveness because, even if the central bank raised interest rates, if it was forced to buy government debt because of excess government spending, the effectiveness of rate hikes is lost. That is what happened to poor Dr Subbarao. He was more a victim than a villain of India's inflation and currency problems as many made him out to be then and still think so.' (V. Anantha Nageswaran in a blogpost on the gold standard site: https://thegoldstandardsite. wordpress.com/2015/03/04/indias-inflation-targeting-regime/)

'How will history judge Subbarao? As a governor who fought fiercely for the central bank's independence, one who had a mind of his own and honestly did what was right for the economy? Or will the verdict be less favourable?' ('The man who dared to disagree', *Business Today*, 4 September 2013)

'Subbarao has been in charge at a very difficult time, with global instability as well as growing domestic and economic problems. Our view is that his record has been a mixed one and has to be understood against the complicated times in which he was managing the monetary affairs of the nation.' ('Subbarao's mixed record at RBI', *Mint*, 4 September 2103)

'He bequeaths a good tradition to his successor. The RBI and the country have been well served by this scholarly, thoughtful, modest and dignified man. Posterity will be kinder to him.' ('Subbarao—End of a turbulent tenure', *The Hindu BusinessLine*, 3 September 2013)

Change of Guard

Real-life events do not respect leadership transitions. The last couple of months of my tenure went completely off script.

I thought this would be the time when I would travel around and visit many of the Reserve Bank's regional offices and also meet the staff of the central office departments to reminisce and rejoice over our time together. I particularly wanted to reach out to middle- and junior-level professionals of the Reserve Bank whose ideas, insights and perspectives influenced me more than they realized. In the event, I was so fully preoccupied with the rupee tantrums that my last day in office, 4 September 2013, seemed to have arrived almost as abruptly as my first day as governor.

At eleven that morning, I spoke to the entire Reserve Bank staff across the country via a video link-up and told them that I would carry many, many pleasant memories of my association with the Reserve Bank. The challenges and anxieties we went through together and the joy and fun we had together would be enduring memories. I pointed out that in a full-length feature article on the Reserve Bank in 2012, *the Economist* had said: 'The RBI is a role model for the kind of full service central bank that is back in fashion world wide.'[1] I hoped, I added, that in a few years' time from then, everyone watching and evaluating the Reserve Bank would say: 'The RBI is a role model for the kind of knowledge and ethical institution that a central bank should be.'

There was a lunch that afternoon to bid me farewell and welcome Governor Rajan. Gathered there were the directors on the board of the Reserve Bank, serving senior management and retired senior officers of the Reserve Bank, CEOs of banks and financial Institutions, other financial sector regulators—about 200 in all. There was the expected round of speeches—nostalgic, emotional and touching.

I kept my own remarks deliberately quite light-hearted. I told the gathering that there are many things I will miss about being

---

[1] 'The Reserve Bank of India: Pulling every lever', *the Economist*, 4 February 2012.

governor, but most of all I will miss being important. Once I step down, I will enjoy the freedom to open my mouth without the pressure of having to say something profound every time I spoke, that I look forward to spending time with my ninety-plus-year-old mother-in-law and that I will freak out on going to a matinee show of *Chennai Express*. I gave some advice to Raghu. He could, I told him, comfortably delegate to his senior staff less important decisions like interest-rate changes and to whom to issue bank licences, but that he ought to retain with himself important decisions like the menu for lunches to be hosted by the governor, gifts to be given to visiting dignitaries and seating arrangements at meetings.

At a brief ceremony at three that afternoon, I signed off and Governor Rajan signed on. Minutes later, I walked out of the office, went down the elevator—with hundreds of Reserve Bank staff present on the ground floor to see me off, and cameras of assembled press photographers clicking away—got into the car and drove away into life after the Reserve Bank.

Summing Up

In the five years that I was governor, I ran into thousands of strangers who recognized me, complimented me and were generous in their appreciation of what I was doing at the Reserve Bank. Every such meeting was a heart-warming experience as their compliments were so genuine. The most touching experience of all was when a young woman approached me in Mumbai airport, while I was awaiting a flight, and said: 'Sir, you are an inspiration for people like me because you've proved that it is possible for someone from a middle-class, underprivileged background to rise to the top.'

As I conclude this book on my five years at the Reserve Bank, I must acknowledge that I was fortunate to have served in a central bank during a remarkable period. From a central-banking perspective, history will mark that period for two distinct developments. The first is the extraordinary show of policy force with which central banks responded to the global financial crisis. This has generated a vigorous debate on the short-term and long-term implications of unconventional monetary policies, as also on the responsibility of central banks for the cross-border spillover impact of their policies. The second historical marker will be the manner in which, reflecting the lessons of the crisis, the mandate, autonomy and accountability of central banks are being redefined in several countries around the world.

Notwithstanding all the tensions and anxieties of policy management during an admittedly challenging period, I consider myself enormously privileged to have led one of the finest central banks in the world during such an intellectually vigorous period. There were taxing times, testing times, anxious times. But at all times, I moved on with the confidence that there is a great institution behind me that will steer me in the right direction. I was deeply impressed by the professionalism, intellectual agility and commitment of the staff and officers of the Reserve Bank. This is an institution that has served the country with dignity and distinction, and will continue to set exemplary standards for professional integrity and work ethic.

Finally, how would I like to be remembered? As a governor whose every decision and action was motivated by one and only one consideration—the larger public interest; as someone who never swerved from the Reserve Bank's dharma.

Index